PENGUIN BOOKS

FIRST PASS UNDER HEAVEN

Nathan Hoturoa Gray (Ngai Tahu, Rangitaane – Waikato whangai) was born in Wellington, New Zealand. He holds an LLB (Hons) and a BA in International Relations, has explored more than 50 countries and can communicate in seven languages. Nathan is a lawyer and has contributed articles to both print and broadcast media. Most recently, he was a communications advisor to the Ministry of Maori Development.

www.greatwalldvd.com

To the builders (of all great things)

FIRST PASS UNDER HEAVEN

A 4,000-kilometre walk along the Great Wall of China

NATHAN HOTUROA GRAY

Dear Alex + Co.!

Hope the book inspires you guys for the future adventures ahead. Arohanui

Nathan Hoturoa Gray

PENGUIN BOOKS

PENGUIN BOOKS

Published by the Penguin Group

Penguin Group (NZ), 67 Apollo Drive, Rosedale,
North Shore 0632, New Zealand (a division of Pearson New Zealand Ltd)

Penguin Group (USA) Inc., 375 Hudson Street, New York,
New York 10014, USA

Penguin Group (Canada), 90 Eglinton Avenue East, Suite 700, Toronto,
Ontario, M4P 2Y3, Canada (a division of Pearson Penguin Canada Inc.)

Penguin Books Ltd, 80 Strand, London, WC2R 0RL, England

Penguin Ireland, 25 St Stephen's Green, Dublin 2, Ireland
(a division of Penguin Books Ltd)

Penguin Group (Australia), 707 Collins Street, Melbourne, Victoria
3008, Australia (a division of Pearson Australia Group Pty Ltd)

Penguin Books India Pvt Ltd, 11, Community Centre,
Panchsheel Park, New Delhi – 110 017, India

Penguin Books (South Africa) (Pty) Ltd, 24 Sturdee Avenue, Rosebank,
Johannesburg 2196, South Africa

Penguin Books Ltd, Registered Offices: 80 Strand, London,
WC2R 0RL, England

First published by Penguin Group (NZ), 2006
This Print on Demand digital edition created by Penguin Group (NZ) 2010

Designed by Shaun Jury
Typeset by Egan Reid Ltd
Printed and bound in Australia by Griffin Press

ISBN 978 0 14 302067 7
A catalogue record for this book is available
from the National Library of New Zealand.

www.penguin.co.nz

MIX
Paper from
responsible sources
FSC® C001695

CONTENTS

ACKNOWLEDGEMENTS

To the Warriors of the Wall: Rev Dr Sumana Siri, for coming up with the idea; Diego Azubel, for encouraging us to get out there and do it; Paolo Antonelli, for taking the kid out into the desert and teaching him how to survive; Kelvin Jones, for the incredible future that still holds; Polly Greeks, one of the bravest women in the world; and Zhao Weiguo, for getting me home so I could tell this tale.

Thank you also to Michael and Wang Wei Gresham for your laughs and hearty meals, and, in particular, friends to talk with in times of need. Also to Ming Xiaodong, Zhao Weidong, Li Beng, Arthur Liu, Tom Yuan, Jiang Xiaofan and Ambassadors Ming Ming Chen and Zhang Yuan Yuan as names to the faces of countless Chinese peasants and friends, without whom this road would have been no road.

Thank you, Mum, for your beauty and irrepressible *aroha*, and, despite your threats, for not throwing my computer outside the bedroom window. Thank you, Dad, for your strength and unconditional support, in particular your encouragement at three vital times. To Tanemahuta for your inspiration to keep going, Clare Burgess for keeping me sane, and to my wonderful flatmates Ruth, Zach, Alex and Pam, and particularly Caroline McBain who edited the mammoth down to an elephant. Thank you also to Harry Rickett's Creative Non Fiction Writing crew, in particular Fionnaigh, Virginia, Penny and Elizabeth; Jo Lusby of Penguin China; Nicholaas Tieman Franchen of Sunny Side Up for all the website help with the motivational DVD for schools; Ronald Fischer for reading the entire book in one night; Averil of Unity Books for her editing skills; Frankie of AIO

Foundation; Renee Taylor's Whitireia crew; Witi Ihimaera; and, of course Finlay Macdonald, Andrea Coppock, Rachel Wallis and Alison Brook of Penguin NZ Ltd for weaving their magic on the homestraight.

He mihi maioha ki ōku nei tīpuna, kia awhina me ārahi i ahau. Tēnā koutou, tēnā koutou, tēnā koutou katoa.

And one last thank you: to *Chang Cheng* – The Wall. For all your blood, sweat and tears; the creation of a path of such power and infinite majesty, and giving me a glimpse of what it is to be a human being.

Arohanui
Nathan Hoturoa Gray

MONGOLIA

Gobi Desert

Jiayuguan

Zhangjiakou

Datong

Yinchuan   Yulin

Taiyuan

Wuwei

Lake Qinghai

Lanzhou

Xian

TIBET

C H I N A

Himalayas

Chengdu

Guangzhou

Zhuhai   Hor

Hainan Island

The Great
Wall of China
stretches across
Northern
China, from
Jiayuguan in the
Gobi Desert to
Shanhaiguan at
the Bohai Sea.

A band of five men from the west
Meet at the western point where souls head to rest
In pursuit of a dream five egos walk east
A wall, thirteen moons and the beast

Nathan Hoturoa Gray

PROLOGUE

AND THUS WE VENTURE

Brown, parched lands.
Dreary fields stripped of life.
Horizontal scars scour the soiled sands —
Telltale signs of a ploughman's strife.

A land of peasant people hard at work.
Obedient in mind to a reign of moral law.
Hands and hoes, ancient plough and horse.
An era enclosed by a gigantic Wall.

Nathan Hoturoa Gray

Pink and white blossom hangs off scrawny trees. The mud is hard-baked and cracked; the sky grey. A crackle of thunder resonates across the valley as two crows fly east towards the mountains. A drop of rain splatters my cheek. Another taps my wrist. Dust rises as heavy drops form craters in the dry earth.

One hundred and twelve days it's been without rain. Clearly I'm a newcomer to these dry, ancient parts, but it seems like a long time to go without water, even for a cactus. I think about the possible meanings of rain. You get this way after walking 2,000 kilometres. Perhaps these desert lands are finally coming to an end?

Up ahead the gigantic Wall lumbers onwards, extending towards a range of grey mountains. Twelve feet high, six feet thick, I have accompanied this petrified serpent of stone, mud and clay for four months across Northern China. Contracting its spine to make an ascent upon a fresh range of mountains, the Wall transforms to a thin line of granite rocks weaving diagonally up the ridge. It is not the sort of Great Wall I had imagined or seen in tourist photos. However, it is still a tremendous feat considering the size and weight of these boulders. I can hardly lift one, and this mountain slope is getting steeper.

Two hundred crimes carried the dreaded sentence of labour on the Wall, either for life or perpetually. If you got the latter sentence then upon your death your son took your place. A major deterrent to ensure strict obedience to the code of Confucian morals. Heading up the steep mountain shoulder, I imagine the grunts of men hunched under their loads, and the sounds of cracking whips as they drive their mules mercilessly up the eroding slopes. Precipices begin to appear, revealing drops of up to a hundred feet. Winding its way through two granite crags, this 2,000-year-old trail, my guide, has become the only navigable path. Tightening my waist and chest straps for surety, I take a deep breath and move purposefully along the jutting granite path. The wind screeches like a banshee, threatening to push me off the trail as a heavy fog moves in to obscure my path. I feel like I'm caught up in a game of blind man's buff. Suddenly a gust claims my cap and takes off with it into the mist. Distracted, I misjudge a step and an ancient brick dislodges, tumbling down the foggy precipice. I instinctively leap to my right just before a small landslide follows, plummeting below with a chilling crash.

Over a million people died building the Wall, the world's longest graveyard. Viewed by the West with such a sense of awe, this almighty Great Wall is an emblem of oppression to the majority of Chinese. Forced to carry rocks up the steepest of slopes, one falter and the worker was history. Most of the bodies were thrown inside the construction. Bones fill in many layers.

I lower my pack and find my brown cap hanging haplessly at the precipice edge. I am lucky. That hat has been vital in keeping my head warm during the chilly spring evenings spent without a tent. I certainly still need it and am thankful it has not been lost. Yet this is the way with the Wall; you only carry what you need – the rest is either discarded or lost.

Twilight begins to fade. My exposed ears freeze and my nose begins to trickle. This is no place to be spending the night. I quickly retrieve my cap, attaching it safely to the waist belt of my pack, and hastily remount the dragon. If I had known where it was taking me, I never would have ventured. But that's the beauty of the unwritten path. You just never know. And thus we venture.

Ж

Here I sit. A Chinese man sits to my right. Slanted eyes and flat nose landmark his pale and expressionless face. He's wearing a green uniform with two military stripes on the shoulders. The addition of a silver star tells me he's moving up in his world.

Fake yellow and red roses line the oak table where we sit. The table is well polished and designed for reading military maps. The walls are white and decorated with army paraphernalia: the Chinese flag, a couple of old rifles, some trophies and a poster of President Jiang Zemin and Mao Zedong rousing the Chinese army. Their arms are splayed out in a victory salute from the back of an open army truck. Another poster shows a host of rockets being transported into Beijing, probably celebrating China's entry into the space programme. Either that or they're nuclear weapons.

Hand on my forehead, elbow resting on the table, I avert my gaze from my silent companion. Indeed, there is no *Star Trek* solution to release me from this four-walled embrace. Freedom may be a state of mind, but compared with walking all those wide-open spaces I feel claustrophobically enclosed by the Chinese State. Just like much of the Chinese population, locked inside its gigantic Wall.

Twenty minutes pass . . .

'*Lindao shenme shihou lai?*' I ask the recruit when the leader is coming.

'*Ban ge xiaoshi,*' he replies, pointing to his watch.

Yeah right. He's been saying 'half an hour' for the past two hours.

Two more officials enter the room, and more Chinese tea is poured. The young men smile courteously as my white teacup is refilled.

When is this friendly-faced façade going to end? It has been two hours since I was escorted back to the compound with two loaded rifles to my head.

I eye the refilled teacup suspiciously. Is this their tactic? To play it nice so that I fill up with fluid and when it comes to play hardball I'm desperate to go . . . ?

'*He pijiu ma?*' The recruit looks to me, offering a beer.

'*Bu yong, xie xie.*' I decline the green bottle with a terse smile.

Forty minutes later I hear the sound of squeaking brakes as a green army truck arrives. Soon after, an army general appears. Unlike the fresh-faced army cadets – young boys in dark green uniforms – there's no friendly smile on this man's face. Smoker's wrinkles bank below his cold steely stare. The leader talks quickly to his assistant and then looks back to me with a frown. I rise to greet him, shaking his hand firmly and returning his stare. I've done nothing wrong and am not intimidated even though he neglects to take off his general's hat.

'You're not supposed to be here,' he says shaking his head. 'Big trouble.'

Before I can respond he performs an about-turn and leaves the room.

Ж

I am on my own, four days out from Zhangjiakou, a city of three million about 250 kilometres north-west of Beijing. The evening fog engulfs the mountain peak I am hiking. Spurred by the mini-victory of reclaiming my cap, I continue up the narrow pathway of rocks. I reach the summit, and break through the fog. A three-quarter moon watches silently from above. It illuminates a giant golf ball about ten times my height. I'd spotted it earlier in the day when walking towards the range – then but a tiny white speck 15 kilometres or so ahead.

'Go there for food and shelter,' a local peasant had pointed out as we crossed paths. Having no idea where the next village was, it had become my goal.

The Wall runs up a flat grassy hilltop towards a brick house, then makes a right-angled diversion down the other side of the mountain. With minimal food and water, I head hungrily towards an open window. Inside are four Chinese: two in civilian clothing, two in green uniform.

Army. Not good.

The two recruits notice me scuttle past and run out. To my surprise their young faces glow with excitement.

'*Wo shi xinxilan ren, zou chang cheng — wo keyi he shui ma?*' I force out my stock Chinese phrase: I'm from New Zealand, am walking your Great Wall, and wonder whether I can have some water before going on my way.

One of the soldiers leaves and returns carrying a pale-red furnace filled with boiling water. I gulp down the last drops from my one-litre green army bottle while passing over my 750-millilitre reserve. It is always such a relief to get resupplied.

'*Huzhao!*' The other recruit holds out his hand, requesting my passport.

I obediently show it to him, feeling uneasy. To get it black-marked or confiscated will be disastrous. It's my sole sense of identity in this Mainland wilderness. He flicks through the pages as the other recruit fills my bottles. I wait patiently while he reads my three-month tourist visa. He looks up and returns my passport with a nod as ten other soldiers walk past. They, too, approach excitedly. I am told to wait while the leader of this new group conducts a brief talk with his troops just out of hearing. The conference of hushed whispers ends, and the platoon again surrounds me. Their smiles look ominous.

'*Zou ba.*' Come with us.

We march towards the garrison, which is a collection of white concrete buildings. The soldiers are happily chattering amongst themselves, so I relax and resign myself to the experience in store. We walk through the central headquarters past a window behind which a group of civilians are enjoying a luxurious banquet in the main hall. The table is stacked up with plates of food two, even three, tiers high, and the gathering includes two women. They are laughing and drinking, sharing in a good sense of camaraderie. My stomach belches delightedly at the prospect of being invited as an honorary guest. I am absolutely starving and, after 30 kilometres of walking, this meal is reminiscent of the Last Supper. The soldiers hurry me straight past, my hopes sinking as we enter the garrison.

> *It doesn't matter whether the cat is black or white,*
> *So long as it catches the mouse.*
>
> Deng Xiaoping

We enter a cold, grey corridor. It leads to a spartan room, which contains two beds, a desk and some books. Like most things in China, it is small. More soldiers appear at the doorway. They, too, are excited. It is unlikely they have come face to face with a Westerner before. They stare unashamedly, prodding me with expectant eyes. The status of 'main attraction', or perhaps more aptly, 'zoo animal', is the everyday norm on this journey. The curious troops are itching for a performance. I casually unzip my fleece and am tempted to launch into a *haka*. They suck in their breath in anticipation. Alas, I will probably be killed if I attempt such a passionate rendition: they will just have to content themselves with watching me wash.

The gathering of soldiers makes way for a recruit who comes in with a giant enamel cup. It is filled to the brim with hot steaming noodles. Another carries a silver basin of warm water. I take off my grubby white t-shirt, grab the dirty cake of soap offered, and begin scrubbing my upper body. Thirty eyes peer closer. I certainly am not getting my scrotum cleaned this evening.

I look into the mirror provided. My whiskered face is tanned and smeared with desert dust. Although I like my tan, most Chinese avoid the sun because browning denotes the peasant class; white is more attractive to the Chinese than black. I use the muddying water to clean my pores, and swish my hair back in a rare moment of vanity. It is nice to see my face again after several days without it. It looks older than I had imagined.

Drying off, I escape the cool air, putting on my tight blue thermals and grey polar fleece. I immediately head to the table, pick up the chopsticks and with three swift swipes swallow the entire bowl of noodles.

'*Hei ooooohhh!*' The recruits applaud, absolutely delighted. What a treat to watch this foreign barbarian so skilfully wield the chopsticks. Their very own travelling circus! I plead with Oliver Twist eyes for seconds, and two more mugs of noodles appear. The crowd hushes as they gather closer to watch the next culinary onslaught.

'*Hei ooh!*' they again shout in absolute hysterics. I deal to both bowls within ninety seconds, slurping up the dregs, and cheekily ask for a fourth. The boys jump at my request; my body ecstatic with the nutrition it is getting. It is nearly two days since my last proper meal. Yet despite the air of entertainment, China's sketchy human rights record lies at the back of my mind. What is going to happen next?

After dinner I am transported down the same corridor to sleep in another room. It is again white, the same size as the other, with three beds. Some wooden cupboards lie in the corner filled with clothes and there is a more extensively-filled bookshelf. I unpack and stretch out to sleep on a hard mattress as two other soldiers enter to take the other two beds. As the lights are turned off, I realise my first foolish mistake: I have forgotten to ask where the toilet is. To have done so would have given me the knowledge that I could leave the room as I wished. Instead I lie there stiffly, too scared to wake the others. Half an hour later I really need to go to the toilet. This is like living hell. It gets worse.

Lying there in the dark, my ears suddenly prick on full alert. Synchronised footsteps pace down the corridor with the distinct cocking of two rifles. The heavy boots stop outside and the door handle is jerked down. My heart seizes and a squirt of urine leaks. Yet the door does not budge. I lie there in shock while one of the soldiers gets up drowsily to unlock it. He goes outside with the guards, exchanges some hushed whispers, and comes back a minute later. Nothing comes of it.

The guards remain outside the room all evening. The waft of cheap cigarettes seeps through the door cracks, accompanied by occasional whispers. Four times through the night heavy footsteps approach the room. Each time I lie there frozen, trapped in my cell. Yet no one comes in.

No matter how much cats fight, there always seem to be plenty of kittens.

Abraham Lincoln

Morning comes. I am up immediately.

'*Cesuo ʒai nali?*' I ask the two soldiers. They point down the corridor. I head outside and down some steps to a concrete landing where the toilet is situated. The Wall trails down the mountainside 150 metres further along a gravel road. I exuberantly relieve myself, then mark out a potential escape route while returning to the room to repack. Just as I am set to leave, two soldiers enter with a breakfast of eggs and more noodles.

'*Chi fan!*' they insist, showing me to my seat. I eat quickly, but just before I finish they refill my plate. My water glass is also filled every time it approaches half-empty. They keep on doing this.

An hour later, packed and having overeaten, there is no further excuse for the soldiers to keep me inside. I shoulder my pack.

'*Wo yao ʒou yinwei taiyang tai re le. Wo jintian yao ʒou shi gongli.*' With an urgent smile, I explain that I have to head off immediately because it is going to get above 30 degrees by midday. I want to make a good 10 kilometres before the heat sets in.

'*Bu xing!*' the soldier replies. You can't go.

'*Weishenma?*' Why not?

He is beginning to look angry. '*Ni yao deng women lindao lai.*' You must wait. Our leader is coming.

I ignore his protests and turn to leave, but he grabs my wrist. I desperately shrug him off, my body quivering in shock. I take a deep breath and stare back stiffly at the recruit, slowly backing my way out. He scowls but stands his ground. I sense he can't keep me here against my will.

I make my way into the corridor, turn around and nervously walk outside the barracks. The recruits follow at a distance. I head down the steps towards the toilets. Halfway down, more soldiers come out.

'You can't leave, you have to wait for our leader.'

Fear-stricken, I force another smile, one of feigned incomprehension, and keep on walking. As much as their leader must be a respectable guy and all – covered head-to-toe in honorary stars and battlefield stripes – I have absolutely no desire to meet him.

Walking past the toilet, I can sense the whole garrison's eyes on me. I stumble down the rocky path, my limbs malfunctioning with fear. I regain my footing but dare not look back. The scene behind is clear in my mind. A pack of Chinese hounds, saliva drooling, hungrily awaiting release from their wrought-iron leashes.

Just get out of here, Nath. Get back to the relative safety of the Wall. I look out anxiously towards the serenity of the Great Wall traversing the next two ranges. The gravel path leads to a crossing over the Wall, which will enable me to slip out of view. I reach the top of the 8-foot barrier, turning around to give a cheerfully composed wave. They all stand at the top of the hill, watching. Although I want out of here, I feel strangely incomplete for leaving filled with fear, not getting the army's blessing for my journey. It is too late for that now.

I take the path across the Wall, and once out of view sprint down the mountainside with all the speed I can muster. A scream emanates from the garrison above, a piercing Chinese war cry that shakes my soul to a state of trembling. The pursuit is on . . .

Here I am, twenty-six years old, alone, with a 20-kilogram pack, walking through China and being chased along the Wall by the Chinese army. Fuck. Realising the futility of attempting to out-run the military, I slow to a walk lest I be seen running from the garrison.

Three soldiers appear on the mountain rise.

'Stop where you are!' they scream.

I walk on, again feigning incomprehension, but freeze when they shout with added intensity and run towards me with their rifles.

'If you were in New Zealand, you could just go and walk as you please.' I tremble. 'Please let me walk, I just want to enjoy your Great Wall.' Tears blur my vision.

The three recruits flank me with their rifles but look uncertain what to do next. They are young boys, probably drafted from some remote village. I stand watching their minds gradually tick over as they simultaneously decide to aim their rifles at my head. I sit down, resigned and dejected.

How on earth did I get myself into this crazy situation?

Best I take you back, right to the very beginning . . .

MOON I

BIRTH

Something I owe to the soil that grew —
More to the life that fed —
But most to Allah who gave me two
Separate sides to my head.

I would go without shirts or shoes,
Friends, or tobacco or bread
Sooner than for an instant lose
Either side of my head.

Rudyard Kipling, *The Two-Sided Man*

Umbilical cord cut, my limp wrinkly body is raised triumphantly to the adoring view of my lifegiver, Tiahuia Te Puea. Lungs and thorax are immediately put to use, screeching like one does when falling at terminal velocity. I'm guessing it is the immediate onslaught of cold air sweeping over my skin. That or being abducted by alien hands into a bizarre enamel environment; St Helen's Hospital ward, Wellington, New Zealand. I could just as easily be screaming for my life. Four minutes later, my twin brother comes surging on out. Squealing even louder, like a warrior on the charge . . .

Being first out of the womb I am generally considered to be the elder. Not so, it seems, from the perspective of the Maori. They believe the second is the elder because the latter twin 'kicked' the first from the womb. Life began with an eviction. I suppose it does with us all.

A genetic conglomerate of olive Maori skin and tight Scottish loins, I am the sort of guy that wants to buy everyone a beer but to never have to pay for it. Indeed, looking into the mirror and seeing the reflection of both of New Zealand's Treaty partners staring right back, this combination of race is always going to have some impact.

For example, imagine if we twins fell out through a dispute over the family estate? According to the legal notion of primogeniture – where the eldest son receives all the inheritance – from the eyes of both cultures it would be a different twin receiving the prize. Fortunately, this legal anomaly will never feature in our lives. My dad, Neil Edward, was an astute trusts, wills and estates lawyer. We twins were also the youngest of five.

> *Love at first sight is none other*
> *Than twins in the womb.*
>
> Nathan Hoturoa Gray

Sometimes I think that identical twins are the product of a past life of ego and vanity. The test of the present body is to have this clone-like teacher who not only looks and acts in an identical manner, but whose actions – whatever they may be – are going to have an impact on both twins' reputations. This, of course, can have both positive and negative outcomes. However, in the context of a Western individualistic upbringing, where one's progress is often merited by setting oneself against the other, the comparison between twins can cause a lot of competition, envy or simple cricket bat-wielding angst.

My older brother, Fraser Cameron, three years our senior, recognised the natural sense of rivalry early on, and with his dimples radiantly exposed, manipulated this to his utmost advantage.

'Whichever twin first makes my bed 100 times will be my favourite.' Indeed, our having eaten his vegetables for almost a decade when Mum wasn't looking, we needed little encouragement to get this new competition up and running.

The inferiority complex between twins is especially pronounced if one is deemed more successful than the other.

The lesser twin, thrust into the predicament of having strangers look at him with this adoring sense of recognition, yet knowing inside that they are cripplingly mistaken, has to think quickly to save himself from imminent embarrassment.

Fortunately there are plenty of options . . .

1) Just pretend you are the other twin. (Pull it off and claim all the glory!)

2) Do whatever it takes to make yourself more famous, so that the majority is actually thinking that it's you.

3) Greet people courteously, rectify their mistake with minimal mental injury, and then create some ingenious story that makes them consider you to be the better twin. (Wastes a lot less energy than option number two.)

4) Go daily to the gym and take excessive amounts of Body Bulk to make you look bigger. (This has the added advantage of being able to pummel the other twin if he is still doing better.)

5) Just keep following the other twin around for the rest of your life, so as an inseparable unit, no one need make any such mistakes again.

6) Leave the country.

Indeed, terrible at pretending, far too self-conscious to wear name tags, and trying my utmost yet failing miserably to put on any weight, I took the hint eventually and ran with number six. Tane left twin territory a year or so later. Starting in London as a *Les Misérables* usher on the humble retainer of £3 an hour, he overcame the tough artist's odds to become one of fourteen De La Guarda aerialists out of about six billion hopefuls. If he hadn't been so successful, well, I suppose I never would have got the email . . .

15 July 2000, Vilnius, Lithuania

Dear Nathan,

A group of monks are making a walk along the length of the Great Wall of China. I'm going to shoot a documentary about their journey. Do you want to join me on the expedition?

Diego Azubel

A Jewish photojournalist from Buenos Aires, Diego possesses dark intelligent eyes and shoulder-length black dreadlocks. A prolific traveller, he has self-financed expeditions to document the impact of landmines in Laos and Cambodia, and slavery taking place in Mauritania, and has spent a harsh winter with the Reindeer People of Mongolia.

I had met Diego six months prior through my twin Tanemahuta, when in London preparing for a five-month hitch-hiking mission around the northern Mediterranean from Morocco to Cairo. Diego was the photographer for De La Guarda. I had just arrived from the United States. After spending two years completing my Law (Honours) and Political Science degrees, I had interned in the US trust territory of Saipan as a foreign investment analyst and clerked in Alaska's top commercial law firm, Perkins Coie. Having saved enough money to travel for two years, I was halfway through my second major hitch-hiking journey up to Norway's North Cape and on my way through eastern Europe towards Iran, Pakistan and India.

When Diego's email comes, my response is immediate.

No way.

Although the idea of walking the Great Wall sounds totally unique, even utterly tremendous, the reality of tackling the width of China on foot is completely kamikaze. I decide to stick with my original journey heading down through Poland and Czechoslovakia instead.

29 July 2000, Český Krumlov, Czech Republic
Diego emails back two weeks later.

Dear Nathan
In October 2000, a group of men will begin a historic walk.
    The event is historical because it is the first group of our kind to walk along the entire length of the Great Wall of China. Starting from the West in Jiayuguan Pass (on the Badain Jaran Desert in the Gobi) and finishing in Shanhaiguan Pass on the

Bohai Sea, east of Beijing, the length of the Wall is uncertain, although it's estimated at approximately 4,000 kilometres.

Apart from a few tourist-approved regions, the Great Wall has been largely closed to the outside world. It wasn't until 1998 that the Chinese authorities decided to open it slowly, a small area at a time. Thus no Westerner has ever completed and documented such a walk. It simply wasn't permitted.

Nathan, are you sure you're not keen to come? I'm securing sponsors now.

Diego

First Westerners? First Westerners!

> *Narrowing vision, vain spirit gazes.*
> *A curious glow ignites ambition's face*
> *Enticing jaws of the ego fly-trap,*
> *Crashing blindly into a suicidal race.*

I have known Kelvin Gilbert Jones exactly half my life. Since leaving Wellington College and Victoria University he has been training to become a professional golfer in Atlanta, Georgia. Brown curly hair and wide hazel eyes, he recently split up with his New Zealand partner, Janice, with whom he has a son, now four years old. When Kelvin escorted Janice and Lucas to Los Angeles airport en route to Georgia, Janice supposedly heading to Utah to follow her Mormon faith, he discovered that it was likely to be the last time he would see his son. Janice had secretly planned to marry an American Mormon she met while he was on mission in New Zealand.

As Kelvin had no custody or visitation rights, the news cut him up badly. He had spent a lot of time with Lucas over the previous year, and had been enjoying his role as father, despite his absence during the earlier years when he was not ready to be a husband.

Kelvin sends me a despairing email informing me of his desire to drive a car from France across Russia to the Bohai Sea. This is coincidentally where the Great Wall of China finishes. Still indecisive about going, I tell him about the journey. It seems the perfect opportunity for Kelvin given his present circumstances. Perhaps even a chance for fame to win his son back? Kelvin leaps at the opportunity, organising expedition logistics and booking a flight to London to meet Diego before planning to leave for China in September.

> *Pussing blisters, ebola backspins, begging for food*
> *A once-in-a-lifetime — what have you possibly got to lose?*
> *Scimitars and scorpions, hunted by the army and detained,*
> *Don't think of such things — naïvety allows you to choose!*
>
> Nathan Hoturoa Gray

15 August 2000

Hey Nath,

Do you want to be known as the man that almost decided to go on that walk with that Kiwi legend Sir Kelvin Jones?

Kelv

How can I possibly refuse? Competition is endemic in twin mentality, not to mention macho capitalism. Blinded by the allure of ambition, I am drawn towards the expedition not just for the fame, but because a fellow national is going to claim all the glory. I hitch-hike through the Austrian Alps, contemplating my choices, and am picked up by four German men driving a red Lada.

'We've had a little discussion between us,' says John, the bearded driver, 'and we would like to invite you to our cottage. You can accompany us if you wish for a mountain hike tomorrow.'

'That would be awesome!' I reply, loving the spontaneity that hitch-hiking provides. After navigating almost 20,000 kilometres through forty-five countries on the strength of my thumb, it seems that only good-mannered people ever bother to slow down to consider you for a ride. I have learned a lot about a nation's state of mind through hitch-hiking – more from those who neglected to pick me up. The Italians and Spanish openly encourage with a thumbs-up as they drive on by, whereas many of the more conservative countries, such as parts of Scandinavia and Germany, nervously divert their eyes. This is the same for richer car owners and many solo women – those who generally have the most to lose. Generalisations aside, hitch-hiking is all about where you are dropped off. If you are anxious about getting to your destination, you're in for a hell of a ride – the sorts of people you attract, it seems, are equally stressed out. However, if you just allow for the new drop-off point to be the place where the next life experience unfolds, whether it be a magnificent vista, a place to buy supplies, or a pleasant random encounter, the ideal ride just seems to come once that moment has been encountered.

We drive through birch forest and into a grassy meadow towards a smooth, glacially gouged granite cliff. A white cottage nestles below, once a small pastoral church. Sitting around the table, eating barbequed meat and drinking lime juice, I inform my new German acquaintances of my China indecision.

'Apparently there's a new Hillary on the rise,' Xavier announces, his large brown eyes looking at me encouragingly.

'It will be a big challenge, China.' John interjects. 'You seem pretty good at keeping up with what we say in German, but I suspect Chinese will be a whole new system of understanding with no relation to the languages you can communicate in already.' I had already learned Afrikaans whilst on Rotary exchange in South Africa – a good basis for Dutch, Flemish and the Germanics. I had also learned Latin, French and Spanish at school, consolidating the latter two whilst hitch-hiking through those countries. John's blue eyes look deeply into my attentive gaze.

'It will also take at least six to seven weeks for your body to adjust to everyday walking.' He pauses, reflecting. 'But out of your two choices, I'd go for China – it definitely sounds the more unique challenge.'

We spend the next day hiking through the Alps. Walking at the back, I film the four Germans clambering along the sides of a narrow snowy ridge, trying to maintain their balance as an icy wind blows over the steeps. Five souls battling the elements and themselves.

23 August 2000, Geneva
Dear Nathan,
I've managed to score team clothing but I need to tell them whether I need 4 or 5 sets of jackets.
Regards Diego

Get the five.

I am in: one week out from leaving and I have finally committed. Cooking sausages on the barbeque at his London flat, possibly our last Western meal, Diego wears grey shorts and walks around in bare feet wearing a white De La Guarda t-shirt. He has let out his black dreadlocks, and grown his hair down to his shoulders. He also has a gigantic bushy beard. We embrace each other, united by the magnitude of the possibilities that lie ahead.

'Just imagine, walking that fuckin' wall and coming to the ocean.' Diego's brown eyes glaze over at the thought.

'And the full moon rising out from the sea.'

Both spines fizz with the spirit of the dream.

7 September 2000, London
We're gonna go on this journey in search of ourselves and at the end of it we're gonna find . . . we don't know what we are going to find.

Musings from the Wall: Diego Azubel

Kelvin flies into London from America showered in team sponsorship. Wearing a yellow Timberland cap, shirt and black Gore-Tex shoes, he also has two giant North Face duffle bags.

We embrace, having caught up only once in the past two years.

'I wasn't going to tell you this by email, but I never would have come unless you had confirmed,' Kelvin confides.

Indeed, it is good to have Kelvin on the journey given I have met Diego only twice before. Most of my concern, however, is Kelvin's security. He is going into the expedition with less than NZ$2,000 and I am under the impression he is relying on me to finance him if necessary. It is a responsibility I don't want to shoulder given my already shoestring budget.

Diego, however, is rapt. He has signed on not one, but two eager Kiwis to help carry his documentary gear across China. The visionary idea of walking the Great Wall came from Reverend Doctor Sumana Siri, a Buddhist monk from Malaysia. The Reverend is to be accompanied to China by an Italian recording artist called Paolo who is associated with one of his temples in Milan. We are to meet the others in Beijing.

MOON 2

PREPARATIONS

Stirred from my slumber, 30,000 feet below,
I shudder in awe at this sandy planet.
Vast and copper, silently sprawling,
An unfathomable thought to walk this desolate land.

Musings from the Wall: Nathan Gray

17 September 2000, Beijing

Our plane taxies into the terminal, a luggage truck arriving through the hot shimmering air. A Chinese man in white overalls steps out. He snorts deeply and spits out a gob of phlegm. Two more Chinese attendants exit the truck, one of them stepping on the festering yellow globules unawares. Before long he too dredges up his own contribution to the snotty tarmac sewer.

More and more attendants appear, busily attending to their daily duties. All short, with black hair and white overcoats, it's as if Snow White is about to vacate the plane. The chime to unbuckle seatbelts sounds, followed by a hundred swift clicks and a mad race into the aisle. I continue to sit beside Diego as Kelvin looks back to attract our attention. His nervous excitement says it all: we are about to become a minority in the biggest population on the planet.

The airport bus takes us to the hot, grimy streets of Beijing. Catching a public bus for 1 *yuan*, we squash in with the Beijing throngs, stopping about half a kilometre from a cheap hostel where Diego once stayed on a previous trip to China. The three of us lug our packs and the two giant duffle bags along the pavement, attracting the eyes of all passing locals. Diego towers over the Chinese like Arnold Schwarzenegger. Facial hair is rare in the cities here, and his bushy beard and wild woolly hair make him an instant hit in the world's bowl-cut capital.

After settling into our hotel, Kelvin spends the night boasting to other travellers about our plans to walk the Great Wall. He quickly secures the fascination of a Swedish blonde and heads out to party with a new group of travel acquaintances. I find it hard to say what we are doing with any real confidence, simply because I still haven't made up my mind whether I am actually going to walk. My spleen has begun to ache after almost a year now of non-stop travelling, and the idea of the trek is still beyond my mental limits. However, I have resolved to at least take the two-day train journey out to Jiayuguan to see where the Wall commences at the Gobi Desert. My plan is possibly to hitch-hike and play a support-crew role for the team if I don't walk.

Diego and I leave the hotel the next day to explore the back streets of Beijing. They are unclean, and littered with rubbish and old brick buildings. We stumble across a dusty courtyard where six snooker tables are lined up for hire. A group of Chinese males cram around our pool table to watch us play, passing cigarettes to each other. They observe us attentively, giving rousing praise for each ball potted. Ash drops onto the faded green felt.

'I'm loving all this attention: we haven't had to queue once and no one lets us pay.'

'Everyone's just keen to have us around, take a good look, that's all,' Diego smiles.

The same thing had happened at the nightclub the night before. Coming out of a dancing trance, I had opened my eyes to see everyone in the room just staring. China is great for the ego.

Diego's grin wanes. 'The stares aren't always going to be positive, Nathan. Life in China is hard and many locals must wonder why the foreigner receives such good treatment. It is their home after all.'

The colonisation of China by the West was particularly brutal, expressing the sort of colonial arrogance that accompanies most expansionist foreign policy. Entering like a parasite during the Opium Wars of 1840–60, the self-confident colonials craved new markets and raw materials to cater to the needs of the Industrial Revolution. Intolerant of the Middle Kingdom's superiority complex, not to mention China's self-imposed isolation, the Western forces attempted to subordinate their host to their own manner of thinking.

However, unlike the British experience in India, where they took on the responsibility of developing the loose grouping of small independent kingdoms within the subcontinent, mutual jealousy between the Portuguese, French, British and Japanese prevented outright colonisation of China, which was more united under the rule of the emperor. The Westerners couldn't seem to get it together to complete the continental takeover, and were forced instead to accept territorial concessions, ruled under extraterritoriality arrangements. One hundred and forty years later, we too want to conquer the Chinese continent. Can we learn from the mistakes made by China's earlier colonists and, despite our cultural differences, succeed in walking the Wall together?

It is time for the team to come together.

21 September 2000, Beijing

We congregate in the hotel lobby of the South Beijing hotel where Diego, Kelvin and I are staying. Our sleeping quarters are like an underground enamel dungeon. The room contains four beds with rock-hard rice pillows and plain white sheets. It reeks of sewage, and features a barred window with a view of passing feet. The fourth bed is inhabited by a quiet Japanese traveller. At US$3 a night (25 *yuan*), it is the cheapest tourist accommodation available in Beijing. Paolo and Sumana stay in the Youth Hostel Association complex, a big white building ten minutes' walk from Tian'anmen Square. This costs 60 *yuan* a night, its view of the city blocked by the lavish TK Intercontinental Hotel, which costs ten times the price. China caters to all visitors' pockets.

A mural of the Great Wall spans the lobby wall. All five of us are sitting in a circle on wooden seats, eyeing each other. There is a feeling of nervousness in the air.

'How do I look?' Diego asks in a South American twang, piercing the tension by flicking his hair comically in front of the camera.

'You look great,' I reply from behind the lens.

'Do I look cool?' he smiles purposefully.

'Excuse me?'

'Do I look mother-fuckin' cool –'

'Shhhhh!' Kelvin scolds, his index finger pointing towards his lips, dimples betraying a mild feeling of amusement. 'Let's get this show on the road.'

'Diego, I thought you were supposed to be leading the expedition?' I state, Diego shrugging his shoulders. 'You may as well take the camera then.'

'Okay, we need to assess our strengths and weaknesses, and what equipment we still need, and determine our goals and precise roles within the team,' Kelvin says in a deep authoritative voice. His eyes scan the circle of attentive recruits, his gaze stopping at the dark-skinned Sumana. His dimples deepen.

Comfortably filling his wooden chair, Sumana possesses one of the fattest stomachs I have ever seen. Barely 5 feet tall, there seems to be little difference between his vertical and horizontal dimensions. I look on, initially perplexed, but also can't help a wry smile. If the Tegel chicken is willing to walk 4,000 kilometres, then so am I. Sumana's eyes dart about nervously, uncomfortable with all the attention.

'I've already visited fifty countries, making addresses in forty-nine of them,' he blurts out quickly in a manufactured Oxford accent. 'I speak eleven languages, including Chinese.' His head bobs proudly from side to side. Living between the cracks of culture, it is hard to trace this man's soul: a citizen of the International Empire. His light brown robes give him a religious air, but perhaps more importantly a connection to something he can't bring – a solid background.

'My family is very proud of me,' Sumana continues, his voice switching to a slightly Sri Lankan twang. 'I'm the youngest of eleven, and am studying theology at Oxford, a PhD no less. Did you know I am the first Buddhist monk ever to be ordained in Singapore?' His dark eyes look around seeking approval. 'I beat all my classmates, including the class favourite!' He pauses for a response, then takes out a book from his bag. It shows pictures of him with many of the greats including Nelson Mandela and the Dalai Lama.

Sumana surprises me. I had always thought that monks were humble and measured. Instead he is a modern-day go-getter, keen to make an instant impression. His travelling partner, Paolo, is the complete opposite. Endowed with pasta-white skin, he is 6 feet tall, of moderate build and has penetrating blue eyes. He scans the group like a Mafioso assassin, scowling in concentration, light stubble bristling his sombre face.

Kelvin takes out my green diary, which contains the list of equipment we think will get us safely across the Gobi.

'Has anybody got any water purification tablets?' Kelvin asks.

'I have a small bottle of iodine – many tablets,' Sumana responds, raising his hand.

'I've also got some chemical pills,' I reply, 'But each person is going to have to carry their own, in case we get separated.'

I grab the pen and diary from Kelvin and begin ticking off the list of boxes. Kelvin gives me a long, cold stare.

'Right, does everyone have sore-throat pills?' I continue, unaware of Kelvin's protest, the pen top in my mouth, looking round in anticipation. Nobody replies.

'Painkillers?'

'I have some,' Sumana replies, adding hastily, 'I also have a homeopathy doctorate, attained in one year.'

I nod encouragingly. 'Antihistamines?'

'Yes.' The monk continues.

'Stomach-ache pills?'

'Yeessss!'

'How about toilet paper?'

'No.' Sumana looks to his right hand, then hastily to his left. 'No need – I spent last year in Africa.' There is a sustained silence. The thought of traversing the Wall without toilet paper makes the rest of us pensive.

'How about a donkey?' Kelvin asks with a smile.

'A donkey?' I reply.

'Yeah, something to lug Sumana's gear, because I sure ain't carrying it.'

Kelvin leans over towards Sumana whispering, 'And if we can feed it enough. . . perhaps it will agree to carry you too.'

The monk giggles. He had wanted to hire a sherpa from Nepal to carry his gear along the Wall. We had been delayed coming to China for a week while waiting for this to eventuate, but it hadn't worked out. Despite the initial confidence boost that Sumana's stature provides, his stomach poses a significant burden. How are we going to accommodate the fat, hearty buddha?

'We have to know exactly what each person is carrying – scrutinise its value for the team and then make sure everyone knows where everything is stored in each other's packs,' I state earnestly.

The packs are going to be big, especially with Diego's filming gear which neither Paolo nor Sumana are going to be carrying. At this stage the group is to be carrying the following items:

5 backpacks and pack liners
3 two-man tents
1 one-man bivouac
6 sleeping bags
5 sleeping mats
5 rain jackets
5 minus-twenty-degree fleeces
2 t-shirts each
1 long-sleeve shirt each
1 pair of thermals each
2 pairs of trousers each

4 pairs of underwear each
12 pairs of socks each (6 nylon, 6 cotton)
1 pair of gloves each (plus inners)
1 pair of boots or sneakers each
1 pair of walking jandals each
5 woolly hats
5 caps
5 pairs of sunglasses
5 desert goggles
5 face masks each
medical kit
sunscreen
water purification tablets and iodine
2 compasses
6 maps
1 cooker
2 fuel containers
1 pot
5 plates and cups
5 pairs of chopsticks
1 or 2 one-litre water bottles each or 1 camel-back
diary/book/pens
toiletries
17 power bars each
biscuits
dried fruit/scroggin
2 kg of rice
electric shaver
documentary and photography equipment:
2 video cameras
4 photo cameras, films and accessories
1 360-degree camera with swivel head
1 tripod

'Diarrhoea pills?' I continue, working down the long list of supplies.

'I have some special herbs,' the Italian says quietly. Diego focuses in closely on Paolo with the camera. Paolo resists looking for several seconds, then gives a cursory glance into the lens. He does not seem to care too much for being a star on film.

'Toothpaste and toothbrushes?'

'I think that's personal, Nath,' Kelvin responds.

'It's not personal,' Diego interjects from behind the lens. 'I don't want anyone on the expedition with bad breath.'

'We've got a question about rope and carabineers,' I inquire.

'I have rope,' the monk replies.

'Good, we are going to need it for the steep sections where one person climbs up first and then we can lift up the bags,' says Kelvin. He lifts his arms up and down pretending to lug the bags up a cliff, showing off his yellow Oakleys and a US$4 pair of green imitation North Face ski gloves I had bargained hard for at the Beijing silk markets.

'How much rope have you got?'

'It's not that long.'

'What, about 20 metres?' I nod encouragingly.

'Oh, it's about 10 feet.'

Kelvin cracks up in hysterics. 'What in the world are we getting ourselves into?'

First Westerners. (Well, perhaps the first ones to start.)

1 October 2000, National Day: People's Republic of China
Tian'anmen Square is alive with revelry. Like a jail-break gone wrong, white lights shine brightly across the gigantic concrete square. The fountains gush full-bore, surrounded by fake flowerbeds of grass and colourful petunias. Yet the most striking feature is the people. Millions of them, pouring through the streets like a highway of bustling ants.

It took humanity over 200,000 years to reach its first billion. We then went and multiplied this number six times over within the next 200 years. China has doubled her population to 1.3 billion in only the past forty years.

Beijing houses fourteen million, but for National Day it is engulfed by an extra eight million. Swept through the human tide, lifting the legs to let others do the walking, it doesn't take long to understand China's need to curb the procreative crescendo. Fines imposed for breaking the one-child rule average 10,000 *yuan* (US$1,250) and the loss of both parents' jobs. Harsh, given that the average peasant wage ranges around 300 *yuan* (US$37.50) a month. Yet the alternative is incomprehensible. China's history is marked by long periods of constraint littered with fleeting episodes of uncontrollable savagery.

Marco Polo (1254–1324) spoke of Dadu (the ancient Beijing, constructed between 1267 and 1292) as having a circumference of 24 miles (39 kilometres) and streets so wide and straight that it was possible to look along their entire length from one city gate to the other. Today Beijing has expanded to over 150 kilometres in circumference – an ugly urban sprawl of dreary grey apartment blocks. Bright neon lights struggle to give the city colour, but without any obvious city centre the concrete conglomerate lacks character.

The interweaving brick alleyways that once poured into Tian'anmen Square are now being demolished by the metal claws of modernity. You can still lose yourself amongst the winding maze of brick hamlets, but you'd have to start three streets back from the main highways to find them. Sheltered by ornately tiled roofs curled under rotting eaves, the arched courtyards are guarded by statues of welcoming lions. Filled with stone slabs, sprouting weeds and laughing children, these living relics are destined to be demolished for just another McDonald's. One hundred and seventy-six franchises already compete with local fruit-sellers on almost every corner.

An onslaught of flying bullets
Tore upon China's intellectual élite
Army man acts on curse of State
Blood and mind no longer meet.

Nathan Hoturoa Gray

Tian'anmen Square is a mile in perimeter; enough room to contain a million people and still have enough space to accommodate the Chinese army. It seems hard to believe, in the grandeur of colour and lights for China's celebration of Liberation, that this was also the scene of the deadly Tian'anmen Square massacre. One hundred and sixty-four pro-democratic students slaughtered by tanks (or so claims the official State tally) to enforce the might of the Communist State. Public rights to freedom of expression are still severely restricted; permission is needed from *danwei* work units to marry, have a baby or an abortion, go abroad, or even change apartments. All urban Chinese have separate files (*geren dang'an*) kept by local police.

Kitted out in our matching red jackets, the Great Wall team stands proudly near the base of the flagpole – a horde of Chinese tourists lining up to get their photos taken. The distinction that friendship with a foreigner bestows upon a local ensures a steady stream of clicking cameras. I imagine our faces spreading like the diaspora, adorning dusty mantlepieces throughout the continent. Yet how will our young faces look at the end of 4,000 kilometres? What in the world will we all be thinking?

Despite coming to China under the allure of fame and vanity, after an hour of continual photos I begin to tire of the superstar status, yearning for the quiet but smelly solitude of our underground hotel sewer.

4 October 2000, Beijing

The group has been in Beijing preparing for three weeks now. In this time Kelvin has befriended a Russian called Julia. Tall and slim, a figure well suited to the miniskirts she wears, she is a curly-haired brunette with brown eyes that, unlike those of most Russian women, don't look at you as if you are constantly doing something wrong. She speaks fluent Chinese and helps Kelvin with team preparations, in particular the buying of much-needed medical supplies, multi-vitamin tablets and a cellphone. Kelvin's eyes shine with the look of new love, gleefully leaving our dungeon cell each night for her plush US$700-a-month apartment.

Diego focuses on preparing his sponsors to organise film and camera equipment. He has secured a 360-degree camera and tripod from IPIX China to take photos, for which the company is going to set up a website en route. He has recently ended a two-year relationship in the United Kingdom to begin this journey and has little time to woo women at this stage.

Paolo is involved in a twelve-year relationship back in Italy, and Sumana isn't allowed women in his life full stop, so both go for walks around the block each day to prepare. They befriend two female university students, Maggie (Zaotijie) and Peggie, to pass the time.

I, too, have met a woman. She is from Kazakhstan, with Asian features and long dark hair. Speaking Russian and English, I accompany Bayan and her sister for a day's visit at the Temple of Heaven, but there is little time to take the friendship much further, as I have to focus most of my time on meeting up with bilingual Chinese to practise the language. At each encounter I write down phonetic explanations for key phrases I think will be necessary for our survival in the desert. English will no longer be an option once we get out onto the Wall. Sumana already speaks some Chinese from living in South China, and Diego has a few words and phrases from his three months spent in the south-western province of Yunnan, but really we are heading out linguistically skimp.

'Many of us do not have proper jobs. We sit and do nothing. Watch pool, chain-smoke, wander about the streets aimless and asleep—many thousands of us. But material incentive is changing all this,' Zhong Wan informs. He is a recent English graduate dressed in an oversized brown suit resembling a Salvation Army hand-me-down. 'The State likes capitalism now, it is loosening its grip on industry, which is fostering competition.'

I look around at the variety of free-market stores lying about on the pavement, selling every imaginable amenity. Cups, fruit, fans, clothes, bird cages, batteries, pots and pans, you name it, they sell it. It reminds me of an eighty-five-year-old woman in Moscow sitting on the pavement selling a pound of butter, a packet of cigarettes and a tin of tuna – her only way of making a living in a transforming Eastern system that embraces capitalism but does not yet have the distribution or infrastructure to adequately cater for the changeover.

Zhong Wan continues, 'The government allows us to get licences to sell goods. If you don't have contacts, though, it's hard to get. Nepotism and corruption are rampant in the cities. The police confiscate our goods if we try to sell them on the street without a licence. That's the worst – when some young boy in army uniform takes away what you have been building up in sale and trade over the past week.' He looks down to his feet, forlorn. 'It's hard not to get emotional. Money is all that is on our people's minds in the cities. Buy this, buy that. Foreigners come for the cheap prices and our people want to be like them.'

I glance across the street to the seven-storey supermarket made of green-tinted glass. The employees, dressed in blue uniforms, are set out in two straight lines outside. Classical music blares out from loudspeakers as they start their star-jump exercises to get their daily exercise and attract clientele. The supermarkets are expensive compared with the local pavement markets on the opposite side of the road, but, like an exercise gym, once the doors are open they are soon packed with obsessed shoppers.

'The State provides holidays especially designed to buy,' Zhong Wan informs. 'The attendants are now receiving commissions on top of their salaries.' He looks to the small stash of curios he intends to sell at the Temple of Heaven later that day. 'We have been locked in our world of closed doors and rigid rules for so long. Everyone now wants to imitate the ways of the West.'

'Imitate?' I reply, 'I don't know whether China will necessarily like this trail. It strikes me as a place better suited to the needs of the community.'

'It's better than Communism. Look where that got us. Millions dead, everyone stagnant – except a privileged few. Now we've all got a chance. Maybe not equal, but at least it's up to you.'

Zhong flicks through the pages of my Chinese phrasebook with well-rehearsed discipline. The Chinese are masters of detail. Whether fine brushwork or methodically laying out their fruit, nothing goes amiss. He flicks through the pages with mesmerising speed to find the more difficult words he wants to use to forge his sentences.

'How did you learn your English?' I ask.

'Like this. From books, although I try to practise with all foreigners I come across. Language proficiency is vital for job opportunities in all the bigger cities, especially with China's entry into the WTO.'

'What is going to be the impact of all that?'

'There is a different sense of urgency and personal motivation now. Many used to have jobs that forced them to come to the office but gave them little to do. Now with initiative rewarded, it's not just the fear of the breadline that motivates. Everyone's eyes are hardening as competition fosters, especially when there's money to be made.' He pauses. 'I can't wait on structural policy changes from the IMF, WTO or Chinese State to come to my aid. In the new China, it's every man for himself . . .'

Relinquishing our friends, women and the big-city comforts of Beijing's hustle and bustle, we set out in pursuit of exploration, freedom and adventure, casting our lives into the hands of the most encompassing lady of them all: Mother Earth. It is time to catch the two-day train ride out to Jiayuguan: the Western Terminal, and official starting point of the Great Chinese Wall.

MOON 3

JIAYUGUAN TO WHO KNOWS WHERE?

Two days sitting on a hard-seat train
Cramping buttocks, back's in pain.
Carriage packed – sleep on grimy floor,
Phlegm and ash, white paper slippers.

Swapping seats, culture and cuisine –
The carriage spirit lives and thrives
Chinese, Mongolian, a six-fingered Pakistani
Turkish belly dancers, and the Western five

Ongoing flux of Chinese townships
Peasants trade apples through train windows
Rice-tiered mountains, lush green vales
Ancient rivers flow through time.

Night takes over and come the day
Vegetation subsides to dusty plain
Chinese man sleeps on washing-room basin
Four hours by plane, two days by train

How long will it take to traverse the Wall on foot?
                                             Nathan Hoturoa Gray

PROVINCE ONE: GANSU
10 October 2000
I stand upon Mount Jiayuguan, a mountain of obsidian driven
up by the rage from within the Mother's crust. Moulded by
time, four Buddhist shrines sit upon her dark protruding peaks.
Delicately crafted with conical roofs, these shrines are a haven

for transcendental meditation. Legend has it that all souls come here to ascend to the next dimension – the Pass unto Heaven. Jiayuguan, 300 kilometres east of the Jade Gate, is also the ancient merchant's entry point into the settled territories of China. If legend and history merge true, my body lies at the ancient silk route thoroughfare into China, my soul at the gateway to the afterworld. I feel like I am in heaven. It is so peaceful and serene. A plateau of pale brown sand lies to the west and north. Waiting in stillness, it stretches far beyond the horizon, exulting in my insignificance.

Only the sound of a distant tractor disturbs this vast sense of quiet. A cool mountain wind communes with my cheeks. I'm having no problems being right here – although to reach this sense of present-moment heaven has been a mental marathon. Two months of worry over the journey that lies ahead have enlarged my spleen and yellowed my eyes. Although life journeys are generally so much longer, I'd chosen to construe these next 4,000 kilometres as a death-row sentence. Precise date of execution: unknown.

To my south lie the Himalayas. Coated in armour of eternal white, at almost 7,000 metres, Qilian Shan towers like a polar bear on hind legs. One hundred and fifty million years ago the udder of India charged in from the oceans, tectonically colliding with Asia to forge the Tibetan plateau. The rooftop of the world halts the Gobi's advance south and provides the backdrop to where the Great Wall will trail.

Tiny in comparison, Jiayuguan Fort lies peacefully in a desert basin. At 6,000 feet above sea level, the fort is known as the soul of the Wall. Stretching 600 by 400 metres, its camel-coloured walls are segmented with 17-metre-high watchtowers. Sumana says the man behind the fort's construction was known as the Iron Abacus. In the middle of the third century BC, the rulers of the Qin Empire tested the architect's reputation as a mathematical genius by asking him to predict how many bricks it would take to build the 36,000-square-metre fortress. If he got it right, he would live. Scripting his calculations onto an obelisk, he signed his family seal so that later generations would know that this stronghold was the product of his mathematical mind. Thirty-six years later when the fort was completed in 214 BC, the bricks were counted. Iron Abacus had got the calculations exactly right.

Merchant caravans travelling the silk route from the West into China would roar in delight at the sight of this fortress. To them the site of Jiayuguan meant they had made it, meant they had successfully navigated the endless dunes of the Taklimakan Depression and re-entered the realm of civilisation.

Vibrant market towns flourished at this safe and busy gate, settled and cultivated during the Han Dynasty. Traders heading to the settled territories dealt in jade, gold, spices, horses, precious gems and silk. Named by the German explorer Richthofen in the nineteenth century, the Silk Road became an artery for the dispersion of trade, knowledge, culture and religion between West and East; in particular dissemination of belief systems such as Buddhism emigrating from the kingdoms of the Himalaya.

The fort's entry arch is named the Gateway to Enlightenment; the exit, the Gateway to Reconciliation – otherwise known as the Gate of the Bravest People in the World. Kelvin, Diego and I left this gate on a 15-kilometre walking warm-up across the plateau to meet the others where the first reconstructed section of Great Wall lies at the top of Mount Jiayuguan's slopes. While it costs 8 *yuan* (US$1) for the entry ticket, the original builders were paid 1 *fen* for each brick they lugged up the steep slopes. With 10 *fen* equalling 1 *mao*, and 10 *mao* equaling 1 *yuan*, 800 bricks needed to be placed to afford today's entry fee. Great value if this ticket was to be valid for the entire 4,000 kilometres.

The first watchtower of the planet's largest open-air museum lies on Mount Jiayuguan's crest. Perfectly manicured with sandstone brick, it contains eight arched windows overlooking the major compass points. Intricate Chinese characters are inscribed on the archway like Elven runes.

Twelve brick turrets
Moulded like a Crown.
The tip of the Dragon's tail
Stands regal and proud.

An ancient archway
Glistening Gobi gold
Like a Dungeon doorway
To tales yet untold.

The spiky tail ambles
Down the mountain's thigh
Out into the desert
Splintered innards soon to die.

And so begins its journey
From the desert to the sea.
Bricks, geography and history
Four crazy men and me.

Nathan Hoturoa Gray

The reconstructed Wall slithers down the mountain's ridge out into the grey plains for about 2 kilometres before disappearing like a worm into the sand. Gone. A small village lies below the pass surrounded by green and yellow poplar trees. I take out the first of five US aviation maps purchased in London for the journey. It unfolds like a picnic mat, 3 by 4 feet in perimeter, the cartographic ratio 5 kilometres to an inch. The village is unmarked, but remnants of ancient Great Wall are marked out further to the north-east. Despite my high-altitude vantage point, I can't see any trace.

The empty horizon inspires. It feels strangely normal to just go out and walk into that sandy expanse. 'I'm going all the way – all the way to the ocean,' I whisper my commitment to the silence of the desert. Suddenly a glint of sunlight catches my eye on a rocky outcrop far to the north. A shiver runs up my spine and I know intuitively this is the direction to head. A *tohu* my ancestors would have awaited before embarking on their sea or land migrations. Standing before the dark archway of the Wall's first tower, the womb of the journey, I take a deep breath and plant the first step. The tower leads through to a brick staircase down towards the mountain's base. It feels good to be heading somewhere.

'What should we do now?' Kelvin asks, lying with his back slumped against the tourist ticket office, basking in the sun.

'I dunno,' says Diego, who is sitting with his elbows on his knees.

'Maybe we should head back to the hotel in Jiayuguan city?' Sumana contributes, glancing hopefully towards Paolo. 'We could stay another night and leave tomorrow?'

Paolo doesn't respond, caught in his own world of thoughts.

'We head this way,' I exclaim, pointing towards the direction of the flash. I pick up my blue backpack, hastily strap it on, and make ready to set off. The rest take their cue and we enter the embrace of the Gobi.

> *Now it turns to the dream.*
> *But that is purely the direction.*
> *It's the multitude of steps and acts.*
> *The actual quest that makes the person.*
>
> Nathan Hoturoa Gray

DAY 1 FROM WEST TO EAST TOWARDS ENLIGHTENMENT
We are starting our journey today – as if it is our only day.
Indian pilgrimage saying

The late-afternoon heat rises off the brown dusty plains that are the Gobi. The sun shines from behind Jiayuguan Pass, a wispy cloud clinging to the peak. It knows full well where its life is most safe. Despite the smattering of snow that had spilled from the peak's bosom that frosty morning, the sun has scored an inevitable victory. It has turned out a desert scorcher.

Down in the world where the humans dwell, a tribe of five, born from all the continents except pioneering Africa, set off in a flurry from the mountain's base, escaping the creeping shadow. The sun dips behind the range to spread its light to the distant lands of the West. Walking east, following the planet's rotation, we will meet the sun again in due course.

A cool desert wind suddenly sweeps over the plain: the solar exhale before the in-breath of night. The cloud releases itself from the mountain's neck and filters outwards into the cooling plains. The setting sun stains the cloud's soft flesh red as it rises high above its dominion and, in a trick of light, the cloud seems to take on the shape of a dragon. Nature is making a powerful statement. The tiny band has commenced its walk along the Great Wall during none other than the Year of the Dragon. The visionary idea, forged by the Buddhist monk one Chinese calendar cycle prior, is today, 10 October 2000, finally being played out. A hue of gold fills the cloud creature's chest. It seems we have chosen well for the journey to take flight.

'Kiwis, look at me!' Sumana bursts out with glee, his small legs powering through the desert like a laden stegosaurus. He is taking two steps to our one.

'Sumana's walking like a man possessed,' I observe to Diego.

'Yes, there's something energising about actually starting.' He pauses. 'We are joined together by a mutual desire.'

'A desire? For what?'

'The desire to arrive.'

Diego's blue and green backpack stretches well over his neck, and, with his dark curly hair and beard, he looks like the Greek Titan Atlas. His pack, almost twice the size of Sumana's, is set comfortably into his posterior. Driven by our ambition we rapidly claim those first few kilometres with little thought to where we are actually heading. The reconstructed Wall soon disappears and we walk along an ancient river-bed following a dusty road. Wilting green scrub flanks the sides, covered in dust. A passing peasant approaches and gives us a handful of pears.

'Water covered in skin.' Kelvin bites into the lush yellow flesh. His eyes close in bliss, the sweet taste soothing his dry throat, which is suffering from the aftertaste of an early-morning dry retch. Walking passionately through the desert, no one would guess that we are both suffering from a chronic bout of food poisoning. Outside her wooden temple hut at the base of Jiayuguan Pass, a Buddhist nun had offered us a plate of thinly-sliced potatoes to share at the end of our warm-up walk. The *tudou si* was laced with red chilli. It tasted hellishly spicy, branding the throat and warming the stomach. Precisely at 3am, Kelvin got up from his tent and gave an almighty groan before spewing up the generous offering in front of the monastery grounds. Sidestepping his leftovers I hastily rushed to the toilet, bowels ready to explode with liquid diarrhoea.

Ahhh yes . . . the Chinese toilet. No getting out of bed, laying your thighs on a comfortably moulded porcelain frame and sitting back to ponder your daily schedule. No toilet paper conveniently placed for the outstretched hand, religiously replaced by an ever-vigilant mum. And, of course, no plastic button to cleanse away those past worries for good . . .

No, first you have to think in your tent about which clothes you are going to put on to combat the below-zero cold. Which pocket contains the toilet paper, and which pocket contains the torch. This must be considered carefully, for any mental stress excites the bowels, leading to the sort of false start that no one in this waterless world wants to be a part of – particularly a supporting role. Clenching your bum muscles, you then carefully check your walking boots for scorpions, then hobble bung-legged to a hole reeking of maggot-infested excrement and covered by two thin icy planks . . .

Emptying my bowels with a liquid splatter, I had used my toilet paper sparingly, hoping this first inauspicious evening was not a sign of things to come. Yet given the consistent outbursts over the past three weeks, our bodies still acclimatising to the alien Chinese oils, this would seem to be more or less the norm for the remaining billion or so steps.

We walk happily. No pains or aches, just enjoying the wide open horizon as we head for the rocky outcrop that had shone from the top of Jiayuguan Pass. It turns out to be a man-made reservoir. Three makeshift canvas tents have been set up by a group of irrigation workers. One tent has its flaps open and is set up as a kitchen. Stirring noodles in a blackened wok, the cook looks up with surprise. He smiles the nicest, most welcoming smile, and waves us towards his open fire – gesturing to share in a meal.

We have arrived.

The workers are dressed in white and grey overalls. After placing the last of the concrete irrigation pipes, they circle around the makeshift kitchen to see all the commotion. Everyone is laughing and smiling, our surprise visit a highlight to their daily labour. The smell of greasy noodles entices my starving stomach. It is amazing to think we had set out into the absolute unknown with little more than simple faith and now a wholesome meal awaits.

Sumana giggles joyously, his hands perched below his paunch. 'If you're willing and eager, the gods will join in!'

Paolo follows him silently to fill up his plate. Kelvin, Diego and I have to first set up our two tents, the second of which we haven't yet tested. We need to learn how to pitch it before darkness falls. I feel relieved when both tents are up, but by the time we are finished we are out of luck with the food.

'Oh well, the trusty old power bar,' Kelvin jokes with a hint of resignation. He reaches into his giant grey pack to eat one of his twenty-seven power bars that Sumana has supplied for our journey. Although it seems an apt punishment for our pre-expedition laziness, I am feeling bitter. Neither Sumana nor Paolo has thought to save us any food. I hungrily deliver my first team lecture.

'From now on in, if anyone gets food, it has got to be shared!'

Day 2

The night is cold. The city lights of Jiayuguan flicker like ⌐ lanterns and a three-quarter moon casts a chalky glow over ti. desolate land. There are four tents in the five-man group. Kelvin and I share a two-man tent. Diego and Paolo each have their own two-man tents, and Sumana uses a one-man bivouac. We all settle in and drift off to sleep – or so I presume. None of us has realised that Sumana lies in his bivouac without getting into his sleeping bag. As the temperature plummets below zero, Sumana begins to freeze. He neglects to wake any of us up to ask for help, and Diego finds him the next morning shivering on a straw mattress in the Chinese workers' tent.

'It never got this cold in Malaysia at night,' the monk trembles, his face blue, the skin dry and cracked. Peering over his blanket like a frightened child, large black wrinkles below his eyes make him look like he has aged a decade overnight.

'Don't worry, Sumana, no one ever forgets their first night out in the desert,' Diego soothes, passing across a cup of hot water.

'Make sure you wake one of us up to ask us for help next time,' I assert. We leave him to rest and inform the others about what has happened while we set about packing up.

'He'll learn,' Paolo says sternly, not bothering to enter the tent and give Sumana any words of encouragement. His attitude surprises me. The two of them had come to Beijing from Italy together, spent the first month in the same hotel during preparations, and headed out on the same sleeper carriage in the train. I thought they were close friends.

'Give me Sumana's medi-kit,' Kelvin contributes. 'I'll carry that to help him out.'

He packs a full-sized biscuit tin into his grey pack which now looks like a concrete block.

'Why are you requesting extra weight?' I ask, massaging my lower back. My pack is thick with Diego's documentary equipment and his tent, as well as my own video-camera gear. Diego had hoped I would leave all my camera gear back in

Beijing to save room for his, but the morning before leaving I called my sister in New Zealand and she said I would be mad not to take out my own gear.

'I'm just trying to make this expedition work, Nathan,' Kelvin rebukes. 'Besides,' he pauses, strapping on his pack and heaving his chest, 'I'm the team workhorse.' Both Diego and Kelvin were very proud when their packs weighed in at 33 and 30 kilograms respectively, especially when mine only came in at 28 kilograms, and Paolo's and Sumana's less than twenty-five.

'I suppose you're right,' I sigh. 'But we haven't yet agreed upon the sharing of profits should the documentary be successful.' I turn to address Diego. 'What's the story with the documentary profits?'

'What do you mean?'

'They should be shared evenly, right? It's only fair.'

'Not so. I have done most of the preparation for this journey, and invested much of my own time and money. There is no way that profits, should there be any, can be spread evenly.'

'But we're helping carry your gear.'

'Some of us are coming to the Wall for work. Others are coming to be just simple walkers. I am here to work, and have to make a living from this to fund future expeditions. Now shut up and don't complain, you wouldn't even be on this journey if I had not invited you.'

I am silenced by my timidity.

Kelvin fills the silence. 'Think about it Nah, five diverse cultures coming together to walk the Great Chinese Wall during none other than the Millennium!' Before we set off Kelvin had passed two of his three greenstones onto Diego and me as a gesture of friendship.

'Don't be so naïve,' Paolo scowls. 'There is no team. There are just five individuals who all happen to want the same thing. That is all.'

Diego and Kelvin glance at each other in disgust.

The word 'Gobi' means gravel and rock debris. It denotes all the deserts and semi-deserts of the vast Mongolian plateau stretching across China. Scientists believe the Gobi Desert was once a sea. A dark red sun rises above the reservoir, laying a cloak of light over the cold, hard earth. The water dances in patterns of chaotic perfection, orchestrated by a chilly desert breeze. The jubilee of light lifts everyone's spirits, mirroring our excitement at finding the Great Wall again. Even Sumana is returning to his normal positive temperature as I help place on his green pack and tighten the stomach straps which he struggles to do for himself.

I head off in the lead, the others trailing close behind. We cross past the reservoir and head along a gravel path straight into the empty desert. Twenty minutes later, Paolo joins me up front.

'Do you actually know where you are going?'

I shrug off his question, walking a little faster. Without a global positioning system, and with Sumana and Diego holding the compasses, it is difficult to calculate exactly where we are on the maps. I also do not want to admit that I am simply following the whim of my intuition. Kelvin has already scolded me that 'signs' were the work of the Devil.

'Where are we heading?'

'I'm not that sure, to be honest, but the way we are going definitely feels right.'

He seems content with my answer. Perhaps it has enough self-belief in it. We walk together in silence, heading towards a small rise in the land.

'Wow!' I gasp, stopping in my tracks.

A ragged spine of baked mud rolls deep into an open valley and onwards into the horizon. A shiver runs up my back, the same feeling I had when accidentally coming across the Coliseum in Rome. It's as if the Wall has a presence – an emblem of uncountable lives. As if waiting with an ancient patience for visitors, its presence feels strangely comfortable. I put away the maps and trust in its silent allure. The long, winding serpent heads deeper into the desert.

The oldest section of the Great Wall was begun in 221 BC not long after China was unified into an empire from a loose configuration of warring feudal states between 475–221 BC. The first Chinese Emperor, Qin Shi, restored the ruins of older walls and linked them with new construction to create a 4,000-kilometre-long fortification meant to protect China's northern frontiers against marauding nomads. Obsessed with the idea of immortality, the emperor was also responsible for building the underground tombs that held the 7,000 terracotta warriors. Guarding his body, it was believed they would accompany him on his next journey. The Immortality Dynasty lasted only fifteen years, but set in motion a course of events that were to shape history through to the present day.

After the collapse of the Qin Empire, China went back to chaos. Suffering from years of neglect, Qin Shi's Great Wall started to fall apart, and China fell to the mercy of fierce outsiders known as the Xiongnu. In 206 BC, a new dynasty, the Han, rose to power and began to move the empire in a new, more open direction. The Han Dynasty was like the European Renaissance, restoring much of China's classic literature, especially the works of Confucius. It also established a strong but more humane central government, set up the first public school system and, in a struggle that lasted nearly seventy years, crushed the Xiongnu menace once and for all.

With this victory by the Han emperor Wudi, a westward expansion into the wilderness of Central Asia saw China's second great campaign of wall-building. His engineers restored the crumbling Qin Wall and extended it 450 kilometres across the forbidding Gobi Desert. As the Wall made its way across the Chinese wilderness (calculated at the rate of a metre a day), its builders were forced to rely on local materials. Much of the Qin Wall was built with dry-laid native stone. Where stone was scarce, however, engineers built the wall from layers of compacted earth. The tamped-earth process began with a simple wooden frame, workers filling the frame with a bed of red willow reeds, loose earth, water and gravel. This was repeatedly tamped solid into a compact layer, a painstaking ten centimetres at a time.

We stop at midday in an abandoned concrete shelter. It is over 30 degrees and it is too hot to walk comfortably. Paolo lays out the petrol cooker ready to impress us with his culinary expertise. With an effeminate meticulousness, he delicately prepares the rice and cuts up the potatoes. Misreading the instructions on the already sketchy-looking silver space-wrapped cooking sauce, Paolo overdoses on the ingredients – four times the norm. He creates a revolting brown sludge, but desperate to eat we hungrily delve in.

'Yuck, this tastes like chlorine,' Sumana complains.

'I refuse to eat this,' Kelvin states, putting his plate to the side and giving Paolo a long stare. The rest of us continue morosely. Ten minutes later the concrete shelter is a disaster site, bodies scattering in all directions to evacuate their running bowels. I just get to my bunker and pull my pants down in time. One squirt comes out black, the other mournfully yellow.

'Never again,' I quietly swear. If only this could be the case.

Paolo, on first impressions, is a quiet and passive individual, unlike most Italians I know. Most of the time he thinks about things while walking on his own. I decide to spend the rest of the afternoon accompanying him.

'What do you know about time?' he asks.

'Time?' I repeat, as I think about an appropriate answer. Indeed, with the Wall parading into the horizon, there is certainly no rush. I reflect on being told once how young children need to be taught to construct time in terms of a chronological sequence of memories. Why the clock hand goes around right rather than left – purely a product of human manufacturing. 'It's a humanly-made construct to enable society to better function.'

'Do you think that the eighty-year lifespan of a human, the seven days of a butterfly and the thousands of years of a mountain are, from their individual perspectives, exactly the same?'

'What do you mean?'

'Molecules in your body live for a very short period. Seconds often, yet they are capable of processing food into energy and transferring it all over your body. Surely a millisecond is like what, say, a year is to a human being when you compare what it can achieve in its minute lifespan?'

'I'd never thought of that,' I reply, scratching my head. 'I suppose you're right.'

'Do you know about the power of mental manifestation?'

'Isn't that visualising some outcome and then asking the universe for it?'

'Yes, kind of. Why don't we set our imaginations to the test?'

'Ah, okay . . .' I reply sceptically.

'What is it that you would really like?'

'Well . . . I'd really like another roll of toilet paper.'

'What would you like to eat tonight?'

'Ummmm . . . anything really, as long as it's not that stuff you cooked us for lunch.'

'Think of something we don't yet have.'

'Okay, *chaomian*, *mantou*, *pinguo*, and *binggan*.' I concoct a smorgasbord of all the possible Chinese delights my limited vocabulary has grasped since being in China – noodles, bread, apples and biscuits. We walk on in alimentary hope.

The desert turns golden as the sun heads towards the horizon. Sumana is at least a mile behind, a tiny red peanut M&M almost ready to melt in the desert haze.

'Wait here for Sumana, Nah. We'll go and find us some lodgings,' Kelvin requests, pointing towards a small village about twenty minutes' walk away. 'One of us needs to stay behind him from now on.'

'I agree, we can't let him get so far behind, especially after last night,' Diego replies, his hands placed on his hips. He pauses. 'Sumana's stomach is going to have to go through some sort of a religious transformation if he is to complete this journey.' He smirks as they both head off.

Twenty minutes later, Sumana wanders wearily past.

'Ahhhh . . . I'm so exhausted,' he gasps, 'but I suppose it's going to save me on liposuction.'

'Breathe through your nose, Sumana, and push your stomach out as you take in the air: it will give you your breath back faster.' There is no doubting it though. The forty-eight-year-old is a living legend.

The clay construction we have been following crashes into the small Chinese village and disappears altogether. Apparently having little respect for the Wall, the peasants have ravished its entrails to build up their small clay cottages. We store our packs in the front porch of one of the local homes, which is piled high with red onion bags. The owner is an old man and has room for one, charging Sumana 10 *kuai* (*yuan*; US$1.25) to stay the night. Diego is off looking for a place to stay, so Kelvin, Paolo and I set off through the village in search of food.

'You go and ask at that house, Kelvin and I will look further down the street,' Paolo suggests, the two of them disappearing down the dusty road.

Sometimes quite shy, I don't particularly like the challenge of asking complete strangers for shelter and food, rarely having done so in the West. Imagine walking from Wellington airport to Cannon's Creek in Porirua one day, waltzing up to one of the State-sponsored homes and asking for something to eat? Hunger, however, propels me through the front gate.

The courtyard is filled with metallic junk and scattered corn seed. An old man in a blue Mao suit is sitting at a table and loudly slurping noodles.

I call out tentatively, '*Ni hao?*'

He does not reply.

'*Ni hao!*' I call again, louder.

Still no reply. After the third time with no response, I gather he is deaf. Stepping through the courtyard I stand before him. He looks up in absolute fright and starts to moan incoherently. He can't possibly have seen a white person before. I feel like a haunting spectre. Three young men come running from the house. They, too, are shocked initially, but their faces soon transform to amusement.

'*Wo shi xinxilan ren. Wo zou chang cheng. Wo yao chifan he difang zhu.*' I carefully enunciate that I am from New Zealand, walking the Wall, and require food and shelter. I have been practising for this big moment now for almost three weeks. The men look back blankly. I repeat the phrase, nodding expectantly. The men still say nothing, blinking silently. With four tones to each spoken word, I may as well have been speaking Hindi. My communication is about as competent as my toiletry. Giving up on the linguistics, I place my left hand on my paunch and make eating and sleeping gestures before passing across a card which has the request written in Chinese. They all nod their heads and invite me in.

I sit down at a table in their lounge. The floors are concrete, the walls painted white with a poster of lotuses. The dominant feature is a black-and-white television with hazy reception playing in the corner. A dirty jam jar full of used tea leaves is placed in front of me and is filled from a green thermos of boiling water. I take a sip. The steaming hot water stings my parched lips, yet surprisingly quenches my thirst. It has the same effect on my throat as guzzling down a gulp of ice-cool water.

Another Chinese man appears. He passes me an apple and a packet of biscuits – just as I'd mentally requested with Paolo in the desert. It feels weird being given food by complete strangers, totally unconditionally, expecting nothing in return. Effectively I am begging. However, it doesn't feel like it. Living off the culture rather than transacting to participate gives me a sense of being connected to a higher sense of kinship. Like a saddhu's pilgrimage, reliant on the generosity of others to survive, giving, it seems, is the basis of the desert people's psychology. It bodes well for the journey.

The men sit around, passing cigarettes amongst themselves, crouched over and staring curiously as I eat. Uncultured in a conventional Western sense – as a bowl of steaming noodles is brought to the table accompanied by a chorus of smiles designed to make even the most outlandish stranger feel welcome – they are certainly no less civilised.

My nostrils flare, taste buds drooling over the divine concoction of fresh white spaghetti salted with spices. Without ceremony I begin to gorge like a starving animal, my first proper meal since the spicy potatoes two nights prior.

'Five-star treatment for the sneaky Grayboy,' Kelvin sniggers, his face widening into a brimming smile. Suspicious at my absence, Paolo and Kelvin have retraced my lucky footsteps and entered the house. I look up from my steaming bowl with both mischievousness and guilt. I haven't forgotten my food-sharing lecture of the night before. Yet it just seems that I would be offending my new-found friends to take off for five minutes, go and grab four others and expect the same treatment. Far simpler to just ignore these considerations and keep on stuffing my hungry face.

The Chinese family immediately embraces the two additional whiteys. Seated on wooden stools, we are presented with a mountainous buffet of noodles, tea, apples, biscuits and bread. I wonder whether the same treatment would be afforded to other Chinese travellers.

Friends of the house owner push through the bead curtain into the dining room as word of our presence slowly trickles through the village. Five new pairs of curious eyes appear, eyeing the house owner proudly for supplying the year's best entertainment.

Our hosts are itching to engage. Kelvin takes out a photo of his son. They look upon the bright-eyed, curly-haired boy with love. The peasants' lives revolve around family, its moral structure providing the foundation for communal unity, caring and nurturing. It creates a viable system for sharing the limited resources. Perhaps this is why they make us feel so welcome, given we are so far from our loved ones.

I take out a photo of my family. My proud parents surrounded by their five children: three boys, and two girls.

'Are these two women your brothers' wives?' The astonished hosts point to the photo then to their wedding-ring fingers.

'*Mama, baba, gege, jiejie. Wo de shuangbao tai.*' Mother, father, older brother, sisters. And my twin. I reply pointing to each member in the portrait.

'*Wu ge haizi?!*' Five children?! they state with a mix of excitement and envy.

'I am not yet ready to marry,' I explain, pointing to the absence of a ring.

'*Ni you dou da?*' How old are you?

'*Ershi liu.*' Twenty-six.

Our hosts are again surprised. Chinese males are usually married with their first child by twenty-four, women at twenty. It is a sign of good virtue and character to have your own family at this age, as you are focusing your energies on the next generation rather than solely on yourself. The word for 'good' in Chinese is a combination of *nü* (women) and *zi* (child) to give *hao* (good).

Kelvin begins to play Chinese chess with the old man of the house.

'No, no, no, no . . .' the Chinese laugh as Kelvin makes an illegal move. The game is incredibly complex, pieces shaped like draughts with a different character etched in red or black on the top. The board has a series of horizontal, vertical and diagonal lines. We move on to a more simple game of strip poker, soon learning the wiles of the cunning Chinese poker face. I lose many rounds early on because of their ability to hide their emotion. Yet in the same vein they seem to have an enhanced capability to read mine, as if reading my mind. It seems a necessary skill to master given I don't know how to properly communicate.

Two days into our excursion eastwards we are already learning about the benefits of stripping down on our material items. We have already offloaded a box of gear at the post office in Jiayuguan before setting off, pots and pans and the electric razor the first victims, and are already thinking about what can go next. Our presence, however, seems to have the opposite effect on the Chinese, in particular the way they wistfully look upon our modern backpacks, cameras and watches. As they say in science, you can't measure something without altering it. I only hope our Western presence won't transform them too much, especially towards a hoarding mindset or one that is fearful of losing one's material accumulations. As another cup of tea and biscuits are brought around, it seems unlikely in these remote lands that this will be the case.

Day 3

We set off early to the farewells of the whole village, families lining up with their kids to wave us off. Hospitality is only ever going to be a series of one-day affairs.

'Which way do we head, Nah?' Kelvin shouts from down the dusty street. There is no Wall visible outside the village. A Chinese boy guides us through the next village and out into the wide open grasslands. Green swampy lakes dot the landscape – homes to ducks, stilts and herons. The depression in the desert accesses subterranean water passages stored up from rains over 10,000 years prior when the land was green and lush during the Ice Ages. Countries like Libya have already begun to drill these underground lakes, pumping the water 3,200 kilometres north through subway-sized pipes to Tripoli. Given that only scant amounts are annually replenished in the current climate, such resources are soon exhaustible.

Behind the swamps lie the fingers of the desert – pestering life like a provocative bully. Our guide leads us along a dusty wagon trail heading through dry tussock. Kids walk to school, and an aged peasant approaches.

'*Chang cheng ʒai nali?*' Where is the Great Wall? Diego mimes, raising his arms high above his shoulders.

'*Ni ʒhen ʒai ʒou chang cheng,*' the peasant replies, pointing to the road we are using.

Spurred on by the scenery, I walk well ahead of the others. Diego is about 50 metres behind, and Sumana is again out of sight. Misjudging a step, I slip on a dent in the road and roll all 28 kilograms of my pack onto my right ankle.

'Ahhhh!' I wince, falling down in agony. The swelling is immediate, the foot thickening against my boots. It is the same foot that received a similar injury a month earlier, rendering me immobile for five days.

'Bugger, I'm out . . . and it's only the third day,' I curse as nausea sets in. Everything seemed so rosy the past three days. My fears of tackling the Wall have been faced and I am enjoying every step and looking forward to the millions that lie out in front. It has never even occurred to me that something like this could happen and ruin the Great Wall party – for everyone. I take off my boots and socks, elevating my injured ankle on top of my blue pack.

Ten minutes later, Sumana joins us. Head down, languidly pacing, he looks up to see my demise and a look of pure glee sweeps across his face.

'Goody, goody, now we can all slow down and Nathan can be the last.' He can hardly contain his excitement. 'Stay positive, it's all part of the faith healing,' Sumana continues in a more serious tone, taking off his pack and sitting at my side. Rubbing his hands earnestly, he applies them to my foot, his warm fingers moving with dexterity as he massages the side of the ankle. His movements look painful, pressing the swelling out towards the heel of my foot, but surprisingly, considering the tenderness of the recent injury, I feel very little pain.

Meanwhile Kelvin sets off to the nearest reservoir to fetch some cold water, then carries my pack to a convenient stopping point and comes back for his own. Paolo gives me his walking stick whilst Diego films the whole episode. Adversity, it seems, is bringing the group closer together.

'There, take three Panadol,' Sumana suggests, passing the tablets across when he's finished.

Miraculously I am able to stand up on my feet with the help of the walking stick within twenty minutes. Within an hour I am able to lift my heavy pack again and keep walking.

'The injury is a warning, Nathan,' Diego asserts in a soft but serious tone. 'Don't rush ahead.'

Hobbling slightly, taking up the rear, I revel in the view of the other four braving the journey. Kelvin is in the lead, scouting out the trail like a ranger. A gaggle of ducks waddles out across his path and he turns around to laugh. Diego is next, an illusionist capturing Mainland life with his metal contraptions. Paolo, with his back straight in a stoic walking posture, is like a paladin, forging his future with his philosophical musings, and Sumana, the robed Buddhist monk with the ability to heal.

The land rises 20 metres to the normal level of the desert, the depression ending along with its soothing clear waters. A watchtower lies before a plateau of hard, packed gravel. Engulfed by the shifting tides of windswept sand, the Wall in these parts has long since perished. Nature renders no favourites when claiming back what's rightfully hers. A second watchtower lies on a small rise in the distant horizon. Wolf dung was burned to create the smoke signals that passed on military messages between towers as to invaders' whereabouts. The Chinese were able to communicate messages for hundreds of miles in only a matter of hours. These cellphones of the ancients are now our only guides across China.

A temple lies to the south behind a line of trees.

'This is a Buddhist temple – I checked it with my binocs!' Sumana exclaims. 'Let's rest here for the night.'

Upon arrival we actually find an Islamic mosque, its golden dome sparkling in the sun. Islam spreads her wings far across the plains of Central Asia, small concentrated pockets surviving deep into Han Chinese territory despite rampant Chinese secularism and the destruction of religious practice during the Cultural Revolution. Most of the Buddhist, Confucian and Taoist temples have been destroyed, but with the departure of Mao their inhabitants are slowly restoring their old temples.

Sumana enters the courtyard. He speaks some words in Chinese to the temple's keeper, who nods his head while tying two small white dogs to a tree.

'I told him that I am an Islamic priest. He believed me and is going to invite us in. That is the way, you know.'

The temple owner grins – a smile that would delight my dentist. Two rows of black, crooked teeth, rotted deep into their roots with a front tooth missing. His white Islamic skullcap emphasises his oval head. His grey hair and face wrinkles show the experience of hard-earned age, but his spirit is young – his cheeks etched permanently upwards as if blessed with continuing delight. Flanked by long sultry ears, he possesses a long, generous nose which stands out against his gaunt jaw. Yet it is his deep azure gaze that mesmerises me: a rare exception to a nation of brown. With bushy grey brows and a wispy grey beard, he reminds me more of a goat than a human. He bids us politely through the courtyard, and, with a slightly hunched back, opens up the doorway to his heart and temple home.

He gestures for us to put our bags down, and requests his assistant to help store them away. The assistant's face is almost the complete opposite. A rotund face verging on chubby, with brown eyes, cropped black hair peeking below a glittering silver beret. His bored eyes light up upon seeing us. I walk with him to hang up my pack, and as I turn my back the young monk places his hand upon my unsuspecting bottom. I flinch in shock as he gestures with sex-driven eyes toward the bedroom. I politely decline with a shake of my head, make an about-turn, and hastily rush back to the team.

Three minutes later it's the Italian's turn.

Paolo quietly approaches our table, looking around furtively, as if still deciding whether to let Sumana and me in on his little confession.

'That monk grabbed me!' he reveals.

I leave with Diego to film the sunset and the full moon rising outside the temple. Kelvin comes out fifteen minutes later.

'Bad news, Gray. But I think you've already guessed.'

'What?'

'Well, apparently there are only four beds.'

'Yes . . .'

'And as you were away, the rest of us decided to draw straws.'

'Yes . . .'

'Well, guess who's been chosen as tonight's sacrificial lamb?'

Kelvin had just had his turn with the friendly monk.

'Just think, Nah, this guy has been praying for years for an opportunity like this and it seems all his blessings have come at once – a fresh-faced virgin from New Zealand arriving smack bang on full moon.' He punches his hands together, cracking up at the bizarreness of our situation in the middle of the Gobi.

'Diego should be the one sacrificed. He looks most like a Muslim. A Pakistani Muslim.'

Two hundred years ago, Chinese hosts offered travellers their wives for the evening as a measure of their hospitality. This tradition had changed but could have still been available for homosexuals. Many societies are slow in this day and age to alter their attitudes towards same-sex interaction. It was common in the Middle East for men to walk around hand-in-hand, and I had been propositioned many times by men while travelling alone through Egypt, Jordan and Syria, as if to do so was simply the norm. Indeed, with restrictions placed on interaction between the sexes before marriage in the traditional Muslim strongholds, it became clear to me that one simply begins to desire those whom they see most often. In fact, Muslim society was essentially very peaceful compared with most others I had encountered, receiving a rough deal from the media with their focus on the minority fundamentalists.

We head back to the kitchen area for a dinner of potato stew and rice. Paolo walks in late.

'Paolo, we've had another vote – a second ballot – and guess what?' Kelvin remarks, pausing to pack the punch, 'Looks like you're the lucky Italian!'

Sumana squeals with delight: simply talking about sex is a grand respite to the most challenging of all Buddhist monk rules – the vow of chastity. The Islamic assistant sits around the table, gazing upon us lovingly, oblivious to our comments. I quietly count my blessings that I am not out here on my own.

Day 4

> *I think therefore I am divided.*
>
> Martin Le Veuve

We wake to the aroma of baking bread (*mantou*). Opening my eyes, I see that a plateful of thick dough lies steaming on the table. With the gracefulness of pigs, we set upon the hot white flesh, chopsticks colliding to fill our drooling mouths.

The Chinese are renowned for their ability to shuffle rice into their mouths rapidly; however, our hosts choose not to partake in such an uncouth eating affair. Chewing the food slowly; sumptuously extracting the food's nutrients, is simply not possible without missing out on one's share. With five of us eating, there is pressure, especially when we have no idea when the next substantial meal is going to come.

We leave the temple and head for the first observation tower in the distant horizon. Passing a small grove of yellowing poplar trees, the desert again spans out in an electric silence. The gravestone of a builder lies beside the crumbling watchtower. We continue eastwards, and after several hours come to a boggy marsh that requires careful navigation. Out in front, 10 metres ahead, Diego takes a path heading northwards to circumvent the bog. My gut screws up in knots as he takes it, but I don't call out to him, even when I find a viable pathway across the marsh a little further south. I assume he will find a pathway across the marsh sooner or later.

I don't see him again for two days.

ж

The four of us cross the marsh and reach a small village. Unable to find a place to cross, Diego keeps on heading further north in the hope of finding another crossing. He sees that we have crossed safely, but has gone too far now to consider turning back. Soon he is just a tiny speck heading towards a white house in the distance.

The village we reach is old and derelict; the patios of every home are smothered in corn. Two Chinese peasants are using a hand contraption to strip the cobs of their kernels. They wind each one down through a channel of metal teeth which leaves the cob bare.

Lacking capital for large-scale farming, the Chinese peasants focus on intensive, high-yield gardening by hand. It all comes down to a matter of hands. Many, many hands. Two-thirds of China's population work the fields, penetrating every available inch of soil to procure a yield far superior to that achieved by the harvesting machines of the West. They have to: even in good years, China's growing deserts, eroded mountains, waterless valleys and the sheer space required to house her massive population, provide seven times less arable land than the United States. She also must feed five times as many people.

I take over from the peasants' work duties while they stoke up a fire to boil up some water. We need it desperately for the trip into the desert that is to follow. Kelvin still has some water in his 4-litre camel-back, so he heads off immediately to try to find Diego, who is only carrying 1 litre. He must now be struggling in the interminable 35-degree Gobi heat. I wait with Paolo and Sumana for some rice to be cooked, but again there is a funny feeling in my gut. Once I refill my bottles, I decide to flag the meal and head out into the desert in pursuit of the other two instead.

I soon catch up to Kelvin and we set off together at a tremendous pace.

'Look, there's Diego's footprint,' I notice, on a rocky formation pointing deeper into the desert towards the next watchtower. We follow, but after an hour cannot see Diego anywhere, nor any more footprints. It is pretty clear that he hasn't ventured out this far. Somehow we must have missed him as he circled around to find the others.

'Kiwi boys, first Westerners!' Kelvin calls out gleefully, grabbing the two wooden walking sticks, and begins to pound his way through the desert. I laugh, excited by his words as we egg each other on, trekking towards dusk. Passing small lakes and villages on the desert peripheries, Kelvin and I head for the nearest village as the sun sets. With the next watchtower still a few kilometres away on a small mountain rise, the plan is to find food and shelter, head to the tower the next day, and set up our orange tent so the others can spy us with their binoculars.

The village feels different from all the others we have encountered. The houses contain corn cobs on their front patios as per usual, yet there is an uncharacteristic brick wall separating each home and a perfectly paved concrete road running through the middle. It looks more like a suburban retirement village. Impoverished peasants walk the streets, clad in dirty shirts, trousers and woollen jerseys. However, for the first time on the journey, they are not welcoming.

'Is there a place for us to eat and sleep?' I ask. The peasants recoil into their homes, closing their doors. Kelvin and I come to a standstill in the middle of the main road. A Chinese man approaches, dressed in a tweed jacket. His grimace reveals a silver-capped tooth and he certainly isn't delighted to see us.

'Perhaps this is a closed town to foreigners,' I whisper to Kelvin. The silence is eerie. Kelvin gets out the cellphone and calls up his Russian girlfriend Julia in Beijing.

'We lost the others. Can you help translate to this Chinese official what we are doing and try to secure us a place to eat and sleep?' He passes the phone to the official who looks at it strangely. Kelvin gestures to put it to his ear. He hesitates, so Kelvin places the phone at his ear lobe. The official gets a shock when the words come tearing out at him, quickly removing it from his head. Tentatively, he returns his ear to the phone, listening with an expression of bemusement. The cellphone connects Julia to the expedition: the sixth member.

The Chinese peasants slowly emerge from their homes to look at the cellphone. I pull out my video camera to film them, then turn the viewfinder screen so they can see themselves on the mini-screen. One child notices himself and points excitedly to the camera calling to the others. Seeing their television reflection for the first time, the peasants swarm in front of the lens laughing hysterically. As their reflection laughs straight back, it compounds their sense of amusement. Everyone jostles with one another to get a better look.

'Oooohhh, aaaaah,' they call out in unison. 'Oooohhh, aaaaaah,' the television screen sounds back.

'Quick over here, shoot me!' a kid giggles, waving his arms wildly to entice the lens. And so the reflection continues until both beings stand still in mutual awe. Two times – one forever changing, the other cremated in recorded permanence.

One small, speechless child with dark pigtails and one blue eye barges her way to the front. She has exceptional strength for her size.

'Aaaaaaahhhhh . . .' she gazes, a harsh guttural laugh emanating from deep within her throat. Female infanticide still occurs in China. Thrown into rivers, left abandoned, Chinese females are expendable because they can't continue a family line, which amounts to the greatest possible betrayal of the ancestors. Exacerbated by the one-child policy of the government, as well as sterilisation of disabled people within the bigger cities, this seven-year-old mute had probably made a strong fight for her survival.

Our technology has altered the initial attitude of the village, and we are soon invited to eat. We enter a spacious white room containing the lounge, kitchen, tool shed and bedroom in one. It is much bigger than most Chinese homes, which are generally segregated into two rooms: one containing the kitchen and a long concrete bed (kang) on which the whole family sleep and eat; the other used for storage. The toilet is always outside.

Twenty villagers pour in excitedly, desperately wanting to get on camera. Even the official has joined in on the novelty. The kindly wife and her husband present three bowls of steaming noodles which we eat while everyone looks on. After dinner I spend the early evening teaching the young students to speak English. Some of them have already learned quite a few words. An hour later everyone trickles home, and I am beckoned to a small conference with the silver-toothed official.

'*Huzhao?*'

'What?'

'*Huzhao!*' I figure they want my passport, but I am reluctant to pass it across and pass him my driver's licence instead.

'*Bu, bu, bu, huzhao.*'

I pass my passport across nervously and the official flicks through the pages. He looks up after a minute, shaking his head.

'You're not in trouble, but you'll have to leave now.' His oriental eyes look at me sharply and his silver tooth glitters.

'But our Chinese friends have invited us to sleep,' I complain, not wanting to set out into the night. I look up hopefully to the kind father who had fed us.

'Let them stay,' the father suggests with his head.

The official grudgingly agrees and leads us to a derelict building where he unbolts a padlocked door. It is a dusty classroom, unused and very much like a concrete cell. It has two wooden desks to sleep on.

'Where's the toilet?' I ask. The official shows us to a brick wall outside.

'I'm glad he didn't point to the corner of the room,' Kelvin whispers nervously. 'It feels risky to stay here. He might call the police.'

'Let's risk it. He said he would be back early in the morning to wake us up, and it saves setting the tent up twice.'

Kelvin and I put the two tables together, blow up our sleeping mats, jump into our sleeping bags and crash.

Day 5

14 October, Gansu: It's day five of the trip and my 26th birthday. Nathan and I are woken by a loud knock at the door. I slowly come to. It takes me a moment of reflection to figure where in the world I am ... Oh yeah that's right China, but where in China – well not really sure. The day before, the Great Walk team had its first real challenge. A long story really as to who was at fault, but the team got separated.

Musings from the Wall: Kelvin Jones

We are woken with a start. The official bashes on the door before entering.

'Get up. You both must leave.' His silver tooth glitters. It is 6.30am.

'Come on, Kelvin. Let's get out of here – oh yeah, happy birthday, mate.'

We pack quickly. Once ready, the official opens up his hand.

'*Wushi kuai.*' 50 *yuan.*

'50 *yuan? Bu, bu bu.*' No ways. I refuse, eyeing him out. The official can't quite return my stare.

'*Sanshi kuai.*' 30 *yuan* then, he says hopefully, succumbing to a cheeky renegotiation.

'No ways.' I shake my head. 'I'm giving my money to the mother who fed us.'

'*Ershi kuai.*' 20 *yuan.*

'No!'

Seeing that he is not going to get his way, the official changes tack. Kelvin and I both freeze, fixated by the padlock in his hand as he threatens to lock us both in. Kelvin's eyes widen in alarm and my stomach caves. We glance at each other helplessly, too afraid to move. Everything from then on seems to happen in slow motion. As the official goes to place the padlock in the bolt, both of us wait for the other to act. I snap out of my reverie first and slam my boot into the gap of the door, wrenching it open and muscling my way past the official.

'Come on Kelvin – let's go!' I shout, completely shocked at what I have just done. We vacate the school grounds, shouting loudly to attract the attention of passing peasants. The official follows in pursuit, but the peasants surround us, curious at all the commotion. Knowing they support our cause, we stand on firmer ground against the village head. Kelvin regains his confidence.

'You should pay us 20 *yuan* for trying to lock me up on my birthday!' he jokes, his index finger raised like a discerning parent.

'Happy birthday to Kelvin . . .' I sing to emphasise Kelvin's point. The official turns his eyes away in scorn, but there is little he can do. Our blatant lack of respect for his authority seems to alter the way the other peasants look at him. Perhaps our presence is triggering a mini-rebellion? There is no time to find out.

We walk rapidly up the paved street, passing our hosts' house. The mother is outside sweeping her porch.

'Quick, give her 10 *kuai*,' Kelvin says.

Her eyes light up when I offer her the money. However, she quickly refuses it, lowering her eyes humbly, shaking her head.

'Take it, please, for your kids.' I pass it across.

Although a meagre US$1.25, she looks as if she has just won the lottery. And with this warmth in our hearts, we set off at a run. Fugitives in China.

Walking steadily through the desert wilderness, it takes an hour and a half to reach the next watchtower, perched on a steep mountain rise. Kelvin's calves and back strain as he lugs his heavy gear up the slippery shingle. At the top we settle to wait for the others. The vista of the Gobi spreads for miles. To the west lies the village and the possibility of pursuing officials. To the north lays the open desert; a wasteland of forbidding sand dunes as far as the eye can see. To the north-east lies a small mountain range. There are no more watchtowers; this is clearly the end of the first stage.

Although there is no more Wall on the maps now for many miles, we still have to work out exactly where to walk to reach civilisation. I spy a watertower far to the south-east just before a heat wave engulfs the view. Kelvin places his pack down in the shade of the tower and starts counting out the M&Ms. He also unwraps a plastic-wrapped sausage we have saved for our breakfast.

The cellphone rings.

'Hmmmm . . . could it be my dad? Ringing me out of the blue to wish me a happy birthday?' Kelvin jokes as he lets it ring twice more before picking it up. His dad has rarely spoken to him since he left him as a child.

It is Diego.

'We're on the run!' Kelvin laughs, exaggerating. 'This place is crawling with officials. Where did you get to?'

'We've been arrested,' Diego replies.

'When, just this morning – just now?' Kelvin replies, alarmed.

'The police came in at 1am and bundled us out of our tents.'

'Oh shit. You guys alright? Where are you?'

'We're stuck in some police station in a city I have no idea where. Where are you?'

'You know that last big watchtower – we're just behind it now. Where do we have to get to?'

'Head for the town near the railway station on the maps. We'll try and hook up there once we get out.'

'We need to stay away from people now?'

'Seems wise. Have you got enough supplies?'

'We've got food, power bars, meaty hotdogs, rice and apples – well, not rice because we have no cooker – but we're good for at least three days.'

'Okay, we'd better save the cellphone battery: it must be low. Just head for the city by the train station and I'll give you a call at four o'clock.'

Kelvin turns the phone off and looks up. 'The others have been arrested, and it looks like we just narrowly avoided that, so . . . we're on the road again . . .' We both laugh. 'Well, we're on the run,' Kelvin continues soberly.

'Where are we gonna meet them?' I ask.

'At the town near the station.'

'I don't think there is a town near the station.'

'Well that's what Diego said.'

'It's okay. We've got the phone, so they can contact us later when we each have a better idea of where we all actually are. There's a watertower in the distance – it's disappeared now but I have this feeling we've got to head for it. You happy with that?'

'Yeah.'

'We'd better move now. It's only going to get hotter.'

We scoff three M&Ms each, share the dried sausage, and descend the other side of the mountain into a series of valleys. Two kilometres later we enter a crater gouged by an asteroid.

'Shit, tank tracks. Could this get any worse?' The land is scarred all over by some heavy-duty manoeuvring.

'Keep low, we can take this route here: it's more obscured from those bunkers in the distance.'

'Mate, they look more like missile silos. What is this place?'

On our first day at Jiayuguan Fortress I had stumbled across a *National Geographic* photographer called George Steimetz. He was shooting an article on the Gobi Desert with a State-assigned Chinese crew. He had said to us that there were several army bases and a Chinese missile installation in the area, which he needed special permits to visit. China has an army of 2.5 million personnel, with 3,400 aircraft and a military expenditure set at US$30 billion, although the Japanese and the United States suspect expenditure is actually twice as much. With seventy-five missiles being added annually towards the recalcitrant island of Taiwan, it is difficult to assess whose estimate is the truer.

'I'm going to hide my tapes and camera at the bottom of the pack.'

'Good idea. Let's get out of here.'

We head swiftly through the army zone. There is no one about and we reach the watertower. A blue concrete building lies behind a white brick wall.

'Shall we take a look inside, ask where the station is?' I ask.

'Don't be ridiculous – it's probably an army compound,'

Kelvin replies. 'We mustn't take any foolish risks.' Just as Kelvin is about to set off down a different road, a white minivan approaches the compound entrance. It stops upon seeing us and a heavily-decorated army general gets out. He is completely drunk and looks us over suspiciously.

'Come back to the van,' his wife complains from inside. He returns and they drive into the compound before he can ask any discerning questions.

'Phew!' Kelvin exhales, hardly believing our good fortune. We set off down the road at a canter.

A kilometre or so later, the road comes to a crossroad. The first sign points to a city 36 kilometres back west, possibly Jiayuguan. The other road heads towards some unknown city.

'Let's go east towards this new city. Perhaps that's where Diego and the others are being held.'

The avenue is lined by yellow willows. After a kilometre of walking, we reach a convenience store. The single-storey building is filled to the brim with clothing, shoes, carpentry, food and lollies – a feast for our desert-worn eyes. I immediately purchase some biscuits and two Coca-Cola drinks, along with some double-happy firecrackers to celebrate Kelvin's birthday.

'Here you go, mate. Bet you never thought you'd see these beauties again.' I grin, recalling how the firecrackers were taken off the New Zealand market because of the danger – but naturally, Kiwis just started firing skyrockets at each other instead. 'Apparently the Chinese invented gunpowder when trying to find the elixir for eternal youth.' I smirk. 'In some ways I suppose they were successful.'

We head outside to set off a firework, but just before reaching the door a police car speeds past the shop, sirens blaring.

'Jesus, that was lucky. That was definitely meant for us,' Kelvin suggests, concerned.

'I'm not gonna give myself up. Let's lay low here. Wait till the heat subsides.'

It is now close to 40 degrees. We befriend the shopkeeper, who is dressed casually in gardening trousers and a white singlet.

He takes us out the back. The property is getting cleared in preparation for a new brick building. We help him cut a tree with a double-handled saw. Afterwards the shop owner cooks some noodles in an oily black wok, and invites us both to drink *baijiu*, a forty-percent clear Chinese spirit. He pours it into a series of shot glasses and passes them around, singing a bizarre guttural song that rises to a high-pitched whine.

'*Ganbei!*' he shouts, taking his glass and tapping it underneath the tips of our glasses as a sign of respect. He looks us both in the eye, then throws the shot back in one satisfying gulp, nodding his head approvingly. We follow suit. It is the most hideous concoction I've ever drunk, strong enough to mellow a rampaging elephant. I shake my head to alleviate the internal burning. One is enough for my spleen. Not so for Kelvin, his thirst for alcohol enflamed.

In the late afternoon, the shop owner organises a tractor to take us into town. As we lie on top, hundreds of Chinese cyclists almost ride themselves into the paddy fields as they stretch their necks backwards to get a good gawp. The mother we had dinner with the night before cycles past. She gives us a big wave and smile as she heads down the road to spend her winnings. The tractor stops off at a country market set up along the street. Kelvin plays some pool with the locals while waiting for Diego's call, but it never comes. As night falls, there is still no word. A bus driver whistles for us to get in. He drives us into a cheap hotel in the city about 10 kilometres down the road. It is a chance to lie low, and assess exactly what to do next . . .

Day 6
Age is not assessed by the number of birthdays, but by the number of experiences and the way you perceive them.

Anon

'What will tomorrow hold?' I muse, resting comfortably in the double bed of a plush Chinese hotel room, which is costing us only US$2.50 a night. 'Why did the cellphone ring just then? And why was the watertower sighted just before it became too hazy to see? If the village official had not set us off early that morning, we would have undoubtedly missed it. Is it perhaps that we are being guided?'

'You won't guess what I just saw,' Kelvin breaks my reverie, returning from a feed of chicken at the local markets.

'What?' After a week of frozen evenings, harsh heat, food poisoning, injury, hypothermia, split-ups, arrests, closed villages, flashing sirens, fugitive status and military zones, I can't even begin to imagine.

'Well there's a population of almost a million in this city, but it seems to attract foreigners who are walking the Great Wall.'

'What! There's another group of walkers walking the Great Wall?'

'Yeah, there's an Italian, an Argentinian and a Buddhist. They were all eating in the same market,' Kelvin grins. 'I've invited them around for my birthday celebration.'

'My word, what a coincidence. What happened to them?'

'They were released by the police after questioning. It took a little longer because Diego was pissed off with the way they lugged his pack with all his photo gear onto the truck, and got angry. The police don't like it when you're disrespectful.'

The group reunites for a party, complete with a creamy birthday cake, soft drink, cookies, fruit and nuts. Sumana also invites a couple of Chinese friends he has made.

'I'm never going to forget this birthday, Nah. Damn glad you're here to share it.' Kelvin hangs out the picture of his son Lucas on one of the seats, so his boy can at least be there in spirit. The celebration ends an almost unimaginable week. A dress rehearsal no doubt for what lies in store.

Stage one complete.

MOON 4

THE HUNT FOR RED SUMANA

*Life is like being at the dentist. You always think that the worst is
still to come and yet it is already over.*

Bismarck

Day 7

After six days walking through the desert, Kelvin and I are full
of self-congratulation. We think we've stormed all the way to
Zhangye, a sizeable Chinese city almost 150 kilometres across
the Gobi.

'*Bu, bu bu.*' No, no, no. 'Jiuquan,' the hotel receptionist
informs, pointing to a city about 40 kilometres east of Jiayuguan.
We are not even a millimetre across the map of China.

'I always do this!' Diego fumes.

'What?' I ask.

'Take on too much stuff to do anything properly.'

He has exposed his still photography film when taking it out
of his camera.

'I'm gonna have to return to Jiayuguan to reshoot.' He
replies, looking at both Kelvin and me. 'Who's gonna come
back?'

'Not me,' I reply, shaking my head. 'My ankle's still tender
and we've already been there.'

'Kelvin?'

'Nah, bro.'

'I'll go back on my own then.'

Diego packs up, ready to catch a bus back to Jiayuguan as
Sumana enters the room.

'Where are you going?'

'Back to Jiayuguan.'

'What do you mean? You can't just go back and expect us all to wait.'

'But I've got to take re-shots of the fortress.'

'Where are we going to meet up?'

'Well,' I interject, 'according to the maps, the next major branch of Wall is in Shandan, it's about 100 or so kilometres by train east. Maybe we should head there?'

'No way,' says Diego. 'We have to walk every step across China even when there is no Great Wall to follow.'

'You're mad,' says Paolo, who has also entered the hotel bedroom. 'We should only walk the sections where the Great Wall lies intact. If the distance on the maps is too far in between sections to walk, then we should hitch-hike or find some other form of transport instead.'

'I'm with Paolo,' Sumana says, standing beside him in support.

'But you're a failure if you don't walk every step – it's not being true to the spirit of the journey.'

'Of whose journey? Yours or ours?' Sumana replies.

Diego is silent.

'In a journey such as this it is very important to learn to accept our limits,' Paolo contributes, enunciating each syllable slowly. 'That we're five individuals is good. The friction produces energy and is good for our personal work. However, if we want harmony we must all learn to accept certain compromises.'

'What do you mean by harmony?' I ask.

'Harmony is,' Paolo pauses, searching for the right words, 'being yourself, and allowing everyone else to be themselves.'

'I'm off then,' Diego says, grabbing his pack and heading to the bus station back for Jiayuguan. The rest of us take the train east to Shandan to prepare for the next stage where the Wall commences. Diego arrives two days later. He is disappointed but willing to make the compromise to keep the group together. Besides, he needs us to help carry all his gear.

SHANDAN, GANSU PROVINCE

Shandan perches quietly on the edge of the Gobi. Small tan foothills called the Daihuang Range lie to the north, and the Qilian Himalaya lies as always to the south. Historically, Shandan's strategic positioning at the base of the narrow Hexi corridor made it a prosperous home to over 240,000 people. It was often mistaken by Arabian merchants as Xi'an; China's old capital. Shandan was overtaken by the Mongols under the leadership of Genghis Khan, who made it his capital in 1269.

Today, Shandan's population has shrunk to 30,000. Despite continuing decline, its abundance of raw materials and space to expand business have enabled it to play a dynamic role in the gradual emergence of modern China, in particular the 'Gung Ho' movement invented by Rewi Alley from New Zealand. Appalled at the death-inspiring working conditions the Chinese were subjected to in the eastern seaboard under Chiang Kai Shek, Rewi is still enormously famous in China for creating the polytechnic movement, utilising communist-styled industrial plants to put the masses of Chinese hands to good use. Rewi had found a derelict Buddhist temple to use as his first school to train young Chinese boys in the technical and academic skills that were needed to serve his revolutionary initiatives. His first project was to make ammunition to fight the invading Japanese. This gave Rewi the support of both the Kuomintang and Communist leadership. Backed by overseas funding, he was able to establish thousands of these schools all over China, teaching all sorts of skills. His idea peaked in 1941, when the Americans adopted the Gung Ho workforce idea.

Day 8

Like bees to honey, a swarm of motorbike taxis surges upon us as we vacate the train at Shandan. Red motorbikes with an attached carriage cost a Chinese man 2,000 RMB (*yuan*) (US$250). It forms a healthy transport enterprise throughout the cities, the price usually 2–5 *yuan* each ride.

'*Wushi kuai yige ren dao shandan!*' shouts a poxy-faced man, wearing a black beret. Fifty *yuan* for each person into town.

'*Wushi kuai! Bu bu, yinggai shi meige ren liang kuai,*' Sumana replies, shaking his head. Fifty *yuan*! No, no, it usually costs 2 *yuan* for one person.'

'*You wo gongli dao chengshi, meige ren jiao shi kuai zuo che.*' It is 5 kilometres to the city – you must pay 10 *yuan* each for a bike.'

'*Wu kuai.*' Five *yuan*.

'*Keyi.*' Okay.

The owner of a dusty Datsun, who is also hoping to take us all as one group, shouts angrily. '*Tamen laowai – yinggai duo fu qian!*' They are foreigners, they have to pay us more!

'I hate how they automatically regard us as rich,' Kelvin says. 'I feel stupid trying to convince them otherwise.'

'It's the tourists who cause it,' I shrug. 'In for just a few weeks, spending up large, there is little time available to waste it all haggling.'

'It's no problem, you just have to agree on price before you set off,' Paolo asserts.

'But, remember,' Sumana reminds us, 'travelling through China, like any third-world country, does call for a little bit of charity.'

Most Westerners can live like kings in the Mainland. With accommodation as little as 3–5 *kuai* a day (US40–70 cents), and meals 2–3 *kuai* (US20–40 cents) for a plateful of noodles, one can live very comfortably on the equivalent of a simple welfare or pension payment.

Day 9

> *Either side of the Great Wall*
> *One blinding vastness.*
>
> Mao Zedong

At 7am the team is up, speeding on motorbikes through the cold, grey streets. Wearing white face masks to combat the smell of petrol and the freezing conditions, the Wall recommences 5 kilometres outside the city in a flat tussock plain. The lumbering giant stands 5 metres high, 2 metres thick; impossible for a man to see what lies on the other side. It takes an arrow-straight course and we accompany the northern side in single file, scanning for a crack to find refuge from the cold wind sweeping down from the Mongolian plains. This side, the land of vast open desert is where the nomadic barbarians historically roamed, viewed by many Chinese as no better than animals. The southern, semi-arable side is where the more cultivated Chinese settled and built up their raidable economies.

Unlike a natural border, such as a river or mountain range, man-made divisions have caused many problems throughout the ages. For example, the English surveyor Radcliffe drew up the demarcation line between India and Pakistan for the 1947 Partition without even visiting the area. The resulting division put the headwaters and the control works of the Himalayan canals in Indian territory. This literally gave them the capacity to shut off Pakistan's water.

In Cyprus, the dilapidated capital city of Lefkoshia is a grim scene of bullet-strewn concrete homes. After thirty years of civil unrest between the Greek and Turkish Cypriots, the border consists of a 200-metre no-go zone surrounded by white United Nations barrels stacked two to three tiers high. Yet on either side, both enemies' children eat from identical cereal packets exported by the same multinational corporate. Seeing the festive celebrations between East and West when the Berlin Wall finally came down in 1989, perhaps the Wall being built in Israel is not such a wise idea?

According to historian Julia Lovell, walls are really only useful when there are enough institutionalised super-ideologies to require erection of clear-cut barriers. Examples are Communism, Capitalism and German Expansionism. Yet with smart bombs and napalm preferred over foot troops and cavalry, history has made a mockery of post-1989 Wall-making. Is it still necessary to divide those who can and can't behave?

There is a gap in the Wall at a motorway 15 kilometres' walk later. The tarseal artery has taken its chunk of Great Wall history and replaced it with a line of brick restaurants. We enter one to spend the night. It has been the group's biggest day walking yet and Sumana is exhausted. A giant oak table stands in the middle of the shop surrounded by carved wooden chairs. Comfortable velvet couches line the walls. The building is both business abode and family home. This is common in China, allowing savings on rent, transport and child-care.

The tables and couches are organised to worship the house's main feature: a 21-inch digital television with a DVD player. The concrete highway is like an intravenous drip injecting the Gobi with the latest technology. An aged Chinese peasant, dressed in a blue Mao suit, is staring mesmerised at the screen. Shuffling rice into his mouth he takes no notice of the real-life movie occurring behind.

CCTV *National News* is showing. President Jiang Zemin sits back on his political throne receiving the King of Sweden. The camera focuses on his official guest at an angle that makes him seem like he is leaning forward seeking the approval of one of the world's most powerful figures. Fully aware of the propaganda value of television, the Chinese Government has imposed a law halving the maximum retail price for a brand-new set. Indeed, critical thinking is not a forte of the Chinese peasant. However, this is slowly changing in the cities, with education, the Internet, and exposure to criticism of the State by the outside world. Twenty-seven percent of Chinese in the big cities now look to international news rather than local stations to get a picture of what is going on in China during the most severe domestic crises.

'These DVDs are pirated!' Kelvin observes, flicking through the photocopied covers of *Armageddon* and *Rain Man*.

'Of course,' I reply. 'Street vendors can get around US$1.50 for a pirated DVD.'

Police movements had begun to stem the tide of illegal trade, given China's legal obligations to join the World Trade

Organization. However, it is hard for the State to impose its will on every street corner, especially when local authorities shield factories from raids, opting to protect jobs over the nebulous notion of trademark infringement. Besides, the West has ripped off their inventions, so why should they comply? Copyright would never have existed had the Chinese not first invented printing and paper. We'd also be fodder for the desert without our magnetic compasses.

Day 10

The Great Wall trails take centre stage against a world of sky, desert and Himalaya. Our restaurant host is dressed completely in black and escorts us to the Wall with Sumana's camera to take a photo of the five walkers together. I also hand him my video camera. Unfortunately he doesn't press the button properly but I don't bother to ask him to retake it. There will be many more chances on such a long journey to get a photo of us all together. We set off walking beside the ancient clay barricade for three hours.

'Why have we stopped?' Diego asks Kelvin, who is sitting in a throne-like indentation in the Wall. 'Our last stop was only twenty minutes ago.'

'Sumana's tired.'

'If we stop we should make a proper stop, not two short stops.'

'We've stopped now, Sumana needs the rest, and if we keep on arguing about it, well, we're not exactly resting are we?'

'That's not the point: we should all agree if we are going to stop and then just make a proper stop.' Diego takes off his giant pack, and begins massaging his knees. 'Nathan said at the last stop we were only a third of the way to the next township. We're not going to make it if we keep stalling like this.'

'Look, stop going on about it. You're just being antagonistic.'

'Antago-nis-tic?' Diego's nose scrunches up, offended.

'Don't take it personally, but I think you're in everyone's face.'

'Am I in Paolo's face? Sumana's face?'

'You're constantly in Nathan's face.' Kelvin pauses, looking at me filming the episode. 'In fact it seems you guys *like* being in each other's faces.'

'That's a sadistic feeling!' Sumana laughs excitedly, putting both Kelvin and I into hysterics. 'I agree with Kelvin that you are antagonistic and in everyone's face,' he continues.

'No, you shut up,' Diego snaps.

Sumana lowers his head in shame, then looks back up towards Diego, his eyes narrowing. 'You are harsh, Diego. Very harsh, actually. You are also very arrogant. You can't be a good journalist if you continue to be like that.'

'You're just saying all this because Nathan is filming you on camera.'

'I don't care if there is any fuckin' camera.' Sumana looks straight into the lens and then smiles, 'I learned that word from you guys!'

Everyone roars with laughter, except Diego and Paolo, who is sitting well away from the court of Gobi politics, listening to the serene silence of the desert.

'Sumana, you little monk, you just don't want to be last.'

'No, no, I am just biding for time. You'll see.' His eyes light up.

'Time's up,' Kelvin intervenes. 'Our unallocated rest is over.'

We set off again. Tensions defused. Diego comically does the fingers at the other walkers behind their backs and waves innocently when I capture him on camera. He approaches me slowly.

'I remember you labelling each of us as one of the senses last week.'

'Yeah, that's right. Sumana was the touch sense because of his healing hands; Paolo the hearing sense, with his love for music and harmony. What was Kelvin again?'

'The taste sense because of his penchant for fine women, and you were the seeing sense because you like to lead with the maps and track the trail.'

'Why do you ask?'

'I can't remember you giving me a sense.'

'There's only smell left.'

'Hmmm . . .' Diego pauses, scrunching up his forehead in thought, 'that must make me the in-sense.'

҉

The creation of uncrossable borders has severely restricted the exchange of cultural thought throughout history. The resulting divisions within people's minds are etched out by those with the loudest voices: in most cases the screeching text of the media or the dulcet drone of a politician's drivel. Despite the growth of globalisation and its corporate aim to homogenise, thinking tends to change every few hundred kilometres in wall-less Europe, as shown by the immense variety of culture and language. In China, the majority of the population speak Mandarin, the State recognising that one language is the key to effective political control over the masses. This sense of galvanising a single Chinese identity developed as far back as 1700 BC when the Shang, the first historically verifiable dynasty, included the northern Chinese hordes into the nexus of patriarchal custom and political organisation. With the first common language written on bones, today's Mandarin has been simplified by the State from 60,000 characters down to 5,000. Approximately 1,500 are necessary to gain a grasp of a daily newspaper.

Communication problems are always going to arise when borders come down and two races begin to interrelate. When Abel Tasman first found New Zealand he blared his ship's horns triumphantly to announce his arrival. The Maori welcoming party perceived the Dutch explorer's intentions as threatening, turning what should have been a welcoming *hongi* into a six-man slaughter. Had Abel piped the flute instead, well . . . *dinge kon verskriklik anders gewees het.* (Things could have been very different.)

If neither strain of the newly interrelating species kills the other off straight away (as two competing mosses will initially attempt to do when inhabiting the same rock), then both will eventually learn to coexist, adopting each other's habits from either side. The Chinese in Hong Kong and Mainland China both derive from Chinese roots which prescribe a Confucian approach to leadership. Under this system, governance is hierarchically enforced and guided by ideology and orthodoxy rather than the disharmony of liberal political debate, which is seen as a boon to economic prosperity. However, the influence of 150 years of civil British rule in Hong Kong highlighted the weakness of the Chinese imperial system to the minds of Hong Kong's citizens. Yet, despite using a liberal system to build up a strong State structure, they still see the relationship between individual and State through a Confucian lens. Thus once British rule departed, Hong Kong still had its own currency, laws, courts, and visa/immigration rules, yet was now viewed as a part of China politically. ('One country, two systems.')

We walk through a dull orange canyon, the Wall perched perilously along its edge. Diego, Paolo and I walk together at the front, engrossed in conversation.

'Guys, slow down. Sumana's miles behind!' Kelvin calls out, having taken on the afternoon responsibility to remain at the back. He rushes up to us, breathing heavily.

'Why didn't you stay behind him?' I reply.

'I had to come and make you slow down.'

Indeed, it is hard to slow one's natural walking rhythm when walking with such a heavy pack.

'Let's wait here until he arrives,' Diego says.

We settle our packs down beside the Wall on a flat yellow field. Half an hour passes.

'Strange, I remember passing him by that police car parked just off the highway – it wasn't that long ago,' I muse.

'He was looking absolutely exhausted when I passed him,' Kelvin states.

'Let's just wait.'

An hour passes, and still there is no sign of Sumana.

'Let's go back and find him,' Diego suggests, lifting himself up. 'You guys coming?'

Paolo and I sit back quietly.

'I'll come,' says Kelvin.

They both set off together to look along one side of the Wall. Paolo remains by the packs while I climb the nearest hill to get a panoramic view of the surroundings. Spotting details up to half a kilometre away, I am hoping to use my video camera to focus in on the terrain to spot Sumana. Diego and Kelvin look like tiny specks compared with the vast landscape of canyon lands and yellow fields that fill the wide vista on either side of the Wall. Half an hour later, Kelvin and Diego return without having seen a trace of Sumana. Paolo comes up the hill to join me at my vantage point.

'Look, Paolo, someone dressed in red is hitch-hiking on the highway. Perhaps it is Sumana?'

'It must be him.'

The figure is too far away to properly tell, however, especially in the fading light. We head back to tell the others.

'What do we do?' Diego asks.

'I want noodles!' Kelvin groans hungrily.

'Let's leave the Wall and head to the next small township on the highway,' I propose, looking at the maps. 'Surely Sumana will have made his way there if he is hitch-hiking.'

The four of us head across the desert plains to a roadside village 3 kilometres away. We file hungrily into a dingy roadside restaurant, ordering a feast of meaty noodles while checking the roadside for Sumana. He doesn't arrive.

Day 11
'The Constitution of the Chinese empire is the best in the world . . . the only one in which the governor of a province is punished when he fails to win the acclamation of the people upon leaving office . . .'
Voltaire

At first light we split up to search for Sumana. Paolo and Diego walk back to where we had left the Wall. Kelvin and I search the roadside village before heading across the plains towards the next village at the foot of the first mountain range the Wall crosses. The village streets are dry and deserted. Clay cottages bank against the 3.5-metre-high Wall. We approach the first house. Inside is a family of six who take Kelvin and me in for lunch while we wait for the others to arrive. A man with spiky black hair enters soon after. He looks at us with a knowing smile, then draws a picture of a little fat man on a piece of paper.

'I've seen him,' he mimes, then draws a picture of a bus and the clock at ten o'clock with the words *Hexi Bao*. We eventually work out that Sumana has left the village to catch a bus to the next major city of Hexipu.

'I remember seeing someone down the highway that looked like Sumana as we set off this morning to look for him,' I mutter to Kelvin quietly. 'But he disappeared without coming to see us, so I presumed it couldn't have been him.'

'He could have said something before buggering off. What was he thinking?'

'Probably afraid we'd make him walk this mountain.'

The four of us reunite and share in the news of Sumana. Diego and Paolo seek out another family for lunch while Kelvin and I decide to go on ahead to slowly tackle the Wall winding in increments up the Yanzi Shan Pass.

'Just so we have no more incidents,' Diego pauses, 'make sure you find a camping spot on this side of the summit.'

Kelvin and I head for the summit, racing each other to the top.

'I get to experience the view first,' Kelvin gasps proudly. I cringe inside, our competitiveness worrying. It's good to be like this for a mountain or two to keep things interesting, but not when there's at least a hundred more. We share a packet of M&Ms, sitting to watch the sunset. The Wall curves in a long arc before straightening and vanishing into the horizon behind. It is amazing to see how far we have walked. The mountains beside Shandan have almost disappeared and the bland, lifeless fields are now just patches in an expansive desert quilt.

The giant mural captures each moment of our past; the Wall unravelling through the middle like a linear guide. I can trace all the incidents, villages, arguments and laughter. I can also see where we had gone left, taken a gap in the Wall and spent time in the deserts of ancient Mongolia, or chosen right, wanting to explore the world of the settled Chinese villages. Out in the distance lies the chunk of missing flesh where Sumana had slipped through the cracks. Turning our heads back to the east, the Wall glows red as it winds ahead through a barren valley towards our future.

Cast in an armour of golden light
Lay concrete remnants of my past.
Cowardice and courage all mapped out
The Wall's lessons designed to last.

180 degrees upon the mountain top.
Miles of Great Wall trails
Seeing my future clear ahead
Can I work out what it entails?

Attitude forges the path you take
Past experience influences the stakes.
Breathe in deep to prevent the cyclic mirror
Each step is new to the man who awakes.

Nathan Hoturoa Gray

Day 15
  The art of living is going to one's deathbed smilingly.
Anon

Kelvin walks towards a Chinese man standing beside a camel. Putting his index and middle fingers to his mouth, he gestures for a cigarette. The farmer grins, reaching into his jacket pocket. Kelvin beams, too. He's had a good strike rate in this country. With cigarettes costing less than 50 cents a packet, most males in China smoke; a cigarette the first thing offered on meeting. Few females smoke, and only ever in the bigger cities. Kelvin gratefully bends over to receive the lit match from his new-found friend. Both take in a drag with a sense of relief – the smoker's communion the same worldwide.

According to the maps, the end of stage two at Hexipu city lies behind a brown mountain range that backdrops a glistening blue lake. To reach it, the four of us have walked for four days since we lost Sumana. My ankles have blisters the size of golf balls after climbing the first mountain range in our new boots, which Kelvin says are factory chuck-outs. Each painful step makes me want to quit and hitch-hike instead, especially upon seeing a roadside that says we have 56 kilometres to go after crossing the range. However, I persevere, Paolo lending me his lighter boots and cotton wool to ease things while I make the necessary adjustments to mentally acclimatise to the pain. Indeed, it takes a combination of curiosity and guts to tackle this journey. Curiosity gets us out here quite contentedly before ruthlessly abandoning us to see whether we have the guts to continue.

It seems apt that the stage ends at a large body of water, sparkling like quartz. The hard concrete Wall, representing 2,300 years of physical struggle and petrified time, symbolises the masculine Chinese notion of *yang*. Water is the Wall's antithesis, the feminine *yin*, a sanctuary to cleanse us from the past – wipe away the stains of the dead, and prepare for re-entry into the world of the living. The Wall crumbles away to a few fragments of clay lining the lakeside.

Paolo and Kelvin rush off around the lake to finish the stage and to flag down a passing truck to take us the remaining 10 kilometres along a tarseal road through the mountains. Diego and I take our time, savouring the peace of the wilderness. It is rare to get a chance to walk with Diego. He is often at the back, loaded down with all his gear. While taking photos of the crystal blue lake, he knocks his light sensor mistakenly into the water. Although he is angry at the loss, I can't help thinking it is a blessing. One less thing to worry about on the journey.

It has now been two weeks on the Wall without a proper wash. At first the flies paraded around our faces and bodies, our sweat attracting them like magnets. Now they cease to disturb, as if we have attained the scent of our surroundings.

Day 16

Hexipu is an industrial city situated just off the main railway line to Beijing. Green-and-white-tiled apartment blocks line the streets. They are ugly and resemble the interior design of your average Western toilet. Developed in haste instead of taste, the Chinese would probably regret not taking the time to emulate its ancient culture with its leap into modern development.

The smell of cooking spices, raw meat and fried vegetables fills the streets. People cook in blackened woks, shouting, laughing and negotiating prices. Buses hoot madly and motorbikes whiz by. Despite the third-world mayhem, the city of 40,000 has a homely feel. The four of us settle into a hotel to wash and rest before finding an Internet store.

With two weeks' worth of sweat and grime caked to our skin, we are desperate for a shower. Many cheap hotels do not contain a shower and so it is necessary to find a communal one nearby. The caretaker sits outside selling soap and small packets of shampoo. He unlocks the rusted metal entry door. We pile into the communal concrete enclave, which is surrounded by metal pipes that are heated by a coal furnace. It is grey and dark, and a hot pool lies in the middle, filled with a group of Chinese. A hush falls over the bathers who stare at us shamelessly. Is the legend of the well-hung white man actually true? Their heads slowly turn to Paolo, to Diego, to Kelvin, then to me – and back to Diego. Alas, the legend is now only myth.

The rhythmic slaps of a masseur echo through the back rooms. Lying face-down upon a white stretcher, the victim's body is kneaded like dough before the skin is scraped with a rough gauze cloth. The hot showers feel divine, the water turning desert brown before it even reaches the floor. Afterwards I feel Western again.

We head to the China Telecom Centre. These are State-owned communications towers catering to the rapidly emerging cellphone network. China is adding 5 million cellphone users a month – the total of India's entire network. The building supports a gigantic telephone tower and the towers stand out as an obvious landmark – a good place to meet should there be any further splits.

Sumana has left a message on the cellphone for us to collect a message here as to his whereabouts.

Dear Team,
I have tired of waiting in Hexipu, and have headed instead towards the next major city of Wuwei.
Rev Dr S S

'He could have waited,' Kelvin chides.

'Yeah, Wuwei's at least another 100 kilometres away. There's no way we'll catch up.'

'He's on his own journey now,' Diego says with a sense of finality.

The Telecom centre also contains the Internet. I am surprised to find it so early on in the journey, thinking that once we headed out into the Gobi, that would be it in terms of contact with the outside world. A major motivation for me to agree to carry Diego's gear was his connection with IPIX China – a 360-degree photo company that is creating a website about our journey. The plan is to send all the diary stories and photos by post at each city for IPIX to load onto the website. Now that I am online again I can hook up with all my friends and readers around the world on my own website.

Privately-run computer stores are hiring computers out for as little as 2 *yuan* an hour (US25 cents). This is affordable and popular with Chinese students, who surf the net, ICQ chat, play violent video games, or download music and DVDs. Government-run facilities are three to four times this cost, but, unlike in Laos or Cambodia where Internet rates are set at

US$4 an hour, development of the local knowledge economy is not stunted because of the expense. With 120,000,000 Internet users in China (as opposed to 190,000,000 in the US), the computer rooms are packed with chain-smoking Chinese, and most stores are open twenty-four hours, the owners sleeping in the room beside the shop.

It is difficult for the Chinese to travel. Even if they have the financial means, it is almost impossible to get a passport, and the State only ever allows them to visit one country at a time. The Internet opens up a window to the outside world; ideas from all cultures, darting across the continents like longitude and latitude lines superimposed onto a world map. Neither the Great Wall nor the mighty Himalaya can stop this exchange of information.

'One day everyone's going to be speaking the same language,' Paolo muses as he watches the Chinese students use the English computer keys to translate their thoughts into Chinese characters.

'English?' I query.

'No, Microsoft.'

The Internet has jolted China from its fifty-year slumber, and most students display considerable humility in their eagerness to catch up with the technological advances of the West. Very few of the older generation are interested in learning about this new age of computers: it's as if the Cultural Revolution has killed off the desire to learn something new. Perhaps it is also fears over censorship. All emails sent are automatically programmed to be copied to the State.

'I hate you writing about our journey, Nathan,' Kelvin scorns, looking over my shoulder.

'But I like to write about it, get it all recorded.'

'Well, don't write about me, then, especially telling everyone about what happened on our first night in China.'

I had already sent an email out to my list of readers explaining our first night in Beijing. Exploring the back streets of Tian'anmen, Kelvin had spotted a stunning-looking Chinese woman sitting on a chair outside a hair salon. She was wearing black stockings, a miniskirt and a tight black lycra top accentuating her nipples. Brushing her long dark hair, she enticed us inside with a wink and a smile. Once inside, two other Chinese women, less beautiful, showed us to our chairs.

I got myself a haircut for $2, which included a head and shoulder massage. Squeezing out cerebral tension with her fingertips and tapping rhythmically with a gun grip upon my shoulders, she located hidden pressure points all over my neck and back. Even my finger joints were clicked outwards and loosened. It felt very sensual. The hairdresser rubbed her body against mine, hoping I would embark upon the next and more expensive stage of the massage. I declined, but Kelvin decided to go for it. He headed behind a curtain into the back room with an even uglier employee and came back out fifteen minutes later, blushing.

'They charged me 60 *kuai* for the massage,' his shoulders shrunk, 'and 90 *kuai* for the clean-up.' It was his whole week's budget.

There isn't much potential for female contact out on the Wall. Well, not unless you are willing to incite a herd of angry pitchfork-wielding peasants, or never want to get anywhere. It is more of a pilgrimage or monk's journey, where one's sexual energy gives way instead to creativity and physical survival. Untainted by fashion media or explicit magazines, I am gradually finding that I do not miss sex at all – that instead I am moved by deeper things: Nature, the cosmos, the massiveness of the planet.

The peasant women are the same. Their beauty is innocent, untainted by make-up or the latest fashions, and they never seem to instigate encounters of a sexual nature. I am attracted to this serene sense of purity – being just who they are.

This is in significant contrast to the cities, where the sexual energy is immediately felt, in particular between Chinese women and the white male foreigner. Prostitution is common in hair salons and hotels, necessary for those who have come in from the villages with no skills or money, and who are unable to find a working husband. AIDS is a big problem in the cities and has begun to spread to all the provinces, because public awareness and prevention campaigns have been minimal, the leaders in denial about HIV. This has led to the establishment of the disease among two large groups: drug users and the peasants in Central China who had readily sold their blood to dealers to get by in the 1980s and 1990s. Using unsterilised needles and mixing everyone's blood together to cut costs, the technicians would then extract the necessary plasma before transfusing the remaining blood corpuscles back into the peasants. With SARS, and its ability to paralyse the country economically, the State is taking the AIDS epidemic more seriously. Government health reports state that 0.5–0.8 percent of the population is infected, although it is estimated that eighty-five percent of HIV carriers don't know that they have it at all.

Day 17
The best use of life is love. Seventy-two muscles are used to frown while only fourteen are used to smile.

Anon

Kelvin and Diego return to the hotel from the hairdresser's.

'I got some great shots of you,' Kelvin says excitedly as he follows Diego inside to recharge the video camera.

'Yeah, some magic footage,' Diego replies, now clean-shaven and with short hair. Diego's modern hairstyle makes him look like a movie star, but I don't like it as much as his previous style, which had a humble air about it. The three of us head down for a cheap meal of rice and noodles at our local hotel restaurant. The restaurant owner is in his mid-thirties, his dark hair smartly groomed in a side parting. He is dressed in a black suit, and with a warm smile waves us to the main table to celebrate his birthday.

The restaurant staff have laid out a banquet. The table is brimming with plates of raw beef, lamb, pork, noodles, vegetables and a number of unidentifiable green leaves. All the ingredients are chopped thinly in preparation for the Chinese hotpot – a specialty derived from Sichuan province near Tibet. A metallic basin filled with water and mixed spices is slotted into a crafted hole in the table above a gas cooker. Once cooked, the food is fished out with chopsticks and placed into a tangy brown sauce with garlic, vinegar and peppery spices (*lajiao*).

'*Chi fan! Chi fan!*' Eat, eat! The staff encourage, grabbing the food out of the pot and putting it onto our plates as we bumble about with our chopsticks. Their generosity mirrors that of the Mainland peasants. The major difference in the cities, however, is the wastage of food. Social affluence is judged by the amount of food left over from a meal. It is a disgrace to the host to clean the plate entirely.

'*Shengri kuaile . . .*' the staff all sing the Happy Birthday tune to Chinese lyrics as the lights are dimmed and the candle-laden cake brought out. The candles are blown out and stripped, but, before it can be cut, the cake is picked up by the celebrant's best mate and hurled into his face. With a massive grin covered in sponge and cream, the birthday host, Jiayu, commences his birthday speech.

'We like very much that you have come to our city – famous for its sponge pudding.' He smiles, 'Meaningful friendship is important to us and it is our privilege to host you.'

He scrapes some cream from his face, attaches it to a giant piece of spinach and hurls it back at the instigator. No further encouragement is necessary and, as a full-on food fight ensues, an infantile side to China emerges that I would never have imagined possible. Harsh living conditions and human rights abuses take up most of the international press and literature about China, but this is far from our reality as a dollop of cream splatters Diego's cleanly shaven face. We launch a counter-attack but go down in a blaze of culinary glory . . .

After dinner the group heads up to the local jazz club. Red velvet couches surround the stage, which is set up with a microphone, piano and drums. A wedding party awaits their drinks for a *baijiu* toast. Everyone laughs as the bride, dressed in a traditional red silk dress, aims the bottle of white spirits into their glasses while being piggybacked by her new husband. A drunken guest sings karaoke with a high-pitched wail, insisting on returning to the podium again and again. Kelvin and I take it upon ourselves to perform a Maori *haka* to provide some respite. The Chinese are awed by the strength and energy imbued in the Maori culture, as is Paolo. The Chinese chew on sunflower seeds, spitting out the shells onto gradually growing piles about the floor. No one can leave until the celebrant either calls it a night or is comatose.

Day 18

'There's a small section of Wall on the map up in Northern Gansu,' Diego informs the team.

'It's too out of the way,' I whine, soothing my two open blisters. 'I reckon we should skip it and head straight to Wuwei where the main trunk line of continuous Great Wall begins. It will enable us to catch up with Sumana.'

'I think Diego is right,' Paolo contributes. 'We have to do this section because even the great English marathon runner William Lindesay neglected to run it on his journey across China. No one we know has ever been there.'

'Yes, it would be a shame to miss it out just to keep rushing towards the finish.'

I agree. To skip actual sections is not in the spirit of the journey. My lack of mental preparation, having joined the journey at the last minute, is starting to show. I haven't realistically considered how long this journey is going to take.

When we are packed and ready to go, the restaurant staff clump together at the hotel entrance waving like the Beverly Hillbillies as we pile into a taxi to leave Hexipu city. The thought of flying food is still clear in all our minds, and the connection of friendship runs deep despite our short visit.

The taxi-van stops 10 kilometres from town at the first sign of the Great Wall. At 4 metres high and 2 metres thick, the Wall curves northward through a dry featureless desert like a giant worm from Arrakis in the *Dune* novels. The engine is cut and the silence is immediate. The vastness inspires. After three days, it feels good to be away from the hustle and bustle of city life, especially the reek of coal fumes and pollution and the eyesore of litter.

Paolo and I walk together at a brisk pace. Diego and Kelvin begin to merge through their desire to stop at regular intervals to film and photograph the Wall. Having to take the video and camera gear out from their packs each time, they begin to slip further and further behind. By the end of the afternoon, Paolo and I are way out of sight. We sit talking in a field filled with yellow flowers.

'The Dark Ages were a cruel era in human history,' Paolo teaches. 'If you were spotted alone by a group of three or more men, you would be killed for what you carried.'

'I hope this place isn't like the Dark Ages,' I reply, pointing to a ramshackle village desecrated as if hit by the plague.

'In an attempt to stop such a destructive age, the Arabs inserted people from the Middle East into the plazas of Europe to play music.'

'Music?'

'Yes, they were trying to create some kind of new emotion and feeling in the people.' Paolo pauses. 'Most people laughed at the Arabs, but it eventually had an impact on the thinking of the time.' He looks up, his blue eyes shining. 'It led to the culturally enlightened phases that followed.'

The complexion of the flowers turns gradually golden as the sun lowers into the horizon.

'It's getting late. You head into that village, and see if you can find us all some shelter for the evening. I'll head back to find the others.'

Paolo walks back along the Wall, while I head slowly in. The street is lined with dilapidated houses. Wooden boards hang off windows and two dogs bark viciously, held tenuously by rotting ropes. Saliva drools from their snapping jaws. They jump out towards me, each time contorting uncomfortably as the ropes crudely hold them back. My heart pounds – I don't like it alone on the Wall. I hold my walking sticks at the ready in case the rotting ropes snap.

Continuing through the empty street, I make my way cautiously to a small cottage that is releasing smoke from a chimney in the roof. I knock on the door. The cottage door creaks open. Inside sit six adults and a child. The room is dark and they all have pale skin and are dressed in muddy clothes. Their smiles expose half-rows of rotting teeth, flesh from a recent meal of meat hanging from their gaps. I feel like I have stumbled upon a group of extras from a *Dawn of the Dead* movie set.

'*Wo keyi shuijiao ma?*' I ask. Sleep available? Their pupils light up as they offer me a place to sleep, and set about boiling a cauldron of water. I rush back to get the others, rounding them all up for dinner. The peasants stoke the fire, providing a generous serving of thick white noodles. After dinner we are led to a dark smoky room. The walls are thick with carbon, and a smoky fire lies in the corner. We settle into sleep, coughing and spluttering through the night, in particular when Paolo attempts to combat the smoke by pouring water over the fire. Despite our clogged lungs, we awake the next morning fully intact and set off early, deep into the far northern reaches of the Gobi.

Day 19
Diego waltzes merrily towards the group wearing a straw hat.

'It's bad luck,' says Paolo, unimpressed. 'The Chinese are far too meticulous to leave anything desirable lying around. You must have taken it from a grave site.'

Kelvin and I nod jokingly in agreement.

'You're being pathetic,' Diego mutters. 'It's just a silly hat.'

Five minutes later, Diego's camera starts to malfunction. Paolo raises his eyebrows.

'I told you so.'

'It's just the cold and batteries, stop hexing me.'

Half an hour later, Kelvin and Paolo enter a village to ask

for a place to sleep. They walk back out perplexed, refused accommodation for the first time on the journey. Forced to walk into the late twilight, Paolo's and my torches simultaneously stop working. Again we are refused entry into a home.

Hungry, we find a spot to pitch our tents, and await a feed of rice from Paolo. However, now even the cooker will not work!

'You're definitely getting rid of that hat, Diego,' Paolo commands. At the hat's very mention, a big gust of wind blows, growing in ferocity. A Chinese farmer earlier in the day had looked up to the clear blue sky and gestured to us that there was going to be a storm. I thought he must have been mistaken. However, these people have senses that only a lifetime on the land can procure. They are very in tune with the elements. Diego leaves the hat lying outside his tent.

'Please take away the evil spirit that lurks and mourns for his stolen hat,' Kelvin prays with a deadpan expression. As he takes out his Mormon Bible I have to stop myself from laughing. Usually the quintessential party boy, I've never seen Kelvin praying before – Mormonism being a relatively new fad of his. Certainly so far as the sex, coffee, drinking and smoking rules go, he's a tad rough around the edges.

When working in the States, I had spent a few days in Salt Lake City, Utah, befriending some Mormons who showed me around the Tabernacle. Thinking me a likely recruit, they shared their views on life with me. I listened with interest but had to be frank with them when they explained the taboos, to which I, like Kelvin, wasn't prepared to subscribe. When they realised that I wasn't going to change, they proceeded to reject me – something my notion of God would never condone.

Upon utterance of Kelvin's prayer and Paolo casting away the hat far from Diego's tent, a group of Chinese villagers appears outside our tents to invite us to have dinner at their home. The cooker, camera and torches also begin to work again. I am flabbergasted, the timing a little more than eerie. As we return to our tents after dinner, the icy wind increases as our first major snowstorm blows in.

'I hope Hefty burns down his tent,' Kelvin snarls, referring to Paolo by his nickname. Paolo is attempting to keep warm by using his fire stove at the tent entrance – the flames leaping up sporadically towards the flapping material.

'He's so self-centred, doesn't go out of his way to help anyone,' Diego complains.

'I helped him lower a fence for him to climb over. Do you think he stopped on the other side to help me?' Kelvin grimaces. 'Not a chance.'

'Let's get some good sponsorship photos so we can try and request another cooker. Then we won't need Paolo.'

I don't like that they are scheming in such a way, even though I am not necessarily in disagreement about the nature of Paolo's character. Kelvin and Diego want me to be part of their unit, but I am not comfortable with just them either. Such talk makes me uneasy.

The storm closes in, so we hastily batten down the hatches and get into our sleeping bags to protect ourselves from the onslaught of snow. The wind shakes our tents sideways, but the tent pegs hold. We have been lucky with the weather thus far, yet the sheer power of the desert and its ability to transform in a matter of moments take our understanding of the surroundings to another level. Nature is in control of the flow of this journey.

Day 20

The storm has ceased by the morning, leaving the land covered in snow. Chalky mist fills the air, but a growing gap of blue sky is approaching. I am up at 6am, ready to go at sunrise as is the case every day with the journey.

'I'm freezing, Kelvin. Come on, let's get going.' My sleeping bag, good to minus-5 degrees, has reached its threshold.

'Nah . . .' he replies drowsily, 'I can't be bothered walking in that cold.' He turns over and sleeps on – his fluffy yellow North Face sleeping bag being good to minus-20 degrees. Kelvin had secured two North Face sleeping bags, keeping one and giving the other to Diego. Diego also has a sleeping bag that is good to minus-15 degrees from other sponsors. Strangely, although he has kept both in his pack, he does not let Paolo or me use the spare one even though ours are inferior.

'I hate how Diego carries the two best sleeping bags. What on earth would he want with them both anyway?'

'He's saving it for his German friend Graham who might still be coming.'

'Yeah, right. Sure, we'll see that guy out here in the middle of the fucking Gobi. I'd give it back if he came.'

Diego had hounded me in Beijing when I had tested out the minus-15-degree sleeping bag, presuming I could use it after Kelvin had given Diego one of his. I am bitter because I am also carrying Diego's tent and documentary equipment, supposedly to save him space to fit in his personal camera equipment. It's okay to be generous for the first 100 kilometres, but with all this extra weight my body is starting to get battered.

'Come on mate – get up. I'm really cold and Paolo's probably even colder. Once we can stir Diego into action then I can get his tent packed up and we can set off to keep warm.'

Kelvin turns over; both he and Diego sleep on. I'm angry but there is little I can do but wait. The group eventually sets off at 11am.

By late afternoon, the snow has already melted. We reach a small farmhouse, which is filled with four Chinese peasants sheltering from the bitterly cold wind that is sweeping down from a series of ice-laden mountains in the distance. The peasants are wrapped in goat-skin blankets and offer us shelter for the night.

'I think we should push on while it's still light,' Paolo suggests, giving up the option to sleep. Paolo is also concerned about the laziness creeping into the group. We brace ourselves for yet another effort walking through the cold. The desert land glows reddish orange and the wind whistles through our limbs as we pace the land. The sun bids a hasty retreat behind the Himalayan fortress, and a hut made from reeds and desert mud appears in the distance just before darkness encases the land.

The shepherd owner watches us walk in with our walking sticks, mimicking our walking style to his enormous amusement. Initially sceptical, I have now embraced the use of the two walking sticks. First, they transfer thirty percent of the weight of my pack onto the forearms, taking pressure off the back and legs. They also help power the body up mountains, and are used as breaks when descending to protect the knees. After a couple of weeks of use, they are becoming an extension of the body, meandering like four-legged game across the planet's surface. I am also able to enjoy the scenery without having to watch out for my feet, covering a third more distance with the same use of cardiovascular energy. It makes the 30-kilometre walking day manageable.

The shepherd wears a blue cap with grey overalls. His face is olive, and he has a healthy-looking set of teeth. With few possessions and no need for locks, he welcomes us in with the sort of trust one finds in a bird sanctuary.

'Our modern Western culture is considered advanced, but it is not as genuine as that of this shepherd of the Gobi,' Paolo suggests as we lie down in our sleeping bags on the shepherd's wooden *kang* to watch him prepare a basin of water over the fire. 'Our personalities have been repeatedly moulded to fit into the ways of the city environment, taking us far away from the essence of natural human reality.' The shepherd goes about his duties merrily, laughing to himself, talking to the fire that he tends. The fire crackles and dances, as if responding.

'It is a weakness,' Paolo continues, 'where a personality that wants to fit in, be liked and accepted, shows off with all sorts of unnatural expressions rather than simply being.'

Kelvin and Diego wash their feet in the basin of warm water provided, Paolo using the muddied water to wash his socks. I head outside to watch the stars.

'You don't ever get stars like this in New Zealand,' Kelvin gasps as he relieves himself outside the hut. I have spent most of the past few hours just watching. With no moon and electricity for hundreds of miles, the night is spread with a blanket of pinpricked light. Stars and planets rise out of the long flat horizon.

Day 21
Tatai whetu ki to rangi, mau tonu, mau tonu. Tatai tangata ki to whenua, ngaro noa, ngaro noa.
Companies of stars in the sky last forever, forever. Companies of men on the earth are lost, lost.

Maori proverb

The shepherd comes into the hut at 5am, speaking loudly and stirring us all into action. It is good to have a kick-start, because no one, as yet, has taken on any sort of leadership role to impose team structure and discipline. He begins cooking up another load of noodles that he has specifically gone out of his way to secure from one of his mates on a neighbouring farm. The generosity is simply astounding, and, in spite of our offer, he has no use for our paper currency in this moneyless realm.

'Oh my God, my dear God,' Diego says as he leaves the hut to film the sunrise. A faint line of orange pierces the base of the star-studded horizon. Drawing gradually above our heads, it is like a giant black curtain being lifted off the face of the Earth by some heavenly force. We thank the shepherd, who lights a fire outside to keep our fingers warm, and then laughs uproariously as he picks up my walking sticks and imitates my keen walking style. We set off again into the unknown.

The Wall is just a mere speed hump of mud. There are still 17 kilometres on the maps to the next lake where the Wall again terminates. We hope to polish it off by lunchtime.

'Let's see how far we can go in an hour,' Kelvin suggests. We race for a clump of trees in the far distance. At the end of the hour we have covered 6 kilometres – a record. Yet Kelvin has strained his calves and both of us are exhausted. We rest while waiting for the other two, and are surprised to see how fast our bodies are recovering. Three weeks in the desert and the body is beginning to adapt to our daily wandering.

The lake is visible in the distance, sparkling blue. A grey Chinese temple stands at the opposite end and a sandbar parades through the middle. Kelvin charges off ahead to reach the lake first. Paolo heads off, close behind in pursuit. Diego and I hang back together, as usual come the end of the stage.

'I hate it how everyone takes off at the end. Look at this place, we could be filming wonders for the documentary.' Fragments of the Wall lie buried in untouched sand dunes with yellow desert flowers and thorn scrub giving the place an archaeological feel.

'There's nothing you can do about it, Diego – just enjoy the scenery for yourself.'

By lunchtime Kelvin, Paolo and I have circled the lake and lie in the sun waiting for Diego. Quite fortuitously, given the remoteness of the terrain, a blue truck comes in from a dusty road in the mountains. It contains two Chinese men. They stop as we wave them down, inviting us to hop on the back. We have to stall the drivers from leaving though, because Diego has not yet arrived. After half an hour they are itching to leave, and we all agree that we can leave Diego to enjoy his lake view and get him to hook up with us later via the cellphone in the next township. It is only by pure luck that Diego appears around the dam corner in time.

The truck drives us out of the reserve and down a tarseal road.

'I can't believe we are leaving here so early,' Diego mutters. No one responds, preparing for the next challenge. Instead of turning south towards the next major city of Wuwei, the truck turns north towards the small city of Minqian, site of the Gobi's northernmost garrison. The truck drops us off in the middle of the city beside the open markets. Before we even get out we are surrounded by over 100 curious locals. Staring and laughing excitedly, it seems pretty clear that these guys have never seen white people before. The police are forced to divert traffic to cater to the increasing audience with their bovine stares. I speed the camera around in circles, catching their looks of awe. After being at the most isolated lake on the trip, the immediate contrast – superstar status – is exhilarating.

We spend the late afternoon in the city, experiencing the local cuisine and markets. Beheaded cows and sheep lie in the outdoor meat works, covered in flies. The Chinese play games with small hoops and fishing-rod magnets, trying to fish out prizes like cigarettes and toy cars. Kelvin takes a bus down to Wuwei that afternoon to settle into a hotel. His calves are still sore and he needs to find a quiet place to rest – if that ever is possible in China. We have all been together for twenty days and tensions have been exacerbated. It will be good to get some independence from each other. Kelvin takes his cellphone with him so we can get in touch when the rest of us arrive in Wuwei.

Paolo meets a schoolteacher with perfect English, who invites Diego and I over for a meal of *jiaozi*, dumplings filled with lamb and dipped in vinegar. They have a son. Sometimes three kids can be seen in families in the more remote farming regions where the one-child policy doesn't apply to ethnic minority peoples or is unlikely to be enforced. Two children are completely legal in rural districts, as well as if the parents are both only children. However, this rarely occurs in cities; the consequences of a 10,000 *yuan* fine and both parents losing their jobs are too risky to contemplate.

'Would you like to have brothers and sisters?' I ask their teenage son.

'Of course, but instead I have a very close group of friends – pseudo-brothers, if you like. We spend all our time together, with a connection as strong as blood.'

Day 22

'I don't want to go to Wuwei straight away,' I complain to Paolo and Diego from our dingy hotel room outside the bus stop in Minqin. 'My plan is to head down to Lake Qinghai first, for a two-day break.'

'There is no guarantee that we will still be in Wuwei when you come back,' Paolo states firmly. 'It's at least a two-day trip just to get there and back.' He pauses, looking suspicious. 'I think you should give us the maps.'

'Yes, Nathan, the Wall is the priority, you can't go off and just take a holiday. You'll have to pass the maps over to us.' They both tower over me like the Wall at full strength. I reluctantly hand over the five maps I had purchased in London before the trip, and prepare to pack my bags to catch the bus to Lanzhou city, which lies at the eastern gateway to the Himalaya. Whether by fate or simple misinformation, I am given the wrong departure time and miss my bus. I ask for the maps back as Diego, Paolo and I take the bus to Wuwei instead to meet Kelvin and hopefully Sumana.

Wuwei is the biggest city we have so far encountered on our walk. Small alleyways interweave through the ancient brick buildings that comprise the old city, each corner secured by a giant Ming watchtower. Outside of the old city, rapid developments are taking place in the typically sterile modern Chinese style. Indeed, once you have seen a few cities, you have pretty much seen them all.

Diego calls Kelvin on the cellphone and we all meet up at the China Telecom Centre, bunking down at a hotel by the bus station for the rest of the day. At the Internet office we learn that Sumana has already headed onwards to visit a different strain of the Great Wall, off the main branch towards the city of Lanzhou.

Day 23

The next day we plan to meet at the hotel by checkout at twelve o'clock to catch the one o'clock bus to the next section of the Wall. It is poorly arranged because nothing is definite in everyone's minds. That is, except for Paolo and I, packed and ready to go, waiting outside the hotel lobby for the others at 1pm.

'Let's go — they should have been here by now,' Paolo suggests, itching to get back out on the Wall. 'We can find the Wall and hook up with them later tonight or tomorrow.'

'Let's wait. They must be coming soon.'

We wait patiently until the 2.30 bus is set to go.

'Come on, it's been an hour and a half – let's go.'

'No, Paolo, we have to keep on waiting. They'll be here soon.'

The 3.30 bus is set to go, and still they haven't arrived. Before Paolo can protest, I take off through the streets to have a look. An hour later, I come back, having seen no sign of them, as the 4.30 bus is ready to pull out.

'One more bus, Paolo, we've waited this long.'

As the 5.30 bus starts to fill up, readying to leave, even I am now completely fed up. Under the circumstances I take Kelvin's cellphone and leave the others an angry note asking them to call us when they get back.

We don't see each other again for four months . . .

MOON 5

TAKE YOUR MARKS . . .

We few, we happy few, we band of brothers;
For he today that sheds his blood with me
Shall be my brother; be he ne'er so vile
This day shall gentle his condition:
And gentlemen in England, now a-bed
Shall think themselves accursed they were not here,
And hold their manhoods cheap whiles any speaks
That fought with us upon St Crispin's day.

William Shakespeare, *Henry V*

The bus speeds out of Wuwei. Turning a brilliant red, the sky dissolves into darkness as the sun sets behind the eastern edge of the Himalayas. There is a sense of excitement as we race off into the night. Half an hour later, the cellphone rings. The timing could not be worse. The bus driver has just stopped at the spot where the Wall intersects the highway, waving Paolo and me out.

'Hey, Nathan,' says Kelvin, calmly opening the conversation.

'Wait a minute, Kelv, I'm just squeezing through the bus aisle. I'll be outside in a second.' I head outside the bus. It is dark and I have no idea where I am. 'Where were you guys? We waited and waited.'

'Oh, we were just around . . .' His casual tone angers me. I am sick of the laziness. 'That's not important. Why am I paying to be talking to you on *my* phone?'

'It seemed the most practical thing to do,' I reply, fully aware that Kelvin had paid 1000RMB (US$120) for the phone, under the impression that all five walkers were going to go splits, and as yet no one had paid. Paolo and Sumana had decided to pay only for the calls they made, and I hadn't used the phone yet, although it had helped reunite the group when separated in stage one.

'Look, if it's going to come down to a money issue, treat that 200 *yuan* I gave you for your birthday as my part-payment for the phone.' This is not the time to be arguing over money matters. We still haven't discussed how we are going to meet up.

'Nathan, look at the Wall under the stars: it's amazing!' Paolo calls out, undeterred by the conversation.

'Wow, bro, you've got to see this place, it's amaz—'
Kelvin had hung up. Stage four had begun.

Day 24, 3 December 2000

It feels weird with just the two walkers. I have effectively jumped ship, teaming up with the man who until a month ago was a complete stranger. I leave the phone on, hoping that Kelvin will call back. There is no other way for us to remain in contact. Paolo and I catch a tractor to a small hotel 5 kilometres from where the bus has dropped us off. With no return call forthcoming, we set off the next day and catch a truck back down the motorway to where the first signs of Wall are visible.

A solitary watchtower stands in the dry, deserted fields. Its caramel colour contrasts brilliantly with a backdrop of snowy peaks. Looking for the Wall, we stumble across a hidden valley with farmhouses carved into the rock. Chickens roam freely and donkeys lie in the open doorways. No other humans are in sight.

A Chinese man approaches from a distance, riding on a camel-drawn cart. Inside the cart is a young boy. His hair is shaven to the scalp above the right ear and he has a knife-slit scarred across his right eye.

'*Chang cheng ʒai nali?*' Where is the Great Wall? I ask.

'*Zai nali – lu hen ʒhai.*' He points towards a dusty road heading east and comments that the Wall is small.

I am surprised to find that I actually understand him. With no one else with language skills to rely on, I have no choice but to try to communicate for myself and Paolo – my two weeks of language preparation in Beijing are starting to pay off. Rattled and torn, containing scribbles and marks, my Chinese phrasebook resembles something of a spell book. First, as with all components to a spell, I need to learn how to pronounce the sounds properly. If not, the Chinese peasant (another of the spell's vital components) will not understand and the command will be a failure. The first spell I need to master is the level-one magician's spell I never bothered to learn when playing Dungeons & Dragons as a kid. That is, to find food and water.

Paolo and I follow the dusty road that lies just to the north of a series of snow-covered hills. The white contrasts brilliantly with the distant vistas of sandy desert valleys, and shepherds watch us silently from a distance as we pass. The road leads to a grass-covered mound of Wall which trails off into the distance. We follow the Wall all day, and just before sunset reach the bus drop-off point of the night before. A Buddhist temple lies on the other side of the highway, a kilometre in the distance.

'I wonder if Diego and Kelvin have caught the bus today and found a place to sleep up ahead. Maybe they are in the temple already, Paolo?' A bell toll signals the end of chanting, and we are waved in by four monks adorned in yellow and orange robes. The congregation moves from the meditation chambers into dinner.

'*Meiyou biede waiguoren.*' No other foreigners have passed, the monk responds, passing us some bread before inviting us into a private room to sleep. I now have no idea whether Kelvin and Diego are ahead of us or behind.

Day 25
I awake feeling drowsy. In a hurry to get ready, I rush past the pot-bellied stove and knock over a pot of boiling millet with a loud clatter. The contents land on my exposed left foot. Gone is the breakfast Paolo has got up early to prepare; in its place is an excruciating burn. Two monks come rushing in. They scowl and

leave, returning with water and rags. Ignoring the searing pain, I start to clean up the mess; this time, in my frightened haste, knocking over the stove's chimney. The monks return again. They simply can't meditate with this noisy imbecile breaking up their kitchen. I only have time to slip my scorched foot into a silver bucket of cold water for a second before thrusting it into my boot and heading out into the hot sandy desert.

The Wall lies suffocated by sand. The bits of clay that peek through the dunes resemble buried bodies and pained faces. My foot is on fire. It is like walking with a sock of red coals and I need to get to some cold water fast. All that lies ahead is miles of parched sand.

Two hours later the Wall emerges from the desert floor, and with its 10-foot height comes my rescue. A pile of snow lies within the Wall's shade. I hurry off my left boot, and cover the aching foot in snow. The skin is like red jelly, but the snow helps freeze the pain until I can no longer feel my foot.

A passing schoolteacher dressed in a tweed jacket stops and invites us both to his cottage for some food. He asks his wife to start preparing some noodles while he fetches his class of young boys. I immediately take my shoes off again as the mother brings in a basin of steaming hot water.

'Oh no, you don't need that,' Paolo says.

'*Wode jiao buxing, sssssssttt.*' My foot no good, I state, mimicking the sound of burning. '*Wo buyao kaishui, wo yao bing shui.*' Hot water no good, cold water better. I act the words out, but am grateful that my spoken Mandarin is improving. The mother returns with some cold water and a potato. As the young schoolboys circle around closely, the teacher starts to cut the potato up into thin slices. He applies it to my foot. It immediately cools the raw skin, and the starch from the potato gives my foot a new skin. The soothing effect is surprisingly immediate.

Chinese doctors are masters at their craft. Similar to those in India, where Ayurvedic doctors can take one look at the posture, eyes or tongue of their patient to ascertain what is wrong,

Chinese doctors can make a diagnosis by taking the pulse. The Emperor's doctor was never allowed to see the royal daughter, because all men were banned from her presence. Hence a fine silk cord was wrapped around her wrist, extending to the next room, where the doctor's incredibly sensitive touch would feel for the pulse.

By late afternoon, a layer of starched skin has solidified over my burnt foot. With the heat of the day over, I am able to head out again to experience our first night walk. Having received no word from the others, it feels like a race has commenced across China.

We walk through the twilight, stars appearing above the ploughed fields, and we reach the foot of the next mountain range. Its dark silhouette towers forbiddingly, and the air starts to freeze. We have no intention of tackling this terrain by night. At its base lies a deserted brick village. Roofs have caved in, walls collapsed, and ghostly shadows are cast across the dilapidated brick walls from our torches. At the end of the village a solitary light flickers from a small cottage. Several Chinese characters are written on the doorway.

Basic Chinese characters are essentially simple pictures. The word for water originally had two long vertical lines running parallel to symbolise the banks of the river, and a smaller line running through the middle. The word for cigarette shows a stick-figure standing beside a coffin. The word for mountain has a line down the bottom with three vertical lines protruding – the middle one higher than the outer two.

I knock tentatively on the door. A small Chinese man in a brown jacket appears. He is surprised to see us, but without hesitation invites us in. It is a small grey room. A candle is lit on a table, and there is an iron gas cooker on a bench in the corner. There are three beds for the three male inhabitants. One of the men has a big bandage around his head and possesses shifty eyes. Playing-cards lie on the table, and one of the men is cutting up sliced potatoes with a meat cleaver.

'What happened to your head?' I ask, pointing to the bandage.

'I got struck with the meat cleaver,' he replies in Chinese, gesturing to his mate's hand.

'They're probably criminals,' Paolo whispers. 'Be careful with your belongings.'

Our hosts feed us a bowl of potatoes and noodle stew, and after dinner a fresh layer of potato peel is applied to my foot. One of our hosts gives up his double bed for us to sleep on, but I find it difficult to sleep, worrying what might happen to us after the lanterns go out.

Day 26

We wake up to the smell of cooking noodles and salty spices. Paolo and I feel stupid about our paranoia. China is one of the safest countries I have ever travelled in. It is just difficult when we are outnumbered and never 100 percent sure exactly what is going on, especially whether or not we are being invited to spend the night. It's like being constantly on guard, preparing the body to be ready in case accommodation doesn't work out. We set off early and I keep the cellphone on just in case Kelvin rings. As we head deeper into the foot of the mountains, we start to lose reception. Any chance of contact is now impossible.

We follow the Wall along the foot of the mountain range for the next two days. My foot aches with a gentle throbbing, but after hours of walking the pain numbs as if it is simply the norm. Routine is beginning to kick in. Wake up, walk, find food, sleep, wake up and walk the planet again. The days go fast when one is focused on finding the next meal. I must have sung 'The Sound of Music' about a million times in my head. The contagious tune – not to mention the Homer Simpson version – has captured my imagination and become my walking mantra, and I tap my walking sticks rhythmically to its beat. The Wall meanders along white poppy fields, through pyramid-shaped mountains, past coal mines, horse-grazed paddocks, scorching deserts and villages.

Given that the US aerial maps don't illustrate where the small villages are coming up next, it is impossible to calculate how fast or how far to walk in one session. Schedules are superfluous. The logical, rational mind has to be tossed out altogether to embrace the unknown path; creating each step as we come to it. This means having to readjust entirely, to listen more to the needs of our bodies than to our minds. Walking fast when full of energy, and slowly when tired, an innate timing mechanism is beginning to develop that seems to know just what pace is needed to get to the next village in time for the next meal. It is like we are gradually rekindling the hunter-gatherer instincts lost with the supermarket conveniences of the modern world.

We walk approximately 25 kilometres a day; some tally off quickly, others are painfully slow. There are huge cracks in the land that have been created by erosion and water channels at the foot of the mountains and we have to climb down and up each of them. Sometimes it takes up to an hour to cover 500 metres as the crow flies. It is an immense exertion with our heavy packs, and I am not sure how Kelvin and Diego are going to fare. There is no way of warning them what lies ahead. That is if they are even behind.

The Wall continues, relentless. Wallowing in the sun, drying off her clay scales, her spine traces across every peak and valley. Without the distraction of the others, the dragon seems very much alive. Her ancient body lures us deeper and deeper into the horizon, and I've developed an obsessive need to follow her path. All around us lie water shortages, wars, poverty and harsh living, but all I can see is the beauty of this architectural wonder. Firmly entangled in her spell, my daily dose of inspiration lies serenely out in front. Nothing else seems important.

I have fallen in love with the Wall.

Day 29, Huang He: The Yellow River

We crawl our way cautiously towards the cliff edge, peering over into the abyss. There, carving its timeless impression onto the crimson walls is China's Mother, the Yellow River. I stand up, awestruck before this superhighway of sustenance which winds its way through seven provinces from the Himalayas to

(*top*) Kelvin Gilbert Jones charges through the Mainland wilderness in Shanxi province near the city of Jingbian. (*left*) Diego Azubel carries one of his many cameras on his historic journey along the Great Wall.

Loess 'tortoise shell' mountains eroded by a lack of trees give the Yellow River its distinct yellow colouring. Sources say the Yellow River is becoming so low from drainage and irrigation needs, it now only trickles into the ocean.

The Great Wall trails alongside peasant crops and ploughed fields for much of the journey across Northern China. The peasants are forced to feed one fifth of the world's population with seven times less arable land than that in the United States.

A small piglet seeks attention and food from inside its pen. Pork, or churou, is the most popular meat eaten in China.

Two peasants of Hui extraction wearing the traditional white headdress as is custom for the Muslim peoples in Central Asia.

These edible Mung berries taste a bit like sour dates and are a vital source of food in the mountain wilderness.

The Great Wall at Jin Shan Ling with the ominous presence of
Simatai snaking up the next range.

The ancient Qin Dragon is nearly smothered by sand dunes en route from
Jingbian towards Yulin, Shanxi Province. Some of these Walls were built and
rebuilt up to 2300 years ago.

Where it all began: The tip of the Dragon's tail.

Jiayuguan Fort, the western terminal of the Great Wall of China, was first built in 214 BC. In the background looms Qilian Shan, a 7000-metre high stretch of the Himalayas separating China from the Tibetan Plateau.

Spanning some of the driest and most inhospitable terrain on the planet, much of the Gobi Desert has not seen rain for the past decade.

Paolo Antonelli stands before a 50-foot sand dune which swamps the advance of the Great Wall in the Tengger Desert just north of the city of Zhongwei.

Paolo Antonelli stands beside a snow laced wall while walking through a storm on our way towards the city of Datong.

The Mainland peasants and shepherds of the Gobi lead a subsistence existence without electricity or much water.

Using mules, camels and carts to transport their wares, Chinese peasants give me directions.

Buddhist Temple in the heart of the Helan Shan mountain range where Monks from China, Tibet and Mongolia go to commune with the Divine.

Intricately crafted from either clay, rocks or bricks, much of the Wall has been taken by peasants to build up their homes.

Watchtowers were placed in strategic highpoints to quickly pass messages by smoke across China in the event of attack.

Paolo Antonelli and a Chinese hitchhiker walk up an icy roadway towards a Buddhist temple in the heart of Helan Shan Mountain Range.

Paolo Antonelli checks the next step as he wades his way through an ice river four days' walk east of Dingbian City.

Keeping it light: Stripping our gear from nearly 30 kilograms to less than 20 kilograms was the only realistic way to cover the desert and mountain terrain.

Paolo Antonelli and a group of young Chinese schoolboys who accompanied us up the last mountain range before Huang He, the Yellow River loop.

I revel in the joy of having successfully navigated the Gobi Desert.

Yin and Yang: Sunset at the end of the first half of the Great Wall of China.

Chinese peasants comprise approximately 800–900 million of China's 1.3 billion population.

A Chinese dweller in the city of Xuanhua approximately 150 kilometres northwest of Beijing.

The average wage of a Chinese peasant can be as low as RMB 300 a month or US$37.50, even less in some cases.

A motorcycle taxi driver earns his living in the city of Xuanhua.

Snaking up into the mountains, the Great Wall journey becomes a challenge of mental fortitude and physical endurance.

Polly Greeks eyes up the wall at Huanghua Cheng (Yellow Flower City), otherwise known as Jin tang Great Wall, near the city of Huairo.

The top of the section at Huanghua Cheng shows how steep the terrain can be on the Great Wall.

Li Beng, my generous host, runs a deer antler farm approximately 500 kilometres from the end of our journey.

A young Chinese girl living in a small village two weeks' walk north of Huairo city. China's population would now be 1.9 billion had not the one-child policy been instituted.

Built during the Ming Dynasty, 1368–1644, this is now the 'tourist section' of the Great Wall around Beijing.

Sima Terrace leads to the steepest parts of Simatai and on to the infamous 'Stairway to heaven'; a pathway one brick wide with a 2000-foot drop.

Kelvin Gilbert Jones rests in a Chinese home. The picture on the front page of his diary is of his son Lucas.

Sumana Siri and Diego Azubel in Henan Province, where an interior line of Wall goes deep into the centre of Mainland China.

The Great Wall of China here surrounds the northern borders in the mountains outside Beijing.

Zhenbei Tower marks the middle point of the Great Wall of China.

the sea. The Wall ends – mere human-made veins no match for this artery.

Technically, stage four of the Wall is finished. There is no more of the Wall recorded on the maps until the city of Zhongwei. However, we are literally in the middle of nowhere. The desert lies above the sheer yellow cliffs the river has etched out, so we have little choice but to enter the deep valley and follow the flow of the river's current downstream.

We follow a trail down the side of the river. Some of the river walls tower up so steeply that we have to clutch to the sides of the cliffs so as not to fall in.

'Oh no . . . don't film that,' Paolo scolds. A mummified corpse lies on his back with his arms sprawled upwards from a fall off the cliff. We continue, cautiously rock-climbing around ledges, and finally reach a rock goat-pen as a bright orange twilight glow sweeps along the gorge walls. A shepherd screams out to his goats from up a thin side valley. The goats look like they are laughing at him, behaving like unruly children as they run further away. Beside the pen lies a raft consisting of twelve dead sheep carcasses. The wool has been shorn and the bodies have been inflated for buoyancy.

'I'm sure we have to take this raft across,' I mutter to Paolo. 'Let's wait for the shepherd to come. He can't be much longer.'

'No, I think we should try to climb this mountain to the normal level of the desert. There must be a village up there somewhere.'

'But that could be over 30 kilometres away and we haven't had a proper meal in two days!'

'I'm gonna press on.'

'But there's a small village on the other side of the river. Let's wait.'

'No, the light's decreasing; let's go quickly.'

Three hundred feet up the gorge, Paolo struggles with his heavy pack up the dangerously steep slope.

'This route is madness,' I rage. 'We're not going to make it up this mountain before dark. I'm heading back to the raft.'

I tear back, but it has already gone. I swear quietly while the goats eye me indifferently from their pen. It will be at least another day before the shepherd returns to run his goats back up the valley.

In the darkness, across the river, a man waits, watching. It is the shepherd.

'Help!' I yell, waving my arms. The shepherd looks set to leave, but hesitates. 'Please can you take us across?' Again he turns to leave but, for some reason, again changes his mind. 'Please? I'll give you money.' He unties his raft and carries it 200 metres upstream to cater for the current, then powers the raft across the river. Once upon the other side, I have to restrain myself from embracing him. He will have nothing to do with my money.

Just as the shepherd arrives Paolo returns, grumpy at having to turn back. The shepherd has a caring face. He is dressed in blue overalls and wears a grey cap. We all trek back up the river another 200 metres. Before inviting us onto the raft, he takes the plugs out of four of the sheep's arses and blows air into the dead bodies to increase their buoyancy. I wonder whether the raft will be able to hold us with all our gear.

Sitting on the wooden planks tied by rotting rope, we position ourselves tentatively. To tip into the water will mean the loss of my camera equipment, the journey and possibly our lives. The shepherd uses his long stick paddle to push us from the cliff face and out into the current. The flow immediately picks up the raft, and the shepherd puts his head down and begins rowing with strong, methodical strokes. Surrounded by steep cliffs, the raft churns through the water as a three-quarter moon appears above the gorge opening. It feels like viewing space from an asteroid.

At the three-quarter point, the shepherd begins to tire. Water laps at our outstretched feet. Any deeper and the packs are going to get saturated. The shepherd has a renewed burst of energy, frantically rowing like an Olympic champion. The water level lowers, the river of no mind to terminate our journey at this stage.

'The others will never make it across the river with all their weight,' Paolo comments.

'I hope they call us soon so we can warn them. It's been over a week now.'

The shepherd invites us in for dinner and sleep. He shares a ramshackle hut lit by two candles with his wife and daughter. The seven-year-old child is dressed in pink and has plastic earrings. Her name is Venus. She lies on the bed showing off, dying for her father's attention. The shepherd probably spends most of his time with his family of goats.

Paolo takes out his sleeping bag, and puts on his green headband to keep his ears warm. He prepares his cooking stove in readiness for a meal of millet the next morning.

'Ear protection and preparing to cook a wholesome meal is not me – it's my dominant instinctual centre, wanting to manage all my energy.'

'What?'

'There are many "I"s inside of us – in fact each of our thoughts projects a different "I". All the great teachings speak of this.'

'What do you mean?'

'I have the emotional me, the instinctual me, the moving part of me, and the intellectual me. All contribute to the person I am, and fight amongst themselves to dominate my reserves of energy. At this point of time, I am observing the typical dominance of my instinctual centre, whose purpose it is to ensure that my body is clean, well fed, and safe. Once I have all these needs fulfilled, this part of me will contentedly retreat to my inner cave and sleep.'

I had already passed out. Two days without properly eating, a bad cold and over 200 kilometres of trekking have turned the expedition into a test of endurance. We all cram onto the same concrete bed. The *kang* is kept warm by inserting hot coals into a hole underneath. I have to sleep on top of my sleeping bag, the ancient electric blanket is so effective.

Day 30

Arabian music echoes from down the river valley. We leave the shepherd's home, donning our desert goggles and face masks to protect us from flying sand as gale-force winds blow down the gorge. We head towards the medieval sound of pipes and clashing cymbals. Kids are dressed in white sheets and gold belts, and wear long, brown paper hats like chefs. Some ride donkeys as they guide us into their village. We have stumbled upon the funeral of a village elder.

The celebration of his life is a big event. Chinese peasants have set up a white-and-black awning over the courtyard rafters. Colourful crêpe paper, balloons and prayer flags flap wildly in the breeze. The coffin is intricately designed. A red dragon is painted on top, the sides depict a brown flat-top mountain surrounded by leafless trees and the Yellow River. It is the scene behind the village. A black-and-white portrait shows the deceased with a well-groomed moustache and stern eyes, his solid frame dressed in a general's uniform. The picture lies, surrounded by numerous candles and food offerings, at the base of the coffin. On top of the coffin lies a silver tray filled with cigarettes. The scene looks more like a birthday party, the Chinese believing that death is just the next stage of the journey.

The man's wife is dressed in a white-and-black dress. She is surrounded by children and sits in a room with an altar full of candles and bread offerings. Her wrinkled face possesses a calm expression. A room is set aside for a group of villagers to play ancient trumpets. The thud of percussion drums and the clang of miniature cymbals fill in the musical pauses of the main raspy tune set by the pipe horns. Paolo quietly shows me a black-and-white photo of him standing beside his mother. She passed away when he was a child.

After a lunch of black rice, a Chinese delicacy, we continue onwards, catching a large barge back across the river. It is attached to a wire and uses the river's flow to propel its way across. A woman in a purple vest and green trousers accompanies us for the rest of the day. I watch her nurturing brown eyes and long black dusty hair. Her facial features remind me of my mother. I imagine her thinking about our journey. Both of my parents were concerned for my life when I told them I was going to walk the Wall. It took a lot of determination to override their opinion.

Gold autumn leaves drop from poplar trees beside the river in the gusty conditions. The lady accompanies us for 15 kilometres along a dirt track to a tarseal road. Here lies a bus stop which will take us to Zhongwei city where the Wall next appears. Mum's prayers seem to be working.

PROVINCE TWO: NINGXIA HUI AUTONOMOUS REGION
To walk the Path, one must first become the Path.
Goteme Buddha

Day 31, 10 December 2000, Zhongwei City
'Sumana!' I shout with delight, embracing the chubby Sri Lankan waiting at the Zhongwei bus stop. It has been three weeks since he disappeared, and it is reassuring to see a familiar face in a sea of unfamiliar faces. He has called the cellphone twice, leaving messages as to his whereabouts, and has also organised a hotel for Paolo and I to stay in upon our arrival in Zhongwei.

'What happened when we lost you?'

'I couldn't find you guys, so I walked and walked before finally coming across this small village along the Wall at night.'

'Yes, we met the guy that looked after you. What have you been up to since then?'

'I've been visiting other branches of the Great Wall and temple sites near Lanzhou.'

'Weren't you lonely?'

'No, it's a good chance for self-reflection, but I do carry my tape-recorder to listen to my favourite tunes, and a whistle and stick in case the locals get overly excited.' He pauses, looking me in the eye. 'Where are the others, and how are you getting along with Paolo?'

'I don't know. We split in Wuwei, but will hopefully meet up again soon.' I pause, reflecting. 'It's been good to have the break to be honest. Things were getting tense between us, and Paolo and I aren't competitive with each other so we've had no real fights.'

'It's also easier on the Chinese hosts with fewer people,' Sumana replies. 'It is quite extraordinary that some of those remote farms were willing to take in all five of us at one time.'

'Yeah, one lady took the four of us in and fed us about twenty pancakes each.'

Sumana looks down at my foot, visible in the open sandals I used to walk in during the last marathon section.

'How is your foot? It looks bad.'

'It still oozes pus and is painful to walk on, although I generally just forget about the pain.' I look down at the scar tissue. There is a red bruise the size of a fist, and all the skin around it has peeled off. 'It is strange how the mind deals with pain. It is as if I have detached myself from my body.'

'You will have to keep the wound clean with carbonated water so it doesn't get infected. Come on, let's go to the chemist.'

Boxed pills line the shelves. The shop has been infiltrated by Western pharmaceuticals, the latest fad in China. Costing roughly the equivalent of Western-priced medicines, they are generally available only to wealthier citizens. However, even the poorer citizens are forking out personal fortunes to purchase the modern medicines, enticed by the guarantees provided by television advertising campaigns. Considering how effectively the simple potato remedy had worked, it seems strange to disregard thousands of years of tested Chinese remedies. I am also sceptical because I once acted as an extra in an advertisement for China TV for a Hepatitis Remedy, where the so-called doctors presenting their 'international opinions' were merely other travellers like me. Sumana applies some carbonated water to my foot. It eats into my wound, leaving white foam on the skin. I lie in bed for the rest of the day, recovering, but find it very difficult to stay stationary. My mind and body are now completely accustomed to being on the move.

Day 32

Zhongwei is a big industrial city lying on the outskirts of the Tengger Desert. Situated in the western border of the Ningxia Hui Autonomous Region, the city is a stronghold of the Hui people, containing 32,000 of the 60 million minority Muslims scattered throughout China. It is also here that Mao Zedong and his Communist troops rested after their gigantic northward march over the Snowy Mountains from Sichuan Province into Gansu.

Sumana takes me to Zhongwei's main Buddhist temple. Four storeys high, it is meticulously built out of wood, dragon statues carved into the eaves with red, black, blue and yellow calligraphy displayed at the entrance. It is a masterpiece of mindfulness and sits in the middle of a lake, reflecting in the surrounding waters. A golden statue of Buddha sits in the lotus position in the main prayer chamber. Flanked by red curtains and incense boxes, the statue's eyes are closed in earnest meditation.

Red cushions lie around the statue's feet. Sumana has dressed himself in his light-brown monk robes and inserts an incense stick into an offering bowl outside. A Chinese attendant rings a golden bell as Sumana bows several times to the Buddha before making his way into the chamber to meditate. I follow suit, sitting alongside. Closing my eyes, I take the time to feel my breath flowing in and out of my nose. The simple sensation calms my thoughts and brings me slowly into my body. I open my eyes a few minutes later and feel my heart beating peacefully. The Buddha statue seems more happy, as though reflecting my mental perception.

'In the ten-day Vipassener meditation, one focuses the mind solely on the breath running over the top lip for the first three days,' Sumana says after finishing his meditation.

'I can't even imagine sitting down for that long. It seems such a waste of time.'

'It helps to focus the mind. Once you have complete concentration, you then sweep your attention back and forth across
your body from the top of the head to the tip of the toes.'

'Why?'

'It enables you to come more into your body, giving you a
proper sense of your true self.'

'Your true self?'

'Yes, at first when you meditate you will have many thoughts,
each one trying to distract you from concentrating upon your
breath. However, as your body is unable to act on these thoughts
immediately, eventually, if you sit long enough, you will notice
that they will drift on by like clouds. You are not your thoughts.'
Sumana pauses, taking a long, slow breath. 'The same can be
said about your body.'

'What do you mean?'

'There are exercises during the ten days where you are not
able to manoeuvre from your sitting position for over an hour.
The pain on the body can be excruciating. However, if you
abide by the technique and continue to sweep your mind back
and forth rather than solely focusing on the painful part, the
pain too will be forgotten. Of course it will come back again
when you sweep by the same place, but like our thoughts it too
is impermanent.'

Sumana's meditation theories intrigue me.

'All of human misery derives from craving; clasping onto
something we find pleasurable and wanting to prolong it, or
craving to get rid of it if the sensation is unpleasant. Buddhists
realise this and take measures to control the mind to curb this
self-imposed suffering.'

'What steps?'

'There are eight steps: right view, right thought, right speech,
action and livelihood, which are to do with wisdom and moral
conduct. Right effort, awareness and concentration, to do with
controlling the mind. If we learn to observe our sensations
rather than simply relish them, gradually one learns to refrain
from reacting automatically.'

'And if you can't stop reacting or craving a particular past accumulation?'

'You will suffer, because nothing on earth can last forever.'

Sumana guides me around the back of the prayer chamber. Behind the main statue lies the Buddhist underworld. Situated on frescoes lining darkly shadowed walls, unruly humans are being punished by green-faced demons. The torture occurs in gruesome forms: the rack, being hung, or jabbed with a red hot poker. One disobedient being has his tongue pulled out with searing tongs. Another victim is sawn in half, her dismembered body discarded to fester in a bubbling cauldron. A wilted grey devil oversees the horror with crazed diagonal eyes, listening to the human screams with gremlin like ears.

'That's the Buddhist god of Hell, Shittigaga,' Sumana points out. 'He tells us also not to develop too-strong attachments.'

Day 33

'When should we leave?' Sumana asks.

We have been in Zhongwei waiting for the others to call for three days.

Paolo replies: 'I think the others have decided to focus on the documentary. They haven't bothered to email or call.'

'Let's wait until we at least get some word, it's crazy to go through this life-changing journey separately.'

'Everything has a price,' Paolo responds. 'Indeed, it is useful to know exactly what kind of price you are willing to pay and to *whom* you are going to pay.' He pauses, deliberating his next words. 'As we learned in that last section, there were some tricky sections that required us to be carrying lighter equipment. If Kelvin decides that it is too heavy to go on carrying Diego's gear, perhaps he can join us. Even Diego, if he really wants to enjoy the journey, must also think to being a simple walker, not holding anything else in the mind.'

'How much longer should we wait?' Sumana intervenes.

'If they don't call by tomorrow, we'll leave for the full moon,' I reply.

Day 34

Buddhists believe you should only ever keep what you can carry. We spend the next morning paring down, ditching unnecessary items such as deodorant, spare clothing, books and sunglasses, used videotapes, even preventative accessories such as antihistamines. Once gone from the pack, they are not sorely missed. In fact, without the precautionary items in our midst, it also dispels the fear of such an event occurring. Like the Aborigines who travel for weeks through the deserts of Australia with just a loincloth, water gourd, one big stick for hunting and a little one for cutting and starting a fire; little is actually needed on top of local knowledge to survive within their environment. The potato remedy taught me that whatever problems we come across can be solved as we face them. The key is to be light enough to be able to walk our way out of trouble.

We dump another box of gear into the post office to send to Beijing, ridding ourselves of 2 kilograms each. I am now down to 25 kilos. We catch a taxi north of the city, deep into the Tengger: the second semi-desert on our route. A white clay watchtower peeps out from behind a large, golden dune. From the top of the tower we are able to see the Wall skim across the sand like a grey mamba. We trail the path deep into the horizon, awed by the immensity of our silent audience.

Sumana walks very slowly, his stumpy legs fighting their way through the thick sand. He is finding it very difficult to reach the top of the dunes.

'This stage is different from the last one,' Paolo advises. 'It is more about patience, controlling that "I" inside you that wants to rush.' Despite our increasing fitness, attempting to walk fast in the sand is a pointless exercise. Not only does it strain the lower back, it exhausts you and you gain no more than if you take slow, methodical steps. I find our new pace quite unnatural – it's as if I have been rushing all my life. The slower speed enables us to more suitably choose the line of terrain we want to walk, up to 4 to 5 kilometres in advance. With gigantic sand dunes and cracks in the planet to circumnavigate, trail foresight is now vital.

'I have a strong feeling that Kelvin is going to call today,' Sumana says, on our third morning out.

An hour later, the cellphone rings.

'Hello?'

'Hey, bro.'

'Kelvin! It's great to hear your voice.'

'Shit, yeah. How are you?'

'Good. We're in the desert just north-east of a city called Zhongwei. Where are you?'

'We've just got to Zhongwei. Can you tell us where the hotel you stayed at is?'

'Sure, it's up the main road, with the giant watchtower about 50 metres on the left. It costs 15 *kuai* a day. A bit grungy, but good.'

'Guys,' I call out to Paolo and Sumana, 'the others are in Zhongwei. We can hitch-hike back and meet up.'

'We're definitely not going back!' Sumana argues.

'Don't listen to Sumana,' says Kelvin, overhearing his retort. 'Look, I've got to go, but I'll call you back later tonight.'

Diego and Kelvin had left Wuwei two days after Paolo and me, spending the first night sleeping in a hay-filled cave on a hillside. Having had little sleep, and with several unwanted Chinese visitors, they spent the next night with a family, but then got stuck in the mountains, their heavy gear causing injuries to Diego's knee and straining Kelvin's ankle. They decided to return to Wuwei to get medical attention, whereupon they met up with a Chinese acrobatic company that specialises in plate-spinning. The cast welcomed the Westerners as an entertaining addition to their travelling act, and they remained with each other for a couple of days. Then Kelvin and Diego headed off towards Zhongwei, taking rides from trucks as a more manageable way to traverse the mountainous continent. One truck driver was in such a rush that he played chicken with the lane of oncoming cars as Diego and Kelvin sat anxiously in the back.

Ж

By late afternoon, the Wall peters away to nothing as the desert of golden sand transforms into a valley of hard-baked farmland heading into a series of dark, craggy mountains. Sumana is relieved. He tried to escape the Wall earlier in the morning, entering a gap that had been eroded away by a 200-metre flood channel. Oblivious to the next watchtower that lay behind a 30-metre-high sand dune, he walked determinedly towards the highway, ignoring our shouts for him to return. Paolo had to run after him.

We find a road to a highway to catch a bus to the small township about 30 kilometres east of Zhongwei. Sumana laughs contentedly as he stays on the bus to head 50 kilometres further north-east towards the next main township of Qingtongxia. There, he will explore Great Wall sites by taxi and bus as he prefers, until we meet him in the next major city of Yinchuan, the one-third stage of the journey.

The Wall's silhouette traipses over the mountains, cast in a glorious backdrop of pink. I look out the window like a mournful dog.

'You don't want to miss out on it, do you, Nathan?' Paolo says. 'We will head back there tomorrow, after a night in the hotel to prepare.'

'Yeah, we need to stay in cellphone contact to wait for Kelvin's call.'

It never comes. Diego convinces him not to call. The journey continues; two, two and one.

Day 37

I am feeling sick after eating a meal of noodles and pork, my stomach is bubbling. Still, we set off in the morning, past an irrigation channel and up towards a Buddhist temple where an old lady feeds me grey roots to help ease the pain. My throat is dry and parched. She allows me to rest for another hour before I pick my ailing body up and follow the Wall, continuing northwards into the mountains. The Wall leaves behind a vast fertile plateau filled with paddy fields, pool-grown reeds, and wispy willows. Fed by the Yellow River, the Ningxia plain is one of the leading farming districts in China, with its constant source of reliable irrigation. First to cultivate the desert peripheries, the Han Chinese set up four irrigation canals. The Ming and Qing Dynasties created another six, providing some 574,600 *mu* (80,000 acres) of farmland watered by 500 kilometres of canals.

With 400 of the 600 Northern cities suffering water shortage, China's major solution is to divert the Yangtze River running from the Himalayas down through Sichuan Province. Causing significant social discontent, river villages have been forcibly expelled to cater for the rising water levels of the Three Gorges dam. Were the Yangtze to burst its banks, it is said a flood of Biblical proportions would result. This is a real possibility, given the haste with which the government is building the dam and the problems they are having with the cement.

Dynamite explosions are heard in the distance. We trail the Wall for two days through the mountains, passing through various rock and coal quarries. Chinese workers place the rocks into wheelbarrows, and soot-laden miners shovel the coal into blue transport trucks. Covering eighty-one percent of China's energy needs, coal is vital to the internal momentum of the nation. The whole country, it seems, is layered in soot. As the temperature gradually sinks consistently into the negatives, mounds of coal lie on every street corner, waiting to be sold and burned in the pot-bellied ovens situated in each home. China is hard on the lungs. No wonder everyone is so eager to spit it all out.

Coal companies set about making massive annual profits by plundering the carbon-enriched lands. Ten percent of China's needs exceed the imported tonnage of Japan and South Korea combined. As industry expels the guts of the planet, I wonder when the earth will respond with its own bout of seismic revenge.

Ж

Nature is dictating the pace of this stage of our journey. Progress through the rocky mountains is slow as we follow the intricately devised wall of bricks. It is the first non-clay wall we see on the entire journey. Trailing it further across the grassy Mongolian plains and arid desert lands, a sandstorm howls in at 60 knots, casting sleet and sand into our faces. We shelter every time we come across a shepherd's hut to warm our frozen fingers.

The temperature plummets to minus-10 degrees and I am finding it impossible to get to sleep in the tent. Thrashing my legs about in my sleeping bag, I curl up into the smallest ball possible, yet nothing seems to keep me warm. Paolo even lights up the cooker inside the tent – but this is far too dangerous for the short-term respite it offers. By morning, our sleeping bags are frozen solid. We walk now simply to keep warm, and keep going for up to eight hours without stopping to find a safe village in which to sleep before nightfall. I have never felt so fit.

Shepherds build their clay houses perched up against the Wall to shelter from the harsh storms. Sheep and goats fight each other with their horns for the limited supply of corn seeds placed in wooden troughs or scattered over the ground. When food is necessary, a goat has its throat cut and is hung up to dry, its wool stripped by a metal claw with five curving points. Often the shearing is done while the creature is still alive, the goats tied to the ground moaning in pain. The bladder and entrails lie inside the sheared fleece, and the rest of the meat is eaten in stews or as shish kebabs cooked with spices over the fire. Even the hoofs are used, burnt down with a heated file, although I am not quite sure what they are used for. Nothing is wasted.

'I wish my friends back home would give me more support for the journey,' I complain to Paolo.

'You mustn't expect such things, Nathan. People will give you encouragement when they feel like it, but, if it is forced, it is not from the heart and thus means very little.' Paolo considers his next statement. 'When Hercules slew the lion, the statues in Greece show him with a forlorn expression because he doesn't think he has the strength to tackle the next eleven tasks. Still young, he is yet to learn of his full potential.'

A hawk flies ahead of us towards the next watchtower.

'Look to the hawk,' Paolo continues. 'It has been marking our progress for the past week now. It seems the gods are in favour of the efforts we are making.'

'How do you mean?'

'In Hercules' twelfth task – where he is lifting up the earth for the demigod Atlas – the goddess Athena is behind him holding up all the weight.' We continue through the desolate Mongolian plains that trail the Wall faithfully towards the gradually expanding contours of a massive mountain range.

Day 42

Helan Shan swallows the sky. Jutting towards the heavens, the Wall heads halfway up the slopes of the mountain before terminating altogether. The ominous sight of Helan's dark, jagged peaks will do the Wall's work from now on.

As the horizon to the east curves in the manner of a frown, my lips curve the other way. This planet I am walking – horizon after horizon, for forty-two days – is starting to reveal her sheer size. The Earth Mother's form continues on and on. Sometimes, when walking silently through such an utterly deserted landscape, the space around you is so immense it becomes increasingly difficult to keep a balanced grip on your own sense of being. Your mind becomes so diffuse – expanding to fill the entire landscape – that it is hard to keep the mind fastened to the physical self. The expanse makes all human activity seem minute and trivial, and sometimes I am horrified to wake up and realise I have a body at all. I am a mere thought traversing the Gobi.

In terms of physical miles along the map of China, Yinchuan city is technically the one-third point of the journey: the end of the dragon's tail. A host of high-rises shines in the far distance like a small paua fragment reflecting the sun on a sandy beach.

Two large cylindrical chimneys bellow smoke into the air. We spend the night in a small coal station at the base of the mountains with four men who play mah-jong into the early hours. Similar to playing gin rummy, the competitors alternate collecting two white dominoes at a time to make straights or threes and fours of a kind. Their playing is fun but intense. Hands move swiftly around the board, collecting and discarding the tiles with well-rehearsed speed. At the termination of each round, the winner gets to flick his opponent on the forehead.

'Let's take a week off from walking, Paolo. It's been a month and a half now, and I need a proper break.'

'Good idea. We can hitch-hike around the Inner Mongolian side of Helan Shan range and catch up with Sumana later when we get into Yinchuan.'

'Maybe the others will have caught up by then, too.'

Day 43

I smile expectantly at the prospect of hitch-hiking after so many days of walking. Patience is no longer an issue. We can always walk if need be. Before I even put out my thumb, two Chinese truck drivers stop and argue between themselves about who is going to take us. We pile enthusiastically into the front of the bigger truck with our packs. It's such a rush being accepted for a ride. The blue lorry ploughs through the freshly laid snow of the Helan Shan mountain pass, our driver concentrating hard on the icy, grey road. He has puffy cheeks and oversized black-rimmed glasses. The Great Wall journey continues under clear, sunny skies.

The road widens out into the snow-swept basin of Inner Mongolia. The truck turns north, passing white Mongolian tents which line the base of the mountains. Ten kilometres further, the driver drops us off on the main road before veering off down another road. While waiting for the next ride, another Chinese man, wrapped in a grey trench coat and wearing a woolly green army hat, crosses the road to meet us. He has been hitch-hiking in the opposite direction.

'You must go and visit the Buddhist temple,' he says with a knowing glint in his eye. He delays his journey so he can inform the next truck driver who stops where exactly to drop us off. I can't help thinking we are meant to meet him.

The truck driver drops us at the base of a desolate road that heads deep into the heart of the mountains. About half an hour later a four-wheel-drive jeep comes down. Seeing us waiting, writing in our diaries, the driver turns around and goes out of his way to take us back towards the temple.

En route, the driver and his girlfriend pick up a female hitch-hiker. She wears a purple top and green trousers and is an inhabitant of the mountains. It is identical attire to that worn by the woman who guided us out of the Yellow River Gorge into Zhongwei two weeks ago. The driver drops us all off at a spot where the road is too icy to continue by car. With her nimble mountain feet, the hitch-hiker guides us up the winding road.

We walk for nearly two hours, passing colourful paintings of the Buddha etched into the mountain rock. Upon reaching the final bend, we turn to see two cascading peaks. In front is a red temple with a stairway encased in ice. It reflects the colour of a rainbow under the sun.

A strange rock stands alone on a mountain summit to the left. It has the shape of a screwed-up face, identical to Edvard Munch's painting 'The Scream'. It gives me an eerie feeling – as if something is warning me to be careful.

We file into the temple. Buddhist monks and devotees have come from all over the land to commune. The back of the temple has a long table laden with candles, incense bowls, money and food offerings. The candles glow blue. Giant horns, their brass bases lying on the ground, are blown by standing monks. The low note resonates through the valley. Thirty monks, clothed in black robes and capes of crimson silk, kneel on purple cushions. One wears a bronzed gladiator's helmet with protruding red feathers. All circle around the head monk in prayer. Wearing a gold jacket, he sits on a throne, reciting incantations. Incomprehensible chants to commune with the Divine. The temple resonates in a low-pitched vibration. The pull is magnetic.

※

'Can I . . . join you?' a girl from the adjoining table at the restaurant nervously asks, disturbing my daydream. 'My name is Zhu Wei. I can speech a little English.'

'Sure.' I gesture with my hand to a free seat and offer her chopsticks to pick at the flesh of my recently killed barbequed fish. Seated at the table beside are six Chinese men in their mid-to-late twenties. They laugh loudly, drinking cheap Chinese beer and directing haughty comments our way.

'That's my brother, Zhong Wei.'

I look over. He gestures with a wink and a commanding smile for us to both come and sit at their table.

A handsome young man in a dark shirt sits on my right. He introduces himself as Lu Qing.

'*Zhongguo tudou!*' Chinese Pizza! Zhong Wei shouts, placing in front of me a plate of fried potatoes dripping with cheese.

'Ningxia Province specialty. Enjoy!' Zhu Wei states with a smile.

'*Ganbei!*' Zhong Wei shouts.

'Cheers.' Lu Qing pours me a glass of beer, inviting me to scull and begin a hasty catch-up. I scull the fizzy, yellow liquid, enjoying the sweet taste of Chinese beer. It's been a while since I last drank alcohol.

'Let's play a drinking game,' I suggest, filled now with liquid courage. 'Do you know 21?'

'*Ershi yi,*' Zhu Wei translates. We spend a few rounds warming up the gullet, each person consuming a full glass if they are the victim of 21.

'How about musical-instrument concentration?' I explain the game slowly to the group, slapping my hands twice on the table and then clapping them twice to set up a repeatable rhythm.

I show them a range of musical instruments they can mimic with their hands. I do the violin first and then choose another instrument; the owner of that instrument must repeat the rhythm and do someone else's, and so on. We play a few rounds, warming up.

'Each time someone mucks it up, they have to drink and then stand out,' I explain. I have always been good at this game back at home, losing rarely, gradually reverting to just the one clap to keep up with the increasing speed of the game.

'Game over!' Zhong Wei cries – about the only words he knows in English – as one of the less talented players bows out early. Everyone laughs at the next poor victim who must now drink.

'Who's next?' I snidely ask.

My Chinese friends catch on quickly, urged into a fun, competitive spirit, until there is only Zhong Wei on the guitar, Lu Qing on the drums, and me on the violin. We're starting to hit the one-clap pace.

'Game over!' Lu Qing celebrates joyously, taking out the tenth round. Everyone laughs as my champion reign comes to an end. We eat, drink, laugh and play games throughout the long, cold evening. Without Paolo, who is back in the hotel and who never drinks, it's like a memory straight from my college days. This is by far the best night on the journey. The restaurant starts to close.

'How are you going to get back to the hotel?' Lu Qing asks.

'It's dangerous out there you know,' Zhu Wei contributes.

I think twice about arrogantly replying that I've been to enough places now in China to be able to look after myself.

'I'll take you in my taxi-van,' one of the other guys, Zhong Wu, offers.

'Ahhhhh ... Okay then, thanks.' I reply somewhat hesitantly, given how much we have all drunk. It's cold, though, my breath is freezing in the air, and my hotel is about half a mile down the road. Lu Qing opens the front passenger seat for me to get in. The rest enter through the passenger side doors just as another Chinese party approaches.

'Can you take us? We're stranded.'

'No!' Zhong Wu slurs. 'I'm off duty.'

One member of the new group of Chinese enters and stubbornly sits himself inside the taxi-van. Sitting comfortably in the front passenger seat, I am curious to see how my Chinese friends will resolve this. After half a minute of telling the man to leave, my friends are soon fed up, and the obstinate passenger is dragged out of the cab and pushed onto the pavement. Tempers flare and a few swinging fists hit the air. Nothing serious, although I check my door to make sure I know where the handle is so I can make a hasty escape if need be.

Both groups stare the other out on the pavement. Neither group looks particularly nasty. They're all young adults dressed in designer clothes, some even in suits. But the other group is getting desperate. It's at least minus-10 degrees out there. They continue to stare. Suddenly a stray punch is thrown and it's all on, bodies colliding as everyone converges. Fists and limbs flay wildly in all directions. I sit tight in my seat just watching – I am even a little excited and I feel powerless to stop it. Animal grunts and screams start to emerge from the pavement as the fight gets nasty. I certainly don't want to get involved now. About thirty seconds of chaos and body collisions later, Lu Qing takes two slow, laboured steps towards me on the driver's side of the van. He looks up to me with a plea of desperation, his chest heaves as he gasps for breath, and suddenly he collapses to the ground.

'What the—?' I look down. Blood is rushing out of his chest. 'He's been stabbed!'

The brawl instantly stops. Everyone looks down at Lu Qing, shocked. His black shirt is drenched. Zhong Wu gives a cry of agony, while Zhong Wei grabs Lu Qing by his armpits and drags his limp body into the van. Zhong Wu inserts the keys into the ignition and, with a crazed look in his eyes, drives quickly off. I am instantly sober.

We speed through the streets. It seems like only twenty seconds before the van is stopping outside a small hospital. It is grey and dark. Zhong Wu rushes out of the taxi to alert emergency staff. He is screaming incoherently. Blood is all over the passenger floor. The other three drag the limp body out of the van. I'm out in seconds, following the boys with the body. A nurse fiddles nervously with the keys to try and get a free room open.

First key, no.

Second key, it fits . . . shit, it won't turn.

Third key . . . fits in, the nurse nervously wriggles . . . no again . . . the guys are losing it . . . come on, nurse.

Fourth key . . . God, this is crazy.

Fifth key . . . yes, it's open.

The boys drag Lu Qing into the lit room, but one of them trips and everyone falls. The body is unceremoniously dumped on the ground. Lu Qing's black shirt rolls up and I see the wound for the first time. A perfect puncture wound to the heart. I stare for a moment before we pick up his body and lay him on the bed. I take another glance – he's already dead. His face has a green tinge and his open eyes hold an unfocused stare like that glassy look of death the moment my cook ripped out the gills of my fish.

The nurse checks the pulse. There is nothing she can do. It is just her, me and one other in the room at this stage. But it feels like just me and Lu Qing. I take a step back to the corner of the room, but I can't take my eyes off Lu Qing's face. An hour ago his eyes were shining with jovial innocence, he was playing the drums with passion. He was sitting just to my right all evening. Sharing laughs, food and drink, he even accompanied and paid for me to go to the toilet. For some reason he was always on my right. He even opened the door for me to the taxi-van, closing it safely before the event ensued – again on my right. I must have been his Death. Carlos Castaneda always wrote that Death will tap you on your left shoulder when the time comes. Even when Lu Qing walked over to me for that last breath of life before collapsing, his left shoulder was exposed . . . I can't remember whether I touched him . . . shit, my shadow must have . . . Madness . . . Crazy thoughts are entering my mind. I have to combat them. Still staring at the lifeless body, I think of my mum – her role in the Maori world is to take those close to death into the next dimension. Many have died comfortably in her arms.

I look again at those shiny, unfocused eyes. The light reflected in the pupils reminds me of the bright star I saw last night, just above the temple, as the Buddhist monks' chants pierced the darkness of the mountain valley. While focusing on the extraordinary light of the star, I observed a black tunnel projecting from space towards me. It intuitively warned me that death lay very close at hand. At first, I thought it to be a family member, and was relieved to find no such news when getting back on the Internet. Of course I had then forgotten about the experience, heading to the restaurant to eat my barbequed fish.

Still unable to avert my stare, I feel weirdly comfortable; as if Lu Qing has done exactly what he has needed to do in his life before heading where he is now needed next. I smile, and look around the room for any signs of the wonders of death. It is rare to get an opportunity like this, but of course I don't see anything. No bright lights, tunnels or angels. It is just a feeling.

Awaken . . . I'm staring at the lifeless lump.

The good feeling has left. It is definitely time to leave the room. I walk out slowly, speechless . . . never to see the room again . . . although, as I lower myself into a dark corner of the hospital corridor, the scene remains clear in my mind.

I feel hidden within myself. Few people, for once, notice I am actually here. Head down, nauseated, I force myself to look up and observe my surroundings. The other friends express their emotions. Three of them are lying sprawled out on the dark corridor floor. One sobs, another screams and hits his face. Zhong Wei does not cry at all. He stands tall, taking it like a man, scanning the corridor up and down.

A fight begins – shit, I didn't realise the stabber had actually come to the hospital. Three of the friends rush at him. He is a nice-looking guy – tidy haircut, clean-shaven – and is wearing a dark blue suit. Zhong Wei jumps in to separate the fracas, the futility of any more violence apparent. Two minutes later, the police arrive. Three men in dark blue uniforms with white cuffs walk down the corridor. One, bespectacled, takes the lead, holding a folder for the paperwork. They reach the room with the body and take a quick look at Lu Qing from the doorway, unable to hide their curiosity. They return to the corridor, ask Zhong Wei a few questions, and then put the same question to the perpetrator. He nods his head in admission, but crosses his arms over his face and chest to show that it was done in self-defence. The police take him by the arm and escort him away. His fate, in China, I don't even want to imagine . . .

Five minutes later, the mother comes down the corridor. Lu Qing's friends crawl instantly to her feet, sobbing uncontrollably, begging for forgiveness. I lose it at this stage, tears blurring my vision . . .

I rub my eyes to see Zhong Wei dragging his friends away so the mother can go to the room where her boy lies. Pacing down the corridor, she reaches the doorway. All it takes is a look. Yet in that look I see the history of a billion lifetimes.

A mother losing her only child.

I am taken away.

Day 46

A haunted sleep. Lying on my hotel bed, I stare into the dark, images of the past parading through my mind. I quietly grieve, unable to get the picture of Lu Qing out of my head. Friendship is like blood with the one-child policy. I weep at the fragility of life, but the day has arrived and I must face the world. Staying in bed only makes me feel more miserable.

I get out, and feel a burst of good feeling. I can do this. I walk to the toilet and manage to hold the stare of a Chinese man coming the other way. However, the good feeling doesn't last long. The reality of what has occurred sinks back in and I again withdraw, feeling very alone.

People I come across seem a lot more dangerous to me. The man in the grey trench coat who keeps looking at me from across the street. The prostitute with the stutter who wants to take me home. Shoulders dishevelled, the world is starting to scare me. Knives are constantly on my mind and I want to run from everyone. I have to be on my own.

I go back to my room and do some hand-washing. As stupid as it sounds it is the most therapeutic thing I can do. I feel like I am achieving something – getting somewhere. The good feeling starts to return. I find the courage to hit the street again. Still numb and distracted, the plan is to find a supermarket and treat myself. I find one, and spend an hour finding all the chocolate biscuits I can muster. Kit-Kats, Oreos, Hershey's Kisses, Chocolate Chips – a huge shopping-bag full – expensive compared to what I have been used to travelling with, but still only US$5 overall.

Safely back in my room, fighting hard to understand the reason for all this, I reflect on the three days since I first put out my thumb. I cannot help but think that there is a predetermined chain of events that has led to all this. And something has to be learned. What can it possibly be?

Found it.

I'm alive.

And the only way is onwards.

Ready now to take on the body of the beast.

MOON 6

THE BODY OF THE BEAST

*China is all about the struggle forward. Nowhere is there so great
a challenge; nowhere is work on so great a scale, nowhere does the
creativeness of the individual, the strength of the group matter
so much. The very fact that China has suffered from millennia of
deforestation and erosion, flooding or even a complete lack of water
posing a constant threat to millions, makes for man-sized problems
that call for big men to solve them.*

How then does one become a big man?

*Not by any political trickery, nor by trying to make friends in high
places. But by ever struggling to gain the objective view, training
oneself, gathering knowledge and experience, learning how to work
in co-operation with others and all the while retaining humility in
the face of immense tasks that have to be done. A big man is not
proud or arrogant. He is simple and thoughtful, building on one
reality after another, so that the basis for his thinking is solid, and
he develops character and directness. As we learn from theory and
practice, so we can develop these qualities which will make our life's
work more effective. It does not matter whether you are called to high
position or just keep on with an ordinary one; to be really big will
benefit not only yourself but also those with whom you come into
contact.*

Rewi Alley

There is a knock at the hotel door. Two Chinese policemen, well
dressed in plain clothes and dark jackets, enter with a female
translator who is dressed in white. I stare at her long, dark hair.

It is perfectly brushed and she has soft, glowing skin. Her beauty provides me with a sense of solidity.

'We need to check your passports and learn of your travel intentions in China,' she asks in sweet tones. 'How long are you here for, and what is the purpose of your visit?'

'We're visiting the Great Wall and plan to take a bus into Yinchuan city today,' Paolo replies, not mentioning walking the entire wall.

It is not permitted for foreigners to sleep in places other than State-registered hotels. This, Chinese officials assure us, is for foreigner safety. Yet it seems more like a money-making exercise – the majority of registered hotels are linked directly to the State's pockets. The US$15–$100 they charge per day is far too expensive for our limited expedition budget.

'If you decide to stay overnight, you will have to register your presence down at the local police station,' she continues.

We know full well the twenty-four-hour registration rule and have no intention of abiding by it. Staying away from the police is the Great Wall walking doctrine.

'There is a nice temple to visit in the mountains if you haven't had a chance to see it yet on your route to Yinchuan.' The police and translator leave, satisfied, after checking our passports.

'They didn't ask me about the murder.'

'The murder?'

'Yes, it's what I tried to explain to you late last night.'

'What? I must have still been half asleep. We've got to leave this city immediately,' Paolo insists.

We pack and set off straight for the bus stop. A white van waits, filling up with passengers. While sitting in the back seat of the rusting twenty-seater, one of Zhong Wei's friends, Li Jiang, espies me in the bus. He had left before the fight. I come out to greet him. We just look at each other helplessly, eyes filled with emotion, struggling to come to terms with what has happened. The bus honks, it is ready to go. Part of me wants to stay; another wants to run as far away as possible. I hug Li Jiang quickly and leave him to his struggle.

Day 47, Yinchuan City

Yinchuan shines like a beacon for lost nomads, a city of sparkling glass. Bricked pedestrian pathways are barricaded from traffic – and each pathway is lined with tall, green-tinted shopping malls dedicated to every human indulgence. The city brims with giant billboards of Western models. China's emerging modernity subscribes to only one ideology now: money. Working long days, the ultimate release from work is to head to the supermarkets and spend. Even public holidays are set aside to encourage the nation's most popular pastime.

Chinese shoppers carry Esprit bags and wear frilly, dark dresses, mink jackets and black suits. They glance at my face as I pass. On the usual second-take, their eyes scan my shoes. Their looks of dismay say it all: my US$2 karate shoes don't cut the mustard warranted by my million-dollar skin.

I feel insecure, my cheeks reddening with embarrassment. It's an emotion I haven't felt in almost fifty days. The desert dwellers never judged my soul by the state of my attire. I find a grungy hotel to again hide from the world. Prostitutes sit knitting in the hotel lobby. Yet theirs is not the sunshine my traumatised soul needs to borrow. With the group in tatters, no command of the language, and no real friends in China, I must face this homicide experience alone.

I turn to the computer. Email has become my most intimate acquaintance. I direct my fingertips in accordance with my mourning heart. With one click of the index finger my story bursts from its PC seed, disseminating a thousand routes along my mass-email highway. Forwarded by those who receive, the second season's harvest is sown in minutes: 1,000 to their 1,000, and 1,000 to theirs – six rapid crops and we have covered the entire educated world.

The collective global consciousness turns its attention to the recesses of my mind, support flooding in from all over the connected world.

Put your head down and keep going, my dad writes, now in full support of the journey.

Be strong, we are praying for you, a friend of Paolo's passes on.

Your journey is so inspiring — I've thrown in my legal job and am now working for the Red Cross in Venezuela, a lawyer from Paris informs.

In reality, the words are probably a flippant comment, quickly forgotten once the writer pushes 'send' and tends to the next of a hundred little emails or duties in their day. Yet such words are clung to and savoured for days, even weeks, while contemplating life and the journey's meaning when walking the empty deserts of the Gobi. People I have never met start forwarding stories of similar incidents. One father talks about his lost son. Another looks forward to having his first. Ironically, the homicide has made the expedition more alive, fuelling me with a different purpose than before. I walk because I can. I walk because there is only death.

Day 50, 1 December 2000

Paolo and I meet up again with Sumana in Yinchuan to spend several days recuperating. Sumana has befriended the resident priest of a local Christian following in town.

'Don't tell them that I am a Buddhist monk. I am pretending to be a Christian and they have accepted me into their congregation.' He looks to me with convinced eyes, and smiles. 'That is the way you know.'

Invited to also attend, we find the church is half full of devotees singing Christmas psalms and carols. The feeling within the church is open and warm, and the attendees find a natural sense of community and contentedness in the word of Jesus Christ. China is renowned for its secularisation, especially since the Cultural Revolution. However, Christianity is again on the rise, although it has a long way to go to reach the levels of popularity experienced in South Korea, where red crosses mark every street in the suburbs.

After a week in the city with still no word from Diego and Kelvin, we decide to press on. The next township of Yanchi is four days' walk east, and we can check up on the others' progress if they have reached an Internet or telephone by then. We set off by taxi to a small Great Wall fortress that lies on the eastern bank of the western loop of the Yellow River.

The Mu Us is the third and biggest desert we are going to have to cross, terminating at the eastern side of the Yellow River loop 700 kilometres away. The dark peaks of Helan Shan lie at our backs, the Wall trailing like a fishing line deep into a sea of orange and yellow sand. I plant my right walking stick, and set my sights on the first watchtower in the distance. Focusing on the next manageable goal provides me with direction and a sense of salvation. The healing of the desert awaits as the three of us launch into the unknown . . .

Ж

A dead man lies in the middle of the road. Where does one stand on the issue?

Musings from the Wall: Kelvin Jones

Diego and Kelvin set off from Zhongwei city, walking for ten days solid. Wearing two knee-braces over his trousers and without the chance to wash properly, Diego's knee has got infected with a white viral growth. Ballooning into two bubbles, the biggest one pops, causing the most intense anguish.

'Kelvin, we have to find medical assistance immediately,' Diego swears. The Wall winds through the mountains as it has for days, but is different from the Wall of clay, being finely constructed with millions of small rocks and bricks. Heading predominantly northwards through dry river valleys and brown, carbon-enriched ranges, the Wall curves eastwards, fleeing the mountains and moving towards a large concrete factory lying at the base of the Ningxia plains. Kelvin peers through the concrete gateway, Diego hobbling slowly behind. Green army troops run in formation around the empty grounds.

'Army!' Kelvin whispers, pushing his right hand up for Diego to freeze as he approaches his shoulder.

'We've got to risk it,' Diego winces, peering in. As the troops finish their drills and enter the garrison just on dark, Kelvin and Diego quietly enter the garrison grounds. Heading straight for the double doors, they enter the main eating hall. Eighty eyes look up astonished.

'*Chi fan, shuijiao, kan bing?*' Food, sleep, medical assistance? Diego pleads, pointing to his knee. The whole room goes silent.

Both walkers are escorted to an underground room. Two hours later, two black Izuzu Troopers arrive. The four-wheel-drives have red number-plates. Stepping out with a nonchalant surety, chewing gum, wearing black jackets and dark glasses, the Public Security Bureau's intelligence unit has arrived. The agents separate the walkers immediately, two of the six agents meticulously searching through their gear, confiscating all film and videotapes. Kelvin is led two further levels underground by four men and a translator. They enter a bare, white chamber, which contains one table and six wooden chairs.

'You are a foreigner.'

'No kidding.'

'You have no receipts for staying at hotels. Why is this?'

'I'm a pyromaniac – I like to burn them.'

The translator looks to his colleagues, shaking his head, confused.

'You have no receipts. You must be a spy.'

'Not a chance. We're just walking your Great Wall.'

'Walking?'

'Visiting.'

'Why did you go to Yumenguan?'

'Where?'

'Yumenguan. It says so on your train ticket.'

'No, that ticket says Jiayuguan.'

Yumenguan is an area about 400 kilometres north-west of Jiayuguan where remnants of the Wall were discovered only recently. The area also contains a nuclear-weapons testing site.

'Why did you go to Yumenguan?'

'I don't know what you're talking about.'

One of these sites, further north towards the Russian border, was occupied by Russian commandos when Sino–Russian relations were at an impasse. The Chinese authorities telegraphed a message to the Russian president to warn him that they were 'conducting' a nuclear test in the area. The invading Russian troops were never heard from again.

'Why did you go to Yumenguan?'

'I said I don't know what you are talking about.'

'Yes you do, stop trying to deceive us. What were you doing there?'

Kelvin shakes his head. 'What are you talking about!'

'Yumenguan.' The interrogator pauses, passing Kelvin a cigarette with a wry smile. 'Tell me about it.'

'I'll smoke your cigarette only once we've finished,' Kelvin replies, hoping that the questioning will finish shortly. It doesn't. Sweat breaks out over his forehead as the interrogation continues into its fourth hour.

Upstairs, Diego manages to befriend his army guard. Walking without a cooker, neither Diego nor Kelvin has eaten a proper meal in two days.

'Can you pass my friend this power bar? He hasn't eaten.' Attached to the power bar is a small note he has written. *Everything's going to be alright Kelvin. Just hang in there.* It gets taken downstairs.

Kelvin opens up the silver wrapping and munches down the vanilla-flavoured bar. The sugar-rush raises his spirits.

'Come on, ask me more questions, you scrotum suckers,' Kelvin snarls, fired up. The translator is unable to understand the specifics, but everyone can read the emotion. The interrogation continues.

'Why did you go to Yumenguan?'

Two hours later, at the end of the interrogation, eight pages of documents have been written.

'Sign each page with your fingerprint.'

Kelvin places his finger in the red ink-pad, doing what he is told, but not before writing a note in English that says that he will not consent to any of this unless he is given an English translation. He smudges the last fingerprint in a show of petty defiance.

Diego is moved into the room next, while Kelvin is locked in a room with a wooden bed. It has no mattress or heater. He lies there shivering and starving. Diego is processed in two hours, then they are vacated from the premises in the black jeeps, heading towards Yinchuan just as the sun begins to rise.

'Turn the music up!' Kelvin gestures, as Nirvana's 'Come As You Are' resonates from the stereo. Upon reaching the Ningxia capital, they are shown to a hotel and their passports are confiscated.

'Be in the hotel at 10am. We will come and meet you,' one of the two remaining PSB agents states, retaining the tapes and photos for scrutiny.

'Where's the damn hospital?' Diego asks. His knee is still in agony.

'Just past the city centre – you'll find it.'

They wait in their room all day, not wanting to miss the early meeting. The authorities do not return till 5pm.

'We will not be returning your passports until you pay us a 5000-*yuan* fee for the development of all the slides which have been sent to Beijing,' the authorities state.

'They're lying,' Diego muses. 'Slides never cost that much to develop.'

'Let's check the flight times to Beijing and see how much it costs to send something by airmail.'

'Yeah, that's pure extortion.'

Checking the flight times on the Internet, they learn that there have been no flights to Beijing that day.

'I'm gonna call the New Zealand Embassy in Beijing.' Kelvin finds a phone and makes the call. 'Hello? We've been detained by the Chinese authorities in Yinchuan. They've got our passports, equipment and have fined us 5000 *yuan*. We don't have the money and need your help desperately.'

'I'm sorry, I'm playing ten-pin bowling at the moment. Can you call the office back on Monday morning?'

Ж

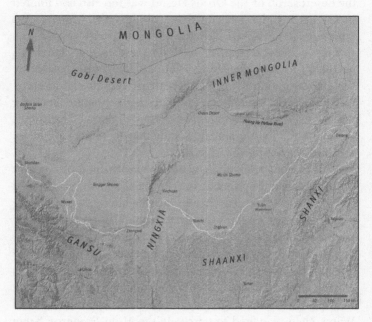

The Great Wall of China crosses the provinces of Gansu, Ningxia Autonomous Region, Shaanxi and Shanxi during the desert sections which comprise half of its coverage of China.

Arthur Waldron writes in his book *The Great Wall of China – From History to Myth* that Mongolian Steppe warfare was dictated by control over one of three areas: the Tarim Basin, 500 kilometres west of Yumenguan; the Orkhon, north of China near Ulan Bator; and the Ordos, lying in the gap of desert within the confines of the Yellow River loop. The loop itself runs northwards along the Helan Shan ranges for 140 miles, then diverges east at the Yin Shan mountains where it ambles through the fertile Ho-t'ao area (the land of a thousand sorrows), and finally turns south towards Taiyuan in Shanxi province 500 kilometres later.

The natural north-western border for China would have most logically constituted the Yellow River Loop; however, the desert scrub of the Ordos Desert was too arid and limited in resources to be consciously secured by the Chinese. Yet limiting their military presence in this area was risky for China's security, so most Dynasties still maintained the eight garrisons necessary to keep the Mongols at bay. This was possible by building irrigation channels where there were small pockets of water, and utilising these to grow grain and prepare metal for weapons. With occasional invasions and diplomatic measures, the Chinese Dynasties were generally able to protect the villages south of the border settlements.

With the enormous drain on resources to maintain these eight outer garrisons, the political court of the Ming Dynasty decided to pull their troops out, thereby establishing an open border policy from the beginning of its reign. This military policy gave the Mongolians, under increasingly unified leadership, the opportunity to re-enter the Ordos and assume control. By the fifteenth century they were in a position to make constant attacks on the Chinese Mainland across the unguarded border.

A powerful and highly influential Ming eunuch called Wang Zhen managed to persuade the Ming Emperor Xuan Zhong that it was necessary to send out an army to help. Ordering up a contingent of over half a million men, he marched them to the border but the omens for the expedition were not good. Storms and torrential rain led to the court astronomers stipulating that to continue the campaign at this time would be ill advised. Emperor Xuan Zhong did not listen and by the thirteenth day of the expedition they came across the blood-soaked battlefield of the Yang-ho, layered in literally thousands of unburied Chinese corpses. Everyone was terrified and by the sixteenth day the Emperor decided to call his men back to make a hasty retreat.

However, the Mongolians had anticipated this response, and prepared an ambush for their return home. Thirsty and starving, not having eaten for two days, the Chinese Army was surrounded and unable to battle with any great conviction. Aware of this, the Emperor hastily sought to draft peace terms, ordering his army to proceed a mile forward to set up negotiations. Interpreting this as an attack, the Mongolians invaded from all sides, the Chinese military breaking ranks and turning into a disorganised mob. 'Throw down your arms and armour and be spared,' the Mongols shouted, whereupon in a frenzy of activity the Chinese soldiers threw down their weapons and their garments and ran towards the enemy cavalry despite their officers' protests. Unable to defend themselves, the Chinese were ruthlessly cut down by their opposition, who captured the Emperor and completely devastated the Ming's fearsome military reputation.

With their army in ruin, the Ming Dynasty were unsure what to do next. Military defence seemed redundant against the Mongolian hordes who had an uncanny ability to synchronise the movement of their troops all over the 4,000-kilometre border despite their nomadic nature. Renowned for their formidable archery skills, little Mongolian boys would first learn to shoot small targets like rats or birds whilst riding sheep before graduating to horses. In fact the word 'soldier' did not even exist in Mongolian vocabulary — so prevalent was fighting as an everyday part of their lives.

The options for appeasing the Mongolians' needs through diplomatic measures were also limited. Nomadic in nature, gravitating from pasture to pasture, it was difficult to draw the Mongolians into the one communicable central authority. Although many villages were able to prevent continual raids by using grain, metals, luxuries and necessary medical supplies as a bargaining leverage, these successes were unknown to the later Ming emperors, raised within the cushy confines of the Forbidden City and having little experience of the outside Mainland. Unlike the earlier Ming leaders, who were heavily involved with direct border fighting, the later emperors lacked a clear sense of military vision, and were easily swayed by the influences of eunuchs, civil dignitaries and palace women.

If they were to attempt to retake the Ordos from the Mongols by force, it would cost the Imperial court approximately 200,000 soldiers, 100,000 transport men, and over 30,000 tons of grain. Having also to contend with a lack of experienced generals after the last major defeat, not to mention the harsh winters of these drought-stricken provinces so far north, another expedition was likely to cause more death and starvation than success.

The remaining alternative, favoured by the Chinese mind, was wall building. Requiring only 50,000 men, not only would it be cheaper and more manageable, but it would cut out many of the enemy invasion routes, curbing the constant confrontation against the villages. Although deemed an exclusionary, even provocative form of foreign policy, this would enable the villages to revive their economies, and continue rebuilding if the strategy flourished.

Day 55

The dark mountains of Helan Shan shrink inch by inch. Within three days, they have already disappeared into the curving horizon. The Great Wall dips into an orange canyon, skimming underground and appearing again on the other side of a small ice river.

'Buddhist monks aren't allowed to jump,' Sumana states matter-of-factly. 'It is one of our 200 rules.'

'How are you going to get across then?' I ask.

'Paolo is going to carry me,' he laughs, and launches into a Buddhist tale. 'One day, two monks were walking back to the monastery when they came across a maiden who was needing help to cross a river. The head monk picked up the lady and carried her across, even though this was strictly forbidden.'

'What happened?'

'When reaching the temple, the younger monk asked the

chief lama why he had broken the rule. He replied: "I may have carried the woman across the river, but I no longer carry her in my mind."'

I like Sumana and his parables. His short walking-stints also serve to break up the monotony of walking with just Paolo. At the end of the day, we reach the township of Yanchi – and the Internet. The others have responded.

Nathan,
We've been detained by Chinese authorities in the city of Yinchuan. They've confiscated our passports and we are unable to leave. If you don't come back NOW – you are out of the Great Walk Expedition for good. Leave all sponsorship gear in the township you are at with details as to where we can pick them up.
Diego

Diego's email comes as a shock. It is virtually impossible to meet up again now unless I am to give up on the others and head back. Neither Paolo nor Sumana has any intention of returning. I feel torn. My friends are in trouble, but I don't want to get involved with their mess – nor the negative tension over the split. I also don't want to return to the homicide zone.

Kelvin emails too:

Nathan, don't come back, it will only cause further problems. In fact, get out of Ningxia region immediately. They have checked our footage and know you are out there. The Police are hunting you down too.
Kelvin

Freed by Kelvin's maturity, I may have been leading the race across China, but I have now lost a vital ally in the Gobi.

Ж

Day 58

Thirty kilometres' walk from the safety of the third provincial border on our route, Shaanxi, I offload almost 7 kilograms of sponsorship gear, including documentary supplies, boxes of spare batteries, the cellphone and Diego's tent. At 17 kilograms without food, keeping only the most basic clothing for survival, I have never felt so light.

'We can share my tent. You take the material, I'll take the poles – half each,' Paolo suggests. We are down now to the following gear:

1 backpack and pack liner
½ tent each
1 sleeping bag
1 sleeping mat
1 rain jacket
1 minus-20-degree fleece
2 t-shirts
1 pair of thermals
1 pair of trousers
3 pairs of underwear
8 pairs of socks (4 nylon, 4 cotton)
1 pair of gloves (plus inners)
1 pair of walking boots
1 pair of jandals
1 woolly hat
1 cap
sunglasses
desert goggles
face masks
3 black plastic bags
medical kit
sunscreen
water purification tablets
1 compass
5 maps

1 cooker
2 fuel containers
1 pot
1 or 2 one-litre water bottles
diary and pens
toiletries
5 power bars each
biscuits
dried fruit/scroggin
packets of noodles
1 video camera and six tapes

I quickly reply to Kelvin's email before heading off.

> We're heading onwards to escape to the next province. Make
> sure you get Diego to sign something on paper to work out a
> deal for carrying all his gear. A photocopy of the maps and the
> rest of the gear are waiting at Yanchi hotel in reception.
> Good luck.

Sumana, Paolo and I take flight through the desert towards the
province of Shaanxi. Battered into increments, the Wall looks
like dragon scales, with the wind blowing golden sand through
the gaps. During a drink break, Sumana reads to us his notes
from Arthur Waldron's book, which we have been reading to
relive the history of the Great Wall.

*Wang Yue, who lived in the fifteenth century, was one of the last
Chinese generals able to fight like a nomad.* He looks up, brushing
his hair to look good on camera. *His strength lay in surprise attacks
on families deep in Mongol territory, and he covered the entire
Ningxia-Yulin area . . .* 'Which we now trail,' Sumana remarks.
He pauses, his dark hands turning the page, *. . . killing villagers,
burning tents and leading off thousands of camels, horses and sheep
– upon hearing of the catastrophe, the Mongols rushed back from
their Chinese raids straight into a Ming ambush. The slaughter
left the border quiet for several years. In this time Wang Yue built*

a 129-mile wall and propelled the Ming Dynasty to complete the entire Great Wall defensive system south of the Ordos. He pauses, getting me to stop recording while he adjusts his monk robes, which, although he is supposed to wear them all the time, he only puts on for the purposes of being filmed.

In 1482 a large group of Mongol raiders found themselves trapped within the fortifications and were easily slaughtered. With their foreign policy vindicated, Great Wall building accelerated, fortifying China on an unprecedented level, terminating the Ming's reign in 1644 as the most comprehensively closed border in pre-modern Chinese history.

We trail the wall for 20 kilometres, heading to a gradual rise in the horizon where an Islamic monastery lies on top of a hill. It is just on sunset and it seems an ideal place to spend the night. The inhabitants wear white robes and headbands. Upon arrival, however, we are refused accommodation.

In general, if a Chinese family rejects you, it will be a great shame on that family if another family in the same village accepts you. In such situations, the whole village will come together to stop the second family from accepting, so as to save face. It takes a lot of strength for the second family to go against the word of the village; however, if they do, the village will accept you in as if they had never protested your presence in the first place.

We continue towards the flickering lights of Dingbian city, 10 kilometres ahead, lying on the Ningxia–Shaanxi border. The Wall's presence is more alive at night. Her dark towers make an ominous silhouette under the gaze of the half-moon.

'Help!' Sumana yelps through the darkness. Paolo eventually finds him: Sumana's foot is trapped in a wire rabbit-trap.

'Are you okay?'

'Yes, it's only wire. But I'm absolutely exhausted. I've never walked so far before.'

'We'll carry your pack between us,' says Paolo.

'Make sure you stick beside us at all times.'

We walk on for an hour, Paolo and I co-ordinating our walk

with the extra pack while Sumana trails behind. It has begun to get bitterly cold. I look back to see if Sumana still follows.

'Sumana?' There is no reply. 'Sumana!' He has gone.

'I can't believe he just ran off again,' Paolo starts, fed up.

'Maybe he's collapsed? Nobody could possibly be so senseless as to take off while we are carrying all his gear. We'd better retrace our steps.'

We look for an hour through the frosty night, asking villagers if they have seen Sumana, but there is no sign. The monk has again vanished.

'It's freezing. Let's get to a hotel in the city. We can continue the search tomorrow.'

Reaching a highway restaurant, the owner's eyes light up upon seeing us.

'*Ni de pengyou shi zai fandian.*' Your friend's gone to a hotel, the owner says, before ordering his son to drive us with both our packs on his motorbike into town.

'That was his last chance.' Paolo leaves Sumana's pack in the restaurant for him to retrieve the next day.

I am fed up with the escaping act too, and can only now begin to imagine just how furious Diego must be.

PROVINCE 3: SHAANXI
Day 63

We track down Sumana around lunchtime. He is resting in a hotel room, exhausted from the night before. We set off the next day. The cold at night is so intense that I have to get out of my tent in the middle of the night to feed Sumana Panadol pills to soothe the pain all over his body. Moaning for his mother, he is simply not as acclimatised as we have become to the cold. Most farmers in the Himalaya are able to spend the night out without a tent, and the Reindeer children in Mongolia run around the snow in bare feet during their minus-40-degree winter. We walk together for another three days before Sumana again decides to leave us at the turn-off to the next major township and continue traversing the Wall as he best knows how.

Sticking religiously to the Wall, Paolo and I trudge along the sand-swept deserts, continuing our uninterrupted line across China. We continue for two more days until the Wall's flow is interrupted by a large, icy river. Paolo attempts to cross the river at its bend. He has his boots in his hands, and is stepping through the freezing ice which breaks up to his knees. Three-quarters of the way across, the river deepens and he sinks thigh-deep.

'Go, bro! You're a legend!' I shout, coaxing him on as I film the scene. Bravely he takes another step, but the ice gives way and he falls to his chest. He looks up to me with sheer terror. I put down the camera to rush out to help, but he manages to wrench himself free, and hastily retreats back towards the safety of the banks.

It is my turn again. It has taken us all morning so far to find a safe route across. I trace a different line along a straighter course of the river further down the banks. It does not get deeper than my knees and, despite cutting my feet breaking through the ice, I make it safely across.

'Come on Paolo, follow my footprints – you can do it.' He hesitates at first, wanting to choose another line. 'Come on, bro. You can do it!' I shout impatiently. He follows the marked-out footsteps carefully and grabs my hand to reach the safety of the banks. Once he is safely across, I shout joyfully at our success. It is the most taxing 20 metres of the journey to date; a threshold keeping out those who are not ready for what is coming next.

Rising steadily from desert elevation, the Wall trails off into the distance towards one of the remotest parts of China. According to the maps, 250 kilometres of non-stop mountains lie before us. A hawk flies ahead, resting on a watchtower in front of us. We are going to need as much help as we can get.

Day 66
After sixty years in China, I feel her greatest gift to me is the idea of making one's life mean something to people, rather than letting the sordid quest for fame, face or fortune dominate it.

Rewi Alley

Good farming land in Shaanxi is scarce. The soil is mostly
– a yellow or chocolate-coloured earth covering thousand
square miles, originating possibly from seabed mud when No..
China lay under the sea millions of years ago. The region was
once covered in trees, but now the forests are gone. Suffering
significant erosion, tons of soil wash into the Yellow River
when the rains do come, giving the mother artery its distinct
murky colouring.

Small clay villages lie scattered through the loess terrain,
hubs of life working the caramel land. There is little water in
these parts, but the peasants seem to get by. Working the fields
with meticulous expertise, there is a sense of pride to the daily
routine: food for the family, sustenance for the community, and
a growing sense of pride for the nation. Each day the Chinese
farmers head out to the fields before sunrise, accepting their lot
– day upon day, year upon year, breath upon breath, until their
bodies can no longer perform and their fate drifts to another
realm. Yet even in death, the peasants never really leave. Their
remains are buried in a mound of dry soil and rock in the very
fields they have tended – refertilising the land that has fed them
for so long. And so the cycle continues.

The Wall, a lumbering clay giant, rolls over mountain-
top after mountain-top. It feels like we are traipsing along a
graveyard of giant brown tortoise shells. Twenty peaks we
have now crossed, and each time we reach a summit another
twenty peaks lie ahead. The erosion in the land is so bad that
there are no connecting ridges, so each mountain must be
scaled from its base. I walk on, exhausted, up and down, up
and down. Coughing and wheezing, my skin is pale and my
guts are bubbling with fits of constipated seizure from a meal
of pig offered the night before.

Leaping over the mountains at the height of two men, had
the Wall not been there to lure me on I would have given up
long before. The turmoil of the Chinese builders drives me on:
the building materials alone extend around the equator eight
times. Yet it is also the pure artistry of filming another human

being facing his life struggle. I follow Paolo's life trail deeper and deeper into the internal and external wilderness.

The Chinese Communists had an initiation process called 'going through the five mountain passes' for anyone who wanted to join the revolution. Devised to inure new members to suffering, the theory behind the process attempted to alter the bourgeois psychology of the educated through adopting a completely new approach towards family, affection, work and lifestyle. By embracing hardship and being exposed to manual labour, the idea was to bring them closer to the unremittingly harsh lives of the peasants who formed the Party's support base.

I am sweating, smelly and close to vomiting. My legs feel like lead, slipping along the snowy trail as I fight off the tears. In the distance a Chinese man lies on a hill-top and suddenly pounces upon an unsuspecting hawk. He captures it in a white sack, and makes a hasty escape before I can chase him to free the bird.

'God, please let this be the last mountain,' I pray silently.

I reach the top and yet another furtive horizon of peaks awaits.

Day 67
Doing the best at this moment puts one in the best position for the next.

Anon

The Wall takes us alongside frozen green lakes and through snow-filled gullies, and it is necessary to rock-climb several steep cliffs. We reach a small township with a tarseal road that heads out of the mountains.

'It must be a military town,' Paolo says, rushing immediately past and towards the next peak that the Wall trails. 'Let's skip it.' He heads on up the next peak as a group of school children dressed in blue uniform rush from their school grounds to sing to us at the bottom of the slopes. I listen to the sweet melody of the ancient tune, looking to the road out, but remain committed to the Wall. When I catch up to Paolo, he looks over at me with compassion.

'This stage is clearly teaching you something, Nathan.'

'What's that?'

'The end will come only when you no longer want it.'

I put my head down, humbled, focusing on my two feet moving forward. It forces me back into the present moment rather than my continual search for somewhere more desirable. Only from this spot can I consciously co-create my existence in accordance with what Fate makes available. I look out to the Wall, which trails behind us over the mountain-tops for miles. Like a lawyer who prepares a case for court, or a builder who constructs a home, each piece of evidence established or brick placed enables the next one to be positioned.

The Wall winds its way for three more days before finally terminating at a massive ice river. Paolo and I cry for joy. According to the maps, we have completed the 250-kilometre south-eastern haul – definitely the most harrowing section so far. Watchtowers line the river-banks on the Wall's 400-kilometre journey northwards to the midway stage of the journey, but there is no longer any Wall visible. A dusty road trails northwards instead.

'Can't we just wait by the side of the road, cook up some potatoes and wait for a passing horse and cart?' We have already walked 30 kilometres to reach this stage by late afternoon and I am exhausted.

'It's time for you to embark upon a super effort.'

'Super effort?' I look up.

'It's when you make a conscious decision to give up your warm, comfortable surroundings, and head out to do battle with the elements at the peak of your exhaustion . . .' Paolo pauses to find the right words. 'When you overcome the fear of death like this, you will access a raw emotional intelligence that will inject your body with energy that enables feats of inhuman endurance.' Paolo looks to me with weary eyes, then turns his attention towards the next horizon. I resign myself to the walk, no longer expecting to finish. What is the end, really? Strangely I feel no more pain or tiredness, just a lightness and revelry at simply being. I walk upright – euphoric in thought as the road comes to meet my desires and a gigantic full moon appears behind the last range of mountains. Two hours later the lights of Jingbian city twinkle enticingly in the distance. As we hit a 40-kilometre walking record, walking the Great Wall of China is simply a matter of existing. I have become the journey.

Day 74, 21 December 2000

'What's that?' I ask, realising I am talking to myself. Paolo is walking past a sand dune some 200 metres back.

'I'm not sure,' Paolo replies, reading my mind. A structure stands out in the distance, shimmering in the desert haze like a golden pyramid. Heading closer, the pyramid grows, inch by inch, filling the horizon until we reach an elaborate brick fortress sitting red against the setting sun. We have reached Zhenbei Tower, the official middle-point of the Great Wall of China.

Built by the Ming in 1607, no one knows whether the tower marks out the precise middle-point of the Wall. Scientists have found that if you measure the perimeter of the great pyramid in Giza and multiply that number by its height, then you will calculate a number just 100 feet shy of the distance from the equator to the North Pole. Maybe the Chinese were on a similar level of mathematical genius? Three days ago, Paolo and I had had a clear intuitive sense that we were heading for the precise middle-point of the Wall, without knowing that such a centre tower even existed.

The fortress lies outside the city of Yulin. The city's name means 'elmwood' because it was forested back in the times of the Qing Dynasty (1644–1911). Now it is encroached upon by menacing sand dunes. The city is dusty, the buildings acrylic white brick.

'My girlfriend back in Milan is saddened that the journey is taking so long,' Paolo warns from our cold, dark hotel in Yulin.

'She wants me to return home to Italy.'

'Are you going to go?'

'Yes, we've been together now for twelve years.'

Marina Zagoborich, the first woman to walk half of the Great Wall, created a documentary with a blind Chinese film-maker and her husband of twelve years. Walking from opposite ends of the Wall towards the middle, their experiences were so varied that, when they did reach each other, they no longer felt like a couple.

'But let's first reach the eastern loop of the Yellow River, and catch up with Sumana for his birthday on January the first,' Paolo suggests. 'Then we can take an extended break over winter.'

'Sounds good.'

It has become impossible for us to sleep in our sleeping bags now, with the weather averaging minus-15 degrees, which means we are under pressure every day to find a village in which to sleep. I don't tell Paolo this, but I am also beginning to get forgetful as my exhaustion increases. The day before, I placed my walking sticks down by a tree to go to the toilet and forgot to pick them back up when I again set off. I walked for 200 metres before I realised I had left them behind.

> *This must be the day*
> *Of all days*
> *The one around which*
> *All the others are bound to gather*
>
> Dinah Hawken

Day 82, 30 December 2000

Paolo and I approach the last mountain range before the Yellow River loop. A group of local school children guide us towards the top of the pass. They have the words 'strive forever' sewn in white onto the backs of their blue uniforms. A few of them had spotted us eating in a local restaurant, and peered curiously through the windows. By the time we had finished our meal, word of our presence had leaked through the township and, with school out, the entire main street was filled with kids. Everyone laughed excitedly as they followed us, while I whistled Beethoven's 10th imagining myself as the Pied Piper.

I can trust Mainland China. That is the biggest lesson I have learned while walking across the Gobi with little more than a will to walk the Wall. I can enter these people's homes, thirsty or starving, and know they will take me in and not ever make me feel ashamed for asking.

Only the ten strongest children remain as we head towards the top. We converge as a group to take photos; twelve pairs of shiny, excited eyes. Before heading home, they wait in a group, sitting upon a ridge as Paolo and I head off to the summit to see what lies on the other side.

'Goodbye!' the children scream, just before we reach the top. Their words carry a cold, chilling depth and a powerful force rushes into my back. It is as if I am listening to the voices of the dead who have been guiding us all this way. Indeed, the children *are* the ancestors. They also hold the reins of the generations to come.

'The world has given us a great moment,' Paolo smiles, his blue eyes shining brightly. With a sense of both loss and relief I turn slowly to watch the boys leave as the sun sinks slowly into the horizon to light the stage of our lives over the past three months. We have traversed half of China. Half in light, the other in darkness. Yin and Yang. Pakeha and Maori.

On the other side of the summit lies a highway of ice. Curving southwards into the dry, purple plains, the Yellow River looks like a border between two different times. On one side, a lone watchtower lies at the top of the mountain's crest surrounded in desert. On the other, a grey industrial city bellows smoke and pollution.

MOON 7

DIVERGING PATHS

Rulers are men, and men are always frightened. A man cannot govern unless he confronts his own fear.

Gita Mehta

Diego and Kelvin remain in the Mu Us Desert following the Wall over winter. Still over a month from the Wall's centre-point, they trudge through frozen sand dunes as the weather plummets to minus-25 degrees. Desert storms are frequent, the sky thick with snow and sand. The peasants have escaped permanently to their huts, and during the more severe storms Diego and Kelvin are forced to barge their way in. Carrying 35 kilograms of gear each, they are also forced to leave all the Jingbian mountainous sections until later.

Reaching the centre-point of the Wall by the end of January, it has become too cold to continue. They hole up in Yulin, awaiting extra thermals and proper gloves from sponsors so they can continue to film in the extreme conditions. During the delay, Kelvin is beginning to feel run-down, and decides to return to Beijing. He wants to propose to Julia and sign custody papers to secure visitation rights for his son, Lucas, whom he has been thinking about constantly. When catching the bus, he starts to develop a high fever. His clothes are drenched in sweat, and he almost passes out as his temperature soars above 90 degrees. Delirious, he drags his shaking body to Julia's apartment, knocks on her door, pops the question, and collapses at her feet.

He has contracted typhoid.

7 March 2001, Overland Journey from Bangkok to Chengdu
Spending the winter recovering on the Thai island of Ko Phang Ngan, I return overland to China from Bangkok via Cambodia and Laos, receiving Kelvin's news by email upon reaching Chengdu in Sichuan province. I can't quite believe what has happened. Paolo and I had planned to set off again towards the middle of March, and we fully expected the others to be at least two months ahead, given their plans to walk with their specialised gear over the winter. My hope had been to catch them up with our lighter gear before the end, overcome our prior misgivings, and reunite to make our way to the sea together. Diego is also back in Beijing, resting his knees and living with Kelvin at Julia's apartment. We haven't seen each other since the initial split four months ago.

Kelvin specifically asks that Paolo not come. I am nervous about this encounter, but know I must face it and am relieved that Sumana is in Beijing and can accompany me.

'Look at me!' Sumana calls out in glee, twirling his body around in delight at our reunion. 'I continued right through the winter, returning to walk all the sections that I had hitch-hiked with you, and I have now reached Zhangjiakou!' he states emphatically.

Sumana's claims are preposterous. Zhangjiakou is a city only 250 kilometres west of Beijing, and it is hard to believe he has come that far, given he has also travelled to Hong Kong to renew his three-month visa. Nonetheless, Sumana is keen to secure a copy of my video footage to prove his feats to the *Guinness Book of Records*. Despite his claims, I still can't believe my eyes when I see him: he is skinny and youthful, having lost almost 30 pounds.

Sumana's transformation to a belly-less Buddha, however, is not quite as startling as Kelvin's transformation. Having lost a similar amount of weight, his body looks malnourished, and his pale face is gaunt like that of a ghoul.

'You've lost your aura – this is not good,' Sumana says with concern as we are shown to the lounge of Julia's apartment.

Kelvin looks to his feet. 'I was unable to afford the travel insurance, so I could only be treated in hospital for the mandatory two-day incubation period. I had to convince International SOS hospital to sponsor me to cover their US$2,000-a-day costs.' He picks himself up like a frail old man, and makes his way to the couch. I am afraid to get too close.

Diego on the other hand looks healthier and stronger than ever. In fact, he has grown in stature. I can't quite work out how there can be such a difference. It is as if he has sucked out Kelvin's life force like a vampire.

Kelvin slowly lights a cigarette, and takes a deep drag, while Diego starts to film. I don't feel comfortable having this moment captured on camera.

'Why did you leave us at Wuwei, Nathan? Something could have happened – you left without finding out.'

'I'm sorry, I didn't even think of that at the time. Taking the cellphone seemed the appropriate thing to do.' I pause, regretfully. 'But why did you hang up? You were the only one with the power to allow us to meet up again. You had many opportunities.'

'Diego and I were pissed off. You had taken the maps.'

'I photocopied them as soon as I knew we weren't going to be together. Even Paolo had tried to persuade me not to when in Yanchi.'

'It's no matter now,' Kelvin responds, taking another drag. 'The split wasn't ideal, but it mirrored our desires at the time.'

'How are you recovering?'

'Slowly, I've been confined to the bed now for almost five weeks, but I don't yet have the energy to watch television or read books. My diarrhoea squirts out jet black.' He stares out gloomily into space. 'That's when you know your body is completely wrecked.'

'Do you think you will head out again when you are better?'

He takes another drag, his face resigned.

'Diego's going out to fill in the sections we both missed, and once I am better we'll do the mountain sections near Jingbian.'

'Go light,' I advise. 'That section was a real bitch – non-stop mountains for days.'

'I am surprised that Paolo and you worked out,' Diego interrupts, staring darkly. A cut on my nose starts to bleed.

'Yeah, we felt sorry for you having to walk with him,' Kelvin continues.

'We aren't competitive,' I reply, 'so there weren't many fights.' I pause, reflecting. 'We just made the most of what we had.'

'But you committed to going on the journey with *us*. I had my obligation to the sponsors.'

'Fuck the sponsors,' I reply angrily, turning to look at Kelvin's wilted frame. I lower my eyes in shame. 'Look how I could have turned out.'

'I predict Paolo and you will separate on this next walk,' Sumana declares.

'You know he won't go back out there without you,' Kelvin responds.

'I know,' I reply. However, Sumana's comment unsettles me. His predictions have this uncanny tendency of coming true and I am in no way ready to tackle this Great Wall journey on my own.

11 March 2001, Beijing

Paolo has changed. Not only physically, having shaven his head and lost a front tooth, but his gaze seems more circumspect, calculating. He has brought with him two Italian friends; one male and one female, married and in their forties.

'They are going to accompany us along the Wall,' he states emphatically, having only warned me about them a couple of days before heading to China. We head back to our usual Beijing hotel, settle in and have lunch in our local restaurant located in the bustling back alleyways behind our hotel. We eat cooked lamb and rice, supplemented with full segments of garlic, which we had become accustomed to eating to stay healthy in the first half of the journey.

'Can you take my Italian friends around Beijing? I have a date with Zaotijie.'

'Who's Zaotijie?'

'She's a Chinese student I met in Beijing before the journey began.'

'You've left your partner back home, then?'

'Yes, I have severed all ties, even those to my father.' He replies without emotion, pausing, before continuing, 'I have to warn you, Nathan. It's not in my heart to walk the Wall any more. I am going to continue only as far as I need to work out exactly what next to do in my life.'

It is risky to take the Italian couple into the middle of as yet unexplored sections of Mainland China. They look fit and healthy, but it is impossible to determine how long it will take to find the Wall again – let alone walk it to the next city, given they are on a two-week deadline. My body protests, riddled with diarrhoea the morning before the four of us are due to set off.

'I'm not ready to go yet,' I admit bravely to the Italians, dashing their hopes. 'I need several days to recover and to properly prepare. I'm sorry.'

'Do not worry, Nathan,' the wife, Tiziana, replies. 'Argostino and I will make other arrangements to visit the Wall closer to Beijing.'

'You're wasting my time,' Paolo cusses, leaving his Italian friends to make their own arrangements.

12 March 2001

'Come and stay with me until you're completely healthy,' Jack suggests. 'There's no point going out half-ready and getting sicker as you go.' With blue eyes and light brown hair, Jack King is a friend from Wellington whom I met at a bar called Tanewha the day I returned to Beijing from the first half of the walk.

Jack knows a lot about long journeys, having just completed a bike trip over the Kharakorum highway from Pakistan into China. Upon reaching Beijing, he met a Chinese girl called Yun, settled and started up a bar in the main nightclub district of Beijing: Sanlitun.

A week later, rested and ready, I bid Jack farewell by the doorway to his home. A Chinese painting hangs beside the door. It shows a dragon transforming, segment by segment, into a snake. I look at it.

'Ahhhh . . . yes – a good sign,' I muse. 'I started the Wall in the Year of the Dragon, and will complete it in the Year of the Snake.'

Jack looks back in shock. The painting has just slipped off its hinges.

'The River'

I followed the greenstones
to China.

The place had changed
reflecting the last journey.

Walking half of history I felt
its weight upon me.

Standing alone before the river
I felt more naked than ever.

My mother
gave birth to the seed

that connected our lives
to the river.

As I walked
across the morning

It would carry me along
in its current.

My thoughts could only be
half the journey.

The greenstone at my heart
made the river strong

The pull of my family
line through my life.

I had never given it
a name.

Tears, breath, river, journey.
The multitude was mine.

Three greenstones
giving each other hindsight.

Fionnaigh McKenzie

When a Maori *taiaha* warrior goes out to challenge an incoming tribe (*wero*), he heads out with a green fern-leaf that he lays sideways at their feet (*taki*). Brandishing his weapon to show off his fighting skills, he demands the visiting tribe to pick the leaf up, as is custom. If they do, they come in peace. If they stamp on it, they come with the intention of war, and the warrior must sacrifice himself, fighting off the enemy while the village gates are locked to save the tribe.

Crossing the Yellow River, my broken greenstone tugs at my heart. I take the pieces out and look at its shiny expanse of concentric circles, the symbol for generational connection, growth and friendship – now in three bits, having broken the night before I crossed the border back into China. The greenstone broke at the same time as my mother, who had given it to me, was hospitalised with a complaint in her uterus. I remember getting this sensation of being sucked back into her womb that very night.

In Maori mythology, the demigod Maui tried to overcome man's mortality by trying to conquer Hine-Nui-Te-Po, the Goddess of Death. Climbing through her womb when she was asleep, he entered her body and grabbed her heart in his arms. He had started tunnelling out feet first when a fantail laughed at the sight of Maui's legs hanging out of the vagina. Hine awoke and closed her thighs, crushing Maui to death.

I cast out the broken greenstone into the river's flow, laying down the *taki* for the journey to meet the river again at the Wall's end at the ocean. In Maori thinking, the *wero* is best done with three men.

PROVINCE 4: SHAANSI
Day 82, 23 March 2001
Every journey has its season . . .

Paolo and I return to the small industrial city where we had finished our first walk. It is ugly and grey, the concrete buildings thick with coal dust. Slaughtered lambs hang up in the streets, and slabs of fresh meat lie on tables ready for sale. The city is packed with market-goers.

'*Kan, kan! Laowai!*' a fat, balding Chinese man shouts, reaching for my balls. Quick, look! Foreigners! The crowd laughs uproariously as I return to an immediate sense of alert. Mainland China is a massive mind-shift compared to the relaxing beaches of Thailand.

We retreat from the Mainland hordes to a dingy restaurant. A group of school children piles in after us, staring over our shoulders as we write in our diaries. Most kids laugh curiously when they see us, although there are still some who are intensely shy, even running away in fear when they see the strange white humans with giant backpacks. One boy in the desert had such a shock when he saw us – it was as if he had never before considered that people could be white.

The amused restaurant owner shoos the school children outside as a plate of steaming brown noodles arrives. The children continue to stare at us through the restaurant window as we eat. I am determined to sample some more food types during this second excursion into China. For the first three months my vocabulary had limited us to a diet of noodles (*mian*), meat (*rou*), rice (*mifan*) and a few vegetables (*shucai*). Usually we choose our meals by referring to the plates of other people in the restaurant or by entering the kitchen to point out to the cook the types of foods we like.

Day 84

When you fully commit to something, serendipity will move on in, the world helping you in ways you could never have imagined.

Goethe

Paolo and I hitch-hike for two days, riding on trucks, motorbikes and cars in our efforts to re-find the Great Wall. The maps are only slightly helpful in this remote region of China. While waiting beside one road, having just been dropped off by a van-load of dam experts assessing the lowering water levels of the Yellow River, a black Audi comes and picks us up. We retrace our steps to an obscure gravel road we never would have thought to take. Leaving us there to wait, a blue truck then picks us up and offloads us in some empty grain fields where the men are heading out with ploughs to commence their day's work.

'This is as good a place as any to start,' Paolo says, looking out into the empty, brown hills towards the east. There is no sight of the Wall. We walk down the hill, and come to a Chinese farmer who stands purposefully in a green uniform at a pathway to the next village. It is as if he has been waiting for us.

'*Dao chang cheng you ba gongli*,' he says pointing up a clay path into the mountains, explaining that the Wall lies 8 kilometres away. I have not even told him that we were looking for the Wall. A group of young children guides us through their village, up a clay road to where she lies. The Wall looks majestic, 10 feet high, thick and brown, as it winds its way down a valley of dry, brown hills and into the horizon where, according to the maps, it will continue to do so for the remaining 2,300 kilometres.

Day 87

Paolo and I ease into the walking slowly: one full day, then one half-day to reacclimatise. Mentally, we know we have the discipline. It is simply a matter of re-finding the fitness. The usual blisters and cuts to the feet occur initially, as we wear in the new sneakers Paolo has secured from Reebok. However, after trailing the Wall for a few days, we are back to our old routine. The journey is more like a job now than a passionate reccie through the desert.

We ease our way for three days through the Yellow River Valley, where the Wall rises up along a range and splits into two branches. The Inner Wall heads south-east down a valley and across a series of fields before heading up another mountain range towards an unknown destiny. The main Outer Wall takes the more circuitous route north-east, looping around, according to the maps, to reconnect with the Inner Wall 1,000 kilometres away, just north of Beijing. There are over 20,000 kilometres of walls scattered throughout China and Mongolia. One certainly can't claim to walk them all. Our journey is more about taking one branch and using it to guide our way across the Chinese continent. We follow the Outer Wall down into a small village that is based in a smoke-filled valley.

A man wearing purple silk robes and pointed slippers waits for Paolo as he approaches the side of the man's temple home, which is etched into the Great Wall. The man has a chubby face and is bald, with eight dark circles branded into his forehead. He moves with a purposeful stride, gesturing for us to enter, and informs us through body language that he has seen us coming during one of his transcendental meditations.

'Italy de,' he states, aware of Paolo's nationality after over-hearing one of our conversations en route. His temple home is small, containing a *kang* to fit two people. Candles and incense surround a bronzed Buddha statue beside a stove and a shrine which lie opposite the bed. The monk proceeds to cook us a bowlful of twenty eggs, sliced potatoes and noodles. As we eat, he sits in the lotus position and begins to meditate. After some deliberation, he invites us to sleep on his *kang* for the night.

It is our first night actually sleeping inside the Wall. Many of the peasants have chiselled their homes into it, or use it as stables. I dream that I am floating outside my body, conversing with Paolo up in the atmosphere. It feels very real, as if I am actually awake. All of a sudden I sense the monk coming, and I warn Paolo that we have to get out of here. Upon waking I feel myself surge back into my body, but I can't move my head because it is clamped down to the bed by an invisible force of energy. I have to wrench myself three times before the force leaves and I can lift up my head from the bed. Paolo sleeps soundly beside me.

Although the Wall was originally devised as a means to ward off invading Turkic and Mongolian nomads from the north, Paolo and I are beginning to question its actual purpose. Many things simply don't add up about the military-border theory. Much of the Wall is hitting mountain ridgelines so remote and steep no Mongolian horsemen would ever consider mounting an invasion from there. Furthermore, the Wall is often not even waist-height, and so would be unable to stop any army except perhaps a platoon of hobbits. The elaborately constructed watchtowers – designed in accordance with *feng shui* precepts – are far too meticulous for mere military need. Is it possible that the brains behind the project secured finances from the emperor on the pretense of building a military border when they were actually marking out the planet's longest ley-line?

When I walk on top of the Wall I never get tired, yet when I take a step off I feel an immediate drain in energy. Lying on a similar longitude as the Camino de Santiago in Spain, do the Wall's towers mirror the Milky Way as many of the pilgrims talked about when following the Camino? One fifty-year-old Frenchman I met completing his three-month *camino* said his walk had healed him of his diagnosis of cancer. Indeed the Outer Wall marked a line of gold reefs throughout Northern China, regarded by writers such as Jamie Sams as the Earth's magnetic tracking system, the removal of which has caused our planet to now slightly wobble on its axis. Has the Wall evolved from a thought base of advanced geomancy and celestial mechanics, common to the ancient Egyptians, that aligned the great pyramids of Giza with Orion's constellation? What were these builders thinking 2,000 years ago? What am I thinking?

Perhaps we are just tuning into the residual spiritual energy present in the world's longest graveyard? Or is this influx of energy in our bodies simply a matter of culminating all the steps taken so far in the journey and transferring it into the strength and determination behind the next? Instituted to keep China's unwieldy population in check, was the Great Wall project a policy directive providing millions with an ordered direction to their existence? This at least justifies all the walls that could not have possibly served any strategic function. The Wall gave the builders a fixed sense of identity rather than finding themselves dislocated with the experience of absolute freedom, and after over 2,000 kilometres of walking, this is exactly what the Wall is providing for me.

The monk wakes us early for another hearty dose of eggs and noodles. Perhaps the surreal dreams are from all this excess protein? I get the monk to write his address on a postcard I have of the Wall in Shanhaiguan, the very end-point where the Wall trails into the sea. I do this with all the people we stay with, promising to send them postcards when I make it to those sections of the Wall. It helps provide a sense of reciprocation and reconfirms my commitment to finish.

Day 94
Paolo and I draw closer towards the city of Datong, approximately two weeks' walk from the Yellow River and only ten

hours by train west of Beijing. Datong is renowned for its hundreds of coloured Buddhist statues etched into a series of caves lying above the city. We have made the city our first walking base of this second walk, leaving the gear we can't carry in storage to prepare us for the next. The city also has a modern supermarket with Western supplies, including biscuits, bread and porridge, and soy milk in small transportable packets. This food is important, given Paolo has now also ditched the cooker to save on weight.

Forty kilometres' walk from the city we come across a medieval village holding an opera festival for Full Moon. The singers are dressed in purple, white and green traditional clothing which is made up to represent wizards and pixies. Their faces are smeared with thick white make-up, their eyes accentuated by black and purple colouring. The musicians play tin percussion drums on the side of the stage as the actors chase each other around, waving wands. They sing in a high-pitched tone, and stretch their voices to guttural wailing. We leave early, not wanting to steal their show, as many in the audience are staring at us instead of the performance.

Spending the night with one of the four men we had met upon entering the small village, we awake to find the windows covered in white. I look to Paolo. There have been several snowstorms in the unpredictable spring weather over the past two weeks, and, although this is the most severe, Paolo still seems keen to go.

'Let's get going now – before it gets too deep to walk.'

We trail the white serpent as the snow gradually rises to our calves. It is exhausting, plodding through the thick snow in our sneakers, thick chunks caking up over our trousers. The valleys are too dangerous to walk up and down, so we trail the watchtowers higher in the mountains where the snow is deeper but where we can avoid the dangerous ditches and canyons below. Despite the cold, we push through our exhaustion threshold, feeling giddy with dreamlike euphoria as the grey cylindrical power-stations at the edge of the Datong emerge through the misty, white land. We cross the railway line and reach the highway to the city.

'I'm heading back to Beijing to be with Zaotijie,' Paolo says. 'I'll be back in Datong in a few days.'

'I'll explore Inner Mongolia and meet you back in Datong,' I reply.

I want to get all the way in one uninterrupted line on foot, not backtrack. Paolo stands on one side of the road, while I wait for my ride on the other.

DATONG

In a country with the saying 'the hills are high and the emperor is far away', edicts from Beijing are routinely ignored.

The Economist

The Chinese Imperial Courts maintained a consistent policy of wall-building in the hope of securing a long-term defensive strategy. However, by cutting off the successful trade relations between nomads and the settled farmers thousands of miles from the decision-making capital of Peking, the Mongols were more desperate than ever to raid through the gaps in the Wall to survive. As the pressure built and the number of raids increased, the thousands of kilometres of Wall were simply impossible to properly defend. The Wall was still being built by the Ming Dynasty when it was conquered by the Manchus in 1644.

The victory by the Manchus made the Wall's purpose redundant both physically and symbolically because they controlled the territory and all the peoples on either side. Establishing the Qing Dynasty, they had now created a vast multi-ethnic empire, precursor to the modern state of 1912. With its essence as a social barrier between 'barbarism' and 'civilisation' dissolved, the Wall, it seemed, had no purpose at all.

After three days' rest in Datong, Paolo and I catch up and head towards the city of Zhangjiakou. We catch a bus to the highway from where we last left the Wall, and walk over a large, muddy river plain towards a mountain range. The Wall drops into a long, dry valley, which is layered with recently ploughed fields. Small temples sit at strategic high-points overlooking the land, ancient villages peppered randomly below. We walk for three days through a series of passes and connecting valleys, remaining close to the mountain paths to avoid the deep canyons that hinder the dragon's advance.

'I'm sorry, Nathan, but I don't want to consider you any longer,' Paolo says four days into our excursion. 'We must ensure that we remain completely unattached so we are free to come and go as we wish.'

'Unattached?' I reply, confused. It was our intimate connection that had enabled us to cross the maze of sand dunes through the Gobi Desert without ever getting lost.

'Yes, Ouspensky says that it's a weak man who considers the needs of others.'

'Don't go quoting those Ouspensky lines again. We're trying to survive a walk across Mainland China!'

'Look, I have a different agenda now. I need to get back to Beijing to sort out my six-month business visa.'

'Suit yourself, but if you want to sever all connection you're gonna have to carry your own tent. It's redundant if we carry half each but are not actually walking together.'

Paolo frowns. 'You could've waited to suggest this at the end of the stage.'

'You're the one who wants to remain unattached!'

'I'm going to make you pay for this.' He pauses, a scowl coming across his face. 'Give me back my sleeping mat.'

'Nuh, you gave it to me, twice now. I've used it for over six months.'

'My old girlfriend back home needs it. It's hers.'

'There's no way she's going to need it right now.'

'I think you should take a look at your attachment to that sleeping mat.'

'Fine, have your sleeping mat!' I throw it from my pack dramatically. He laughs provocatively.

'You're not ready for the teachings of esotericism. You have to be completely willing to bow under your teacher's will before you can learn to change.'

'I don't think I like your teachings any more.'

'Well then, stop following me around, imitating me like I'm your twin.'

I feel a surge of anger so strong I want to punch him. The builders don't deserve this, so I continue along the Wall on my own.

A length of New Zealand to go.

MOON 8

GOING SOLO

Day 105, 8 April 2001
  Ka hinga atu – he tetekura. Ka hara-mai he tetekura.
  When the fern frond drops, another rises to take its place.

Threatening clouds sweep across the plains towards the mountain I'm hiking. With no tent, I have to find shelter quickly. I continue along the Wall, passing watchtower after watchtower, but none provide me with a home. All are filled with mud and clay. The clouds congregate at the base of the mountain.

With no one else to follow, the Wall is all I know. It takes me towards the summit just as the elements close in for the kill. I crouch low to avoid the howls of the wind and look back in the direction I have come from. A spectrum of golden sunlight peers through the clouds, making a diagonal line towards the next peak. It shines on a small cave. There it is.

Paolo has set up his green tent at the mountain's base, sheltered from the wind. I don't have the nerve to go back down to ask if I can sleep. Not after the fight that morning. He has been playing games with me all day, walking ahead of me and then hiding on the other side of the Wall so that I walk past and he reappears behind. One is in more control from behind.

Darkness inks the sky. I push aside my misery and leap into the journey ahead. Each brick becomes my focus: step by manageable step. Diego was right about how much more intense it is to walk the Wall on your own. It's when your relationship with the Wall-builders becomes so much more alive. I walk for an hour before the cave entrance appears. It's a brick stable. I relax upon sighting it, but trip immediately, almost twisting my ankle again. I have to stay alert.

The stable is dark and damp, wet mud and rocks are strewn all over the ground. There is one dry spot just big enough to fit one person. The journey is catering to my needs. I climb into my sleeping bag and lie on top of my grimy, yellow pack-cover and three black plastic bags. I light a candle in an old prayer shrine protected from incoming gusts of wind. As the storm rages outside, the candle flickers resiliently.

'I can do this,' I say to the candle, savouring a handful of salted peanuts and a gulp of water.

The candle burns steadily.

I can do this.

Day 106

I watch the sunrise from my sleeping bag. The mountain I have climbed is clear through the stable arch, surrounded by a horizon of dry fields. Venus shines and gives me comfort. I crawl to the entrance and peer down the slope. I can't see Paolo's tent. He could be anywhere. Without his alarm clock, and one another to egg the other on, my head slumps back to my t-shirt pillow. The concrete ground is surprisingly comfortable, and I fall straight back to sleep.

I awake again, more refreshed. There are no stars now. The wind sings, the Wall's ancestors calling me on. Hunger and the prospect of facing the increasing heat are now the daily motivators. I pack up my small home and move on along the Wall. Surely the next few miles will diminish the problems plaguing my mind.

'What am I really doing here in China?' The separation with Paolo has left me feeling adrift. It's like I've lost a part of myself and I'm not sure who I really am. I've always been a 'we' on this journey.

I walk on and see a shepherd. He is old, and sits looking out over his sheep grazing on the hillside. I spend my time sitting with him, watching the world through his patient eyes. I feel like I can give myself more time to take in China rather than be pushed along by someone else's schedule. The sheep don't do much, so I press on and see Paolo meditating on the next peak. I look again. It's just a rock. I've got to eat.

The Wall heads down to a small village at the base of the range. A dog barks wildly, angered by my foreign scent, as a man in a blue Mao suit looks up from hoeing vegetables in his back garden. I gesture to my empty water bottle. He smiles and invites me into his small brick home.

We enter and are greeted by his wife. She looks loving and sweet – her eye wrinkles point upwards when she laughs. Her daughter smiles, too. She has hair to her waist, a smooth white face, and alert oval eyes. I find her soft serenity a soothing relief after the harsh beauty of the Wall.

The mother passes me a handful of apple slices. I giggle nervously, but have never felt so grateful. It's like I've been sentenced for the crime of self-centredness to a year of strolling amongst some of the planet's most generous people. My hunger compels me to stay. It's been a day and a half since last I properly ate, and I'm sure the mother knows I'm on the verge of tears.

The mother and daughter start to cook bread, noodles, potatoes and tofu. Mixing the water and flour into dough, it is mixed with herbs and spring onions before being moulded into round balls and twisted bread rolls. The process takes most of the day – a significant part of their lives revolving around this meal. The mother likes me filming her work, she laughs happily as I film. Her performance is flawless and I'm going to be invited to eat. I relax properly for the first time since being on my own. We sit cross-legged around the *kang*, gobbling up noodles and bread. Nurturing the body with good food, the soul with community and laughter, these people are giving me the strength to continue.

A dog barks outside and I wonder whether it is Paolo coming past. The daughter is now knitting, pulling the wool from an old jersey to be used for a new one. She has a contented smile as her work slowly grows. It is her meditation. I don't really want to leave these people's home, but reality pesters and I must continue with my project.

I fluster about, readying to leave.

'*Man ʒou,*' the man says in a firm, compassionate voice, providing a focus for my glazed-over eyes: Go slow. He places his hand upon my shoulders. 'The journey is the reward.'

My heart soars at this family's kindness. The prospect of tackling the next 1,700 kilometres suddenly isn't quite so daunting. I look up at the Great Wall, thick and brown, contesting its next range. I look forward to what lies ahead.

Outside the village I see Paolo sitting down beside a brick wall in the ploughed fields. My instincts say to just keep on walking, but foolishly I don't.

'I'm just digesting my meal. Want to buy the sleeping mat off me? I'll sell it to you for $30.'

'Thirty dollars American? Jesus, that's more than they cost brand new.'

'Thirty dollars.'

He knows I need it, so there is no point in bargaining any further. I give him all the US dollars I have left, and watch him walk off, wanting nothing more to do with him.

The Wall meanders along another mountain range and heads into a plateau flanked by two villages. Paolo, still well ahead, takes a quiet back-street to find accommodation. I head instead up the main street. A host of local kids follow me excitedly. I enter a shop to buy some supplies for the next day's walk.

'*Binggan doushao qian?*' How much for a packet of biscuits?

'*Ba kuai,*' the shopkeeper replies hesitantly. Eight *yuan*.

'*Bu shi, liang kuai tian.*' No, no only 2 *kuai*, a young child states earnestly. The kids give me their richest attention, but their smiles fade when I'm tapped on the shoulder.

'*Jinlai, laowai.*' Come with me, foreigner. A fat policeman stands behind me in a dark blue uniform. He has thick, black-rimmed glasses. '*Lai, woman qu gong'an ju dengji.*' Let's take a visit to the police barracks.

'But this villager has offered me a place to sleep in his home.' I look to the peasant hopefully. He lowers his head, quickly retracting his earlier offer. We walk through the main street, turn left and enter the police compound. There are four men inside.

'What are you doing in our village?' a plain-clothes cop with a poxy face asks. 'Are you a spy?'

'No,' I respond icily. 'I wouldn't have had any interest in visiting your village if the Wall didn't trail through here.'

'Are you alone?'

'Uummmmm . . . Yes.'

'Can we see your passport?'

'Yes, of course.'

A bespectacled officer flicks through the pages curiously. He is skinnier than the rest. He looks up.

'You've travelled a lot.'

'Yes.'

'*Meiguo ren?*' You American? He points to my Arabian visa from Jordan.

'No, New Zealander.' I'm glad they can't read my US study visa. There's been quite a lot of anti-American sentiment going on ever since a Chinese military jet collided with a US spy plane, killing the Chinese pilot and sending the US plane down into Hainan Island. The US spies were captured and safely returned to the US, but the media had reported that the US plane had purposely rammed the Chinese jet.

'You're not in trouble — we just want to know which lands you have seen.' His glasses reflect the light. He seems to be playing the good-cop role.

I'd dealt with several police and government officials en route. Most of them would test me, first, with their gaze. If I could counter their suspicions with a forceful stare, I would generally be accepted into their clan and invited to partake in a feast. Only a privileged member of the police or government can afford such a multi-tiered affair. Theirs is high-status living.

The second test was the *ganbei*. If I managed to hold my liquor (my university training suddenly becoming invaluable), I would leave the exchange as a fellow comrade blessed for the journey ahead. If not, I guess I'd wake up hungover in some cell. It is fortunate that Caucasians generally have a higher alcohol tolerance than that of Asians. There had been times when I had done a lot of necessary sculling.

'I smell something fishy – you're not telling us something.' The poxy-faced cop grimaces, sensing my inner distress. I can't look him in the eye knowing that Paolo is still in town. It would be very suspicious for him to be found.

'*Ni you shenme gongzuo?*' What is your job?

'*Wo shi lushi.*' I'm a lawyer. The cop's eyebrows rise. Less than one percent of the population are lawyers, only 150,000 admitted to the bar by 2000. They are generally held in high esteem. Indeed, it is a lot safer than saying you're a journalist – twenty-four having been arrested or reported missing according to Reporters Sans Frontiers already this year.

'Look, here's a photo of my family.' I use my second tactic to get them onside, describing each family member enthusiastically to avoid the poxy-faced cop's questions. It isn't working. His dark eyes scan me scathingly, his nose sniffing for a guilty scent. He opens his mouth to ask another question, when suddenly my attention is diverted to a small silver television playing in the corner of the room. It is showing a CCTV1 news broadcast with an item about the New Zealand Prime Minister, Helen Clark, visiting the Chinese President. They are shaking hands.

'Look, our leaders are making friendship!'

The hard-nosed questioning ceases. I must be the luckiest bastard in the world.

Day 109

Zhangjiakou is a city of three million people, who are neatly boxed-up in concrete apartments. Running through the middle of the city lies a dried river-bed which etches out one of the five main invasion routes used by the nomads into China. If

Zhangjiakou was taken, it was only a matter of time before Beijing would fall. These days, the only breach in the mountain divide is a sewerage outlet – the human manure used for growing vegetables. Housing China's gargantuan population takes up twenty percent of the available arable land, so every available inch of growing space has to be used. The global average of land mass required to sustain a human being is 2.9 acres. The average US citizen uses 31 acres per year, whereas the average Indian uses 2 acres. With the available arable land set at 2.1 acres per person, humanity will soon need another planet to sustain its needs.

Dawn in Zhangjiakou is awash with exercise. Toddlers wander along the riverside, watched by their adoring grandparents. Nappies can't be afforded by the pension-less pram-pushers, so a slit in the trousers is all that is necessary. Some people meditate by the river-banks; others unify body and mind with the soft, flowing movements of t'ai chi. All breathe in the richness of the rising sun.

I fall in line with the aged, the smooth momentum keeping my tired joints young. On the other side of the river, a group of grandmothers lines up in square formation. Groovy 80s music blares from a silver ghetto-blaster as old ladies fling their arms wildly, partaking in a lesson of hip-hop. It's the sort of stuff you'd never see your grandparents doing back home. The Chinese take their classes very seriously.

It is here that I meet Jerry. With chubby cheeks and hair down to his neck, he is quite unlike the stereotypical Mainlander who sports a short-back-and-sides. Renting a small blue shop, he is setting up the first English-teaching franchise in town. The shop doubles as his home, and he's lied to his parents, who believe he is working in an industrial factory. He places two giant speakers outside and blasts Backstreet Boys music to attract clientele.

To Jerry, my foreign face is a goldmine. He feeds me breakfast of soft black rice then sits me outside his shop as unprecedented numbers of parents come in to enquire about signing up their kids for lessons. On the pavement outside is the usual reminder of Chinese history. A peasant in a blue Mao suit sells crafted mats and pipe parts while an old man next door sells ice creams for 20 cents. He passes me a Jelly Tip with a wink. My eating his product quadruples his morning's business, with everyone who passes taking a gawp at the white guy. Peasants edge their wares closer; peppers, carrots, eggplants and tomatoes artistically arranged on sacks. Toffee-apples sprout from a bike carrier, and a metal candy-floss maker spins with a sewing-machine foot-accelerator. Quail eggs are pan-fried, exploding in their shells, while snails are stirred in a wok full of soy. One hapless duck is being dragged home to the pot on a yellow leash, the owner ruthlessly kicking it in the head.

Jerry's friends have written a newspaper article about my walk for the region's local weekly. Each day I sit outside reading, help take classes, and go to the bigger schools to make speeches. It is the perfect place for my next base.

'Why don't you spend the summer here? You can settle for a while, rest and write, and it would be good for my business. I can get you an extended working visa,' Jerry proposes.

'Possibly, it's going to be too hot to walk soon. I'll think about it during this last walk to Beijing.'

Having started in Jiayuguan – 50 hours by train west of Beijing – now I am only five hours away. Beijing: the 3,000-kilometre point has now become my personal walking goal.

Day 110
Kelvin emails.

Diego and I separated. We had a fight and I left him.
*
Same with me and Paolo. What happened?
*
Diego got psycho because he was sick of mothering me.
    I thought it best to just keep on walking on my own.
    Besides, he wanted to walk all the branches of Walls, and I had no interest in covering the same areas twice.

*

Where are you now? How's your health?

*

I'm doing alright. I'm back resting with Julia in Beijing.
   It was getting so hot in the desert. We almost melted.

*

Do you want to come with me for a stint? It's pretty lonely
out here.

*

I know you're lonely, but Sumana has also asked for me to go
with him for a few days. He's just north-east of Beijing and
soon to be finished. Sorry mate, I'm gonna have to put you
down the batting order.

I'm not that disappointed. His rejection completes the cycle of
karma which began with my decision six months ago.

DAY 111

Today's defeats provide the strategy for tomorrow's victory.

Anon

My family and friends back home are concerned that I am
walking the Wall alone. I admit the idea is disconcerting. It
has been hellishly lonely walking those last three days into
Zhangjiakou, paranoid that I will be overpowered by villagers.
This was especially so on the second night when I was offered
a small, smoky room in which five men were playing cards
and drinking into the early hours of the morning. However,
none of my friends in Beijing can just up their jobs and walk
with me on such short notice. I need another nomad. I decide
to email Paolo:

Dear Paolo
Are you still walking? Can we let bygones be bygones and
continue together?
Nathan

I return to the Internet store that night to see if he has replied. He is sitting right there tapping away at the computer.

'Paolo!' I shout elated, rushing him off to meet Jerry and the rest of the English corner clan. Paolo has skipped the last few days to Zhangjiakou, organising his business visa in Beijing instead.

'I'm just walking now until Zaotijie finishes her exams.'

'Great. It will be good to have the company until Beijing!' The time spent apart has rekindled our relationship. We spend another night in Zhangjiakou and eat lunch with Jerry the next day before setting off back to the Wall, which continues up the mountains that surround the city. Unfortunately, we both begin to feel sickly from a green vegetable patty eaten off the street, and once we catch a bus to the edge of the city Paolo can't get the twist screw on his walking stick working.

'Nathan, I think we should take a route around the mountains. I always feel lazy at the beginning of these stages.'

'Sure, let's take this valley up the back, then.'

We head off together, but a group of Chinese kids comes running up to us. 'Go back! The Wall is over here.'

'I think I'll take the Wall, Paolo, it just feels right.'

'Yes, you do that. I'll walk around the mountain and we can catch up further along the ridge later in the afternoon.'

'Awesome.'

We never see each other on the Great Wall again.

I trail the mountain-tops all afternoon. By nightfall the city lights of Zhangjiakou flicker peacefully below, but there is no sign of Paolo, and I spend the night in a concrete bunker. I have no idea whether Paolo is ahead or behind, so at dawn I continue along the trail of grey rocks on my own. Alone in the world's most populated country, I am simply not prepared for such torment. Field upon field, mountain upon mountain, I wander like a lost twin scouring the planet for a mate of the soul. Where are you Paolo?

The landscape I trail is one of grey, rolling hills, but the valleys are crossed within the dark recesses of my mind. I am becoming dangerously automaton, dangerously alone. Birds scatter from the undergrowth, their flushing wings seizing my heart: the Wall's ancestors are stirring me from the slumber of my thoughts. I awaken to notice that another mountain range has been passed – yet I am not quite sure how. It is like walking a grey-coloured dream mapped out by rock. The journey is now a matter of maintaining my sanity, desperately trying to keep connected to this world. The graveyard of rocks soldiers on into the horizon. I clench my fists, breathe in deeply and stubbornly soldier along beside it.

Day 116

Four days' walk east from Zhangjiakou, 250 kilometres north-west of Beijing, the evening fog engulfs the mountain peak I am hiking. I continue along the narrow path, feeling my way through the mist. Debris falls down the cliff sides. This is no place to be spending the night.

Darkness approaches. I reach the summit ridge and break through the fog. To my relief, a giant golf ball lies at the top of the summit. It looks like a weather-forecast or aviation satellite. When I spotted it earlier in the day, walking towards the range, it was just a tiny white speck – 15 or so kilometres ahead. A local peasant pointed it out as a place to eat and sleep. I had no idea where the next village was, so it had become my goal.

The Wall runs up the flat, grassy summit towards a brick house, then makes a dramatic right-angled turn back down the other side of the mountain. My spirits leap. My scroggin and biscuit supplies are diminishing. Even worse, my 1-litre and 750-millilitre water bottles are nearly empty. With only a few prized gulps left, I race hungrily towards the house.

Cautiously, I peer through an open window. Inside are four Chinese: two in civilian clothing – two in green uniform.

Oh shit, army . . .

Day 117

Here I sit. A Chinese man sits on my right. He has stern, slanted eyes and is wearing a green uniform with two military stripes on his shoulders. The addition of a silver star tells me he's moving up in his world.

'*Lindao shenme shihou lai?*' When is the leader coming?

'*Ban ge xiaoshi,*' Half an hour, the man says.

Yeah right. He's been saying 'half an hour' for the past two hours. Two more officials enter the room, and more Chinese tea is poured. The young men smile courteously as my white teacup is refilled.

When is this friendly façade going to end? It is two hours since I was escorted to the compound, with two loaded rifles to my head.

I eye the teacup suspiciously. Is this their tactic? To play it nice so that I fill up with fluid and, when it comes to playing hardball, I'll be desperate to go to the bathroom?

'*He pijiu ma?*' Would you care for a beer? the recruit asks.

'*Bu yao, xie xie.*' No thanks. I decline the green bottle, veiling my terse smile.

Forty minutes later the sound of squeaky brakes is heard. An army truck pulls up outside and the long-awaited general appears. Unlike the other army cadets – young boys in dark green uniform – there's no friendly smile on this man's face. Early fifties, smoker's wrinkles bank below his cold, steely stare. The leader talks quickly to his assistant and then plants me a frown the size of the horizon. I rise to greet him, shaking his hand firmly with a stare of equal strength. I've done nothing wrong and will not let his disdain intimidate me.

'You're not supposed to be here. Big trouble,' he states quickly in Chinese. Before I can respond, he does an about-turn, and leaves the room.

I sit back at the table, which is designed for spreading out military maps. My head slumps as another guard enters with some paper and a pen.

'Write us a statement as to why you are here and please sign it.' I take the pen and deliberate carefully over each word, nervously flicking through my phrasebook for the appropriate characters.

I am visiting the Great Wall ... didn't know it is an army garrison ... just thought it is a weather-forecast station ... asked for water and was invited by the troops to eat and spend the night.

Ten more minutes pass. The room is silent, everyone awaiting the return of the general. I take off my shoes and socks, get out my diary and place the photo of my family on the table. I look down at the family portrait. It is the morning before the wedding of my sister Merenia, our first full family reunion in years.

The general reappears. I sit up straight, anxious, but his face is full of warmth.

'Check your bags.' He nods, pointing to my blue pack in the corner.

I look back confused, thinking that something must have been planted. I look through my belongings. Just as I left them.

'*Chi fan.*' Two soldiers leave and return with a whole heap of noodle packets and beers.

I place eight packets of noodles in my bag, but decline the beers politely, wondering what on earth has happened to change the general's mood. He must have called some central authority in Beijing.

'You four,' he points to a group of soldiers who have come into the room, 'accompany him to the garrison borders.'

They escort me out down the garrison steps, past the toilets and over the Wall where they had hunted me down three hours earlier. The temperature is now 35 degrees. They each take turns carrying my pack and we trail together through the thorny undergrowth.

'No cameras,' the army man scorns, waving his hand at the screen. I can't resist trying to get some shots of the Chinese military carrying my pack for me along the Great Wall. Two kilometres later, they pause at the next mountain summit and return my pack to me. Fuelled with relief, blessed for my journey, I'm fired up to tackle the next challenge along the Wall.

It is to be my hardest.

PROVINCE 5: HEBEI
Day 130, 5 May 2001

The emperor's daughter was a killer for lists. She made a list of superfluous subjects which were debated by the eunuchs in the political chambers of the Forbidden City. She also made a list of the things she could do with her nation's money. Her favourite list, however, was of activities that quickened the heart. I continue walking through a people focused on merely surviving, following the trail of Wall eastwards, deep into the mountainous heart of Hebei province. It is the fifth of seven provinces on the route.

The journey has never been life-threatening. Although in some ways the whole journey is, never before has there been a stage where in the next ten steps I could actually die. I'll never forget this view: a line of limestone rocks a footstep wide – with a sheer 2,000-foot drop on either side . . .

I have spent several days bush-bashing through thick mountain foliage to reach this point. The Wall is about 2 feet high – a redundant gathering of bricks, weaving in and out of the jungle like a fleeing snake. My arms and face are torn, marked with blood-stained scratches. Gasping with hunger, it takes a certain wildness for me to continue.

'First Westerner, first Westerner.' My mind repeats its latest mantra. Indeed, only ants praise my passage, crawling up my shoes and through my pack as I lie resting on the forest floor, longing for the lifelessness of the desert. Three nights ago, sleeping in the open air on top of the Wall, an insect crept into my ear; without a tent I am fodder for all the creatures of the jungle. The little blighter screeched at maximum velocity in my eardrums as I waited for it to probe deeper towards my brain. Fortunately, it got bored with what little lay inside and went the other way. Apart from the ants and the odd snake, everything else has long given up on the place.

It is a pity because the terrain is absolutely majestic. Steep mountainous contours, straight from Chinese paintings, swallow the sky. To the far north lies a dark, ancient volcano, the base of which is being quarried by the Chinese. I am walking the pathway to heaven.

I have begun to learn the ways of the jungle. Orange mung berries are my staple. Found on prickly thorn bushes, blood is the price. I also prey on lietzels, big brown nuts covered in green spiky skin that grow on trees. Sour green apricots, and even the odd apple, pose as alimentary salvation. The berries mildly enhance the limited diet of dried fruit, biscuits, vacuum-packed mint, mince, or orange power bars, and noodles that I secure in the street markets of each city before setting out. This is easier than trying to decipher the packages of unknown goods sold in the supermarkets.

In the extreme heat, now over 40 degrees, and walking through continual mountain ranges, to secure food or water means heading down several thousand feet towards the nearest village. You only want to do this, at the very most, once per day. Animals in the wild become accustomed to having a successful hunt once every two days. It keeps the beast alert, the senses alive as to where the next meal may be. I now carry 4 litres of water and enough food to do the same if need be.

There is no question of turning back, even though I know full well what will happen if I slip. Yesterday, I left my pack on a cliff edge while I had lunch – of mung berries and Kit-Kats – when, with a mind of its own, the pack slowly leaned forwards and plummeted 90 metres below, landing with a solid *thrack*. Surprisingly, my camera attachments remained unharmed. My mind is getting stronger by the day: I have long ago stopped pining for Paolo and I really feel I can do this all on my own.

I walk to the base of the deadly trail. Suddenly, my body gets wind of what is going on and my guts cramp up: I rush off my trousers and release a wave of mung berry diarrhoea all over the Wall. I feel quite awful that I have shat on the Great Wall, but there is honestly no other place in the three seconds I have to prepare. I apologise, accordingly, knowing full well what lies next. After wiping myself with toilet paper (for I am not completely uncivilised), lighter and more balanced, I lift my faded blue Mac Pac and face the limestone tightrope of death.

Again my guts seize. The drop is hideous. How long will it take to fall 2,000 feet? I focus instead on the next manageable step, dragging my mind from the dangers of fear. I slowly lift my right leg onto the first brick, make sure the rock holds solid, then take another step. Concrete fills my calves and I retreat at the sight of all that space down below. How am I going to get across? Momentum is the only way – less time to think about falling. With a burst of will-power, I set my mind to the task and launch my legs upon each thin, white brick as if I have just become a spirit. I don't even bother looking back, and continue alone in my wildness.

Day 150, 25 May 2001
Mao's prison camps were designed to break a man's 'image' before rearranging his thoughts. Walking through China without a mirror also brings one to the imageless plains. I awake early from my grassy bed, set conveniently amongst an otherwise inhospitable rocky terrain. Wearily I make my way along the garden of rocks, clinging onto roots on the steep mountainsides, and squeezing through clumps of jungle trees. The view up ahead causes me to freeze.

Intricately designed Ming towers of thick concrete blocks climb up mountain slopes so impossibly steep that I feel the same overwhelming fear that the limestone tightrope of death elicited. The Wall clings to the mountain's flesh like a limpet, hanging on for dear life to an 80-degree slope. Much of it has already collapsed, unable to maintain its grip against the relentless pull of gravity. How in the world did they carry the rocks to build it up there? This place must have killed most of the builders.

I go to take a photo. My camera is gone! For the first time on the whole journey I have forgotten to strap it back to my shoulder. Fatigue is again setting in. I backtrack almost 2 kilometres to find the camera lying where I had last taken a short rest. My camera is essentially my sole companion on the trip. My testimony, I suppose, and my eyes for the world.

The Wall here is called Jiankou. The Heart of the Wall. It is the point where the Inner and Outer Great Walls meet after trailing 1,300 kilometres from the split where Paolo and I started this second walk. The two veins clash in the most dramatic fashion. The Inner Wall labours up a 70-degree slope along a narrow ridge, reaching the summit at an ancient arch; the Outer Wall trudges up a perilous 80-degree stairway.

The silence is piercing, interrupted only by the occasional cry of the shriku bird. A chilling wind drives up through the green valley. Local postcards call it "the Wall that the fairies built". Looking at it from across the valley, there is no possible strategic purpose for its construction. Untouched by feet, tended to by ghosts, this weaving warrior is nothing more than a wedding aisle of death: to cross this path is to marry one's life to the Wall – a commitment till death do us part.

'Go home, Nathan.' I've never heard my heart talk before. 'Go home.'

Losing my sense of self as exhaustion gradually drags me from life, it is the day before my twenty-seventh birthday. My month walking alone along the Wall has not made me into a man. What lies before me is a lost, malnourished child, driven to walk by a fear of failure – the need to be perfect – to be the first Westerner along the Wall.

A plane turns south, making its final descent into Beijing. I have watched these planes overhead all the way back from Yinchuan: a four-hour jaunt from Jiayuguan against my 150-

day strain. The capital lies out in the plains 80 kilometres to the south. A brown valley lies before the deadly mountain divide. Two villages sit with smoking chimneys below, their lands scoured by the plough. Modern and ancient are now caught on either side of the Wall.

Three thousand kilometres, five months of walking, and I have finally arrived due north of the starting point of my walk. There are still 1,000 kilometres of Wall left, but I make my first courageous decision of the entire journey: I let go of the Wall. Unlike the halfway point, this time I am not afraid to say goodbye. When Peter Hillary climbed Everest on his fourth attempt in 1990 and called his father from the top, Sir Edmund reminded him rather drily that the job was only half-done. The Wall has been here for hundreds of years, and, unless the world nukes itself, it will be here when I return. I cement this view of fairyland into my memory and make my way down a tourist track into the modern world. The vista of floating staircases will haunt me until I fulfil my promise to return.

26 May 2001, Beijing
Money robs the whole world, both the human world and nature, of their own true value.

Karl Marx

On one side, twenty-three percent of the world's population struggles to feed itself with only seven percent of the world's arable land. On the other, lies more wealth than the other world could ever imagine. One side does not have money, but deals in the currency of kinship, kindness and caring. The other side forges connection through transactions, waxed paper and plastic. Averaging ten new millionaires a week, Shanghai and Beijing are far surpassing their main rival across the Pacific. With annual economic growth at 13.5 percent of gross domestic product, the amount of US currency bonds in China's hands gives her the potential to wipe out the value of the US dollar altogether. Nostradamus prophesied that by 2030 China is going to experience world domination unheralded since the times of Genghis Khan. Ruling from Malaysia all the way across Eurasia to Hungary, Genghis Khan's imperial kingdom has never been matched.

China's real strength, however, lies with her people. Her future comes down to the manner in which these people are directed.

Caught in a 2-mile traffic jam, I leave my bus to Beijing and head up a hill to assess the situation. A truck has spilled into a ditch. All the Chinese are milling around, doing nothing, hooting their horns and getting frustrated. I head down and start to take the bricks out of the blue truck. The Chinese laugh at first when they see me trying to help, but my efforts soon build up a sense of trust, especially once they cotton on to what I am doing. They start to listen, as I direct them to heave the truck out of the hole.

Once the truck is out, we learn that it has broken down, so I get the traffic to reverse to create a gap along the side of the road on a grassy flat. It will be a long shot for the buses to take this way past, but, after a tractor successfully tests it, others start to follow. Half an hour later my bus makes its way through, the commuters enthralled that the foreign *laowai* has come to their rescue. I ask the bus to wait until the rest are helped out too, but, despite the praise, as soon as the bus is free they have no desire whatsoever to help the others out.

There are two types of Chinese – those who are caring and helpful, and those who actually enjoy watching other people's misery. It was the latter who were easily swayed to carry out the cruel denunciation and punishment of their people under the mandate of the Cultural Revolution. Indeed, it is every man for himself on the modern side of the Wall.

I leave my policing role lest I lose my luggage, trying to explain to a couple of Chinese farmers that they need to make sure the traffic doesn't close in on the gap created. They are unable to follow my instructions, and the gap is immediately filled by frustrated commuters. I feel for the first time what it is to be a leader. I also feel the emptiness a leader experiences when they are not able to help the whole tribe. Alone, 3,000 kilometres through my journey, I am finally learning what it is all about – you only take your mouthful once everyone else has been fed.

Mao's long march gave birth to a manifesto of 6,000 hard-fought miles that steered over 600 million minds – more than any other leader, ever, on the planet. He asked everything of his people's loyalty: that they endure bullets, malnutrition, frostbite and fatigue. Eighty thousand men began their walk to escape the Kuomintang Nationalists, and only a few thousand finished. Yet these remaining men would march into Beijing to instigate a whole new planetary evolution. I walk into the capital to go and pay my respects to his body.

> *Dying – I die not – the messengers of the sun*
> *Fasten their eager wings upon my feet,*
> *Inviting me to the day – illumined heights!*
> *Oh, then I'll fight my battle over again,*
> *Until my strength is melted in the Sun,*
> *Until the Universe and I are one*
> *Then falls the wall that rears, 'twixt me and men.*
> *Between the good and the evil, the live and the dead,*
> *Then I'll come back, and bring the sun with me!*
>
> Rainis

Chinese pilgrims come from all over the land to pay homage to Mao. His body lies in a rectangular palisade in the middle of Tian'anmen Square. People form serpent queues around his burial throne. Romanticised by his blinding poetry, Mao ensured massive support by exploiting the ancient Confucian brainwashing protocol – the unquestioning obedience to the 'heaven-chosen' emperor. All incumbent dynasties secure their hereditary entitlement with a bloodthirsty battle.

Fostering a cult of personality that the nation was prepared to revere, Colin Thubron writes that Mao disguised his hunger for power with the bewitching words of a deified prophet. In his discerning words: 'Mao saw China as a blank sheet of paper with which to write poems of unending revolution'. Distributing little red books to focus minds both young and old, Mao gathered power like a vacuum suction. The few intellectuals who resisted his charms were oppressed into mental submission through harsh labour in prison camps. He was ingeniously brutal. One hundred million workers were pulled from the fields to set up the steel-making industry. Any remaining grain was confiscated to sustain his relationship with Stalin.

Visitors get only a second to pay their respects to Mao's body, guards ushering them on so they can't even stop walking. Mao's face, heavily powdered, is surrounded by a wreath of red roses. I ignore the guard's instructions and stand before Mao trembling. For those few brief seconds I can physically feel his presence. His strength of spirit is immense and I don't want to leave. Even in death his power oozes.

Mao's giant portrait sits at the very spot where he announced the People's Republic of China in 1949. It is on the Gateway to the Forbidden City, across the road from Tian'anmen Square. Most peasants still celebrate Mao with a strong sense of reverence, unwilling to openly voice dissent against his acts. Yet those connected to the 16 million who died of starvation – forced to eat twigs and leaves, even fragments of brick from their clay cottages – quietly whisper: 'They have neglected to draw in the wart on his jaw.'

26 June 2001
Map life through by setting worthy goals. Main priority – to become a good person.

Helen Keller

Reverend Doctor Sumana Siri completes his historic journey across China at the end of June 2001. None of us others are there to share in his accomplishment, but when interviewed by journalists he claims to have walked the entire 7,000 kilometres to the border of North Korea in a little over seven months, notably wearing out seven pairs of sneakers. Looking at Sumana's stature, the journalist expresses certain doubts about the credibility of his claims.

Yet after nearly a month of walking on my own, I have begun to understand the genius behind the monk's walk. Completely committed, taking no breaks except to renew his visas, Sumana may not have walked every step, but – with right mind and right determination – he is the first of us to make his way safely across the Chinese continent. Sumana, too, had gone on a search for himself, and at the end has found his Realist Buddhist values again. Understanding and accepting his personal limits – just six months shy of his fiftieth birthday – he has completed his journey across Communist China by successfully adopting the middle-way path; a way of living which Buddhists believe is the best way to achieve peace, liberation and personal understanding. I email him accordingly, congratulating him on his enormous accomplishment. He emails back immediately, thanking me for my compassion, and we stay in touch. We both learn through our victories and defeats how hard it is to live up to the initial expectations of our dreams. So long as it is the vehicle to give one the will to walk, the journey itself – no matter how it pans out – is the reward.

1 July 2001, Beijing
> *One step forward. One step back. Is one step closer.*
>
> Triona Gaynor

I bump into Paolo at our local South Beijing Hotel.

'What happened to you? I emailed and emailed, but you never told me where you were!'

'We just missed each other by two hours outside the border to Greater Beijing ,' Paolo says, happy to see me.

'Two hours! How can you possibly know this?'

'I was walking through a police checkpoint and they told me you had just passed.'

'Jesus, I knew something was up that day. I could feel it in my gut.'

Ж

Sixteen days into my solo jaunt across China, a pair of twins circle me like electrons on two motorbikes. They offer to take me for a ride towards a gigantic loop of the Outer Great Wall which curves around from the North. The twins drop me off in the middle of nowhere, having to turn back lest they run out of petrol. I get another ride in a small three-wheeled blue truck, past a diamond-shaped green lake and into an exceedingly remote village. The Outer Wall snakes above the village on the surrounding ridgeline. Upon reaching the Outer Wall again, I spend the night, and in the morning I have this strong urge to walk the Wall backwards. I do for a little bit, wondering why on earth I am doing so, then backtrack and continue up towards the last steep mountain range towards the outskirts of Beijing.

Here the Wall terminates, the terrain is so steep. Unable to cross the intense crags, I am forced to backtrack to walk around the entire range. At the base, a Chinese man completely covered in flour comes up to me and invites me to his home to eat lunch. He takes me past a police checkpoint, and into his village. He has portraits of Stalin and Lenin inside his lounge. I sleep beside his family on the *kang* after lunch during the intense 45-degree heat of the day, then leave at 3pm. I am anxious to set off, even though I sense it is still too early, given the continuing intensity of the heat and tiredness of my body.

I walk through the police checkpoint and along a tarseal roadway down the side of the range. There, I see a pathway back into the mountains which my gut tells me to take, but my fear of snakes in the heat stops me from taking it. A white car comes along and I hitch around the mountain instead – and I have this clear feeling that I have taken the ride off an old Chinese lady who is waiting patiently by the side of the road 200 metres further down. After 16 days' absence, in the middle of the absolute wops of China, by some minute chance Paolo came walking through two hours later.

Ж

'Like the Walls that split and gradually together come, it is good not to be afraid of letting your partner go so you can maximise your life's creations.' Paolo pauses. 'Here.' He smiles, passing me a red basin and some soap powder with which to wash my grubby white t-shirt, as we did at the running rivers. 'If they come back and meet again, it is meant to be.' He gazes into my eyes as I look up towards him. After a few seconds, he looks away and I lower my head in humble silence.

'What are your plans, Paolo?' I ask eventually.

'It is too discomforting to walk in this heat, and there are too many snakes. I do not like it. I'm heading down to South China with Zaotijie to ask her parents for marriage.' He frowns as he concentrates on speaking English again. 'We make plans to return to Italy.'

'Will you return to the Wall?'

Paolo shrugs. 'We will see. This journey has already prepared me for many encounters I will face in the future.'

With Sumana finished, and Kelvin in Zhuhai teaching golf near the border of Macau, Diego is now the only walker who continues the Great Wall dream. Having filled in all the gaps he missed in the first half, he has just crossed the Yellow River on his way to Beijing.

13 July 2001, Beijing

China is on the threshold of fulfilling its own dream as the Olympic Committee settles in to make its decision for 2008. China was deeply ashamed of losing out to Sydney for the Millennium Olympics, and is desperately keen for international recognition during its re-entry onto the political stage. When the Olympic assessors came to town, buses had not been allowed to run for the two weeks before, so the city would be pollution-free. Toronto and Istanbul are now Beijing's main rivals.

It's seven o'clock on Friday night.
Tian'anmen Square is forbidden.
Army are lined up everywhere
It's the night of the big decision.

A big screen is showing in Wangfujing.
The masses have begun to draw.
Galvanising together anxiously
The result, no one can be sure

The decision is set for 10pm.
Only 10 minutes now to go.
A million nervous faces look up to the screen.
Stalled emotion is beginning to show.

'The verdict for the host of the Olympic Games . . .'
The Olympic Committee pauses to add to the sting.
Clenched hands and heaved breaths, please let it be.
'The host for 2008 is . . . !'

MOON 9

TURANGAWAEWAE

China is a sleeping giant. When she awakens she will astonish the world.

Napoleon Bonaparte

With China, the world's biggest market, now approved by the World Trade Organization, and the Olympic bid, the world's spotlight is now turned on this emerging economic giant. Established companies are reaping profits twenty-fold and with foreign investment growing by a world-leading 21.7 percent each year, hordes of multinational entrepreneurs are entering China's gates searching for the idea that will fill their wallets for good. With corporate thinking now the mental mould, and capitalism embraced as the new ideology, what political face is actually going to emerge?

Whereas *perestroika* and the floundering of the Eastern European Communist regimes led to the emergence of democracy in 1991, China's leadership holds firmly onto the reins of power, promising economic prosperity and political stability. Unifying China with a 'Middle Kingdom' mixture of traditional Confucianism, nationalism, patriotism, and a touch of 'Great China-ism', the Great Wall is no longer a divider of peoples but a symbol of national unity. This is aptly expressed by Deng Xiaoping's famous statement: 'Let us love our country and restore our Great Wall!' Semi-capitalism seems a viable third way between Communist central planning and the free hand in the market economy, especially given the psychology of the one-child generation.

Indeed, the nouveau riche see the State as a partner rather

than an adversary, joining the Party to gain influence on financial policies, obtain scarce materials, and secure loans and tax benefits. Although Beijing's bureaucrats often disrupt some capitalist successes through competing political agendas, once inside the Party an entrepreneur is shielded from unfair Party and legal decisions, and from competition outside. Liberal political debate is essentially seen as a boon to political stability, curbing the focus and pace of the Asian economic boom.

Still, while city economies blossom and 300 million people have been pulled from absolute poverty over the past twenty years, the gains are not evenly spread. The average per capita income of the 900 million peasants remains stagnant at the 300–500 *yuan* a month mark (US$35–$60), with 100 million peasants earning as low as 65 *yuan* a year. With estimates as high as 30 million killed during the famines of 1959–61, the Chinese peasant looks at food and energy resources in decade-long and generation-long pictures, rather than the single-year or even single-quarter views that dominate Western corporate decision-making. Yet history has shown that China's long-term restraint has been punctuated with episodes of ungovernable savagery. The rise of the Ming Dynasty in the thirteenth and fourteenth centuries was facilitated by a peasant-led rebellion that toppled Kublai Khan's oppressive Yuan Mongolian reign. When the country's impoverished status hits Mark 4 out of a possible 5, Chinese leaders have learned to proceed with caution because this can be the signal for countrywide mayhem. At present it stands at 3.5 and signs of unrest are evident. Chinese leadership will have to step carefully.

Meanwhile, as the world's best athletes prepare to enter a land historically renowned for shutting everyone out, and Chinese and Tibetan climbers are planning to scale Everest united by the Olympic flame, it seems that all the walls have come tumbling down with the Chinese Government's new-found sense of global inclusion. I head down to Shanghai to see in the flesh just what the new Chinese global empire will be like.

17 July 2001, Shanghai
With over 300 high-rises in Shanghai since her first in 1985, the
Chinese like to joke that their new national bird is the crane.

China Daily

Shanghai, the Pearl of Asia, a city of vibrant diversity rooted
in the colonial greed of opium-hungry Europe. It straddles
the banks of the Huangpu River, and I walk around as if
on Ecstasy, the cloud-stricken skyscrapers forcing my gaze
skywards. Oh the big buildings – it's been so long. My neck
aches under the elation of the modern world; the land that
kisses the sky.

The emerging Manhattan that is Shanghai hones talent from
all around the globe. Brash Americans, headstrong Germans,
romanticising French, analytical Brits, even the Russian mafia
have entered the mix to take part in this cultural resurgence.

Unlike the Chinese of the far North, who stare in bovine
wonder, the Shanghainese contemplate the Westerner with an
assessing eye. How much is his shirt? He's got no watch. I like
his silver ring. Shanghai is a beacon for mass globalisation.

Human and metal traffic condense the narrow streets. Dust
rises below old colonial French mansions, where washing lies
strewn across wrought-iron balconies. Gone are the days of the
drifting currents of cyclists; bike carts filled with fruit, families
or recyclable cardboard are now battling the loud and polluted
charge of the tinted black Audi, red capillary taxis and cram-
packed green buses – the motor market increasing forty percent
each year. The world's fastest train – Shanghai's Maglev – takes
only eight minutes to transport visitors the 40 kilometres from
Pudong airport to the middle of town.

Illegal corrugated structures and concrete Bank boulevards
both find room in Shanghai. Beggars pound the pavements,
hands open; students in miniskirts talk into palm-sized
cellphones.

I quickly discover these two worlds living alongside each
other: the beer which costs me 40 *yuan* (US$5) in a modern bar

costs only 3 *yuan* (US 40 cents) across the road at the Chinese 7-11 store.

We hit the clubs. Oh the clubs. That beat, pulse, and energy – labelled techno or house, it doesn't really matter – my body screams to get amongst it. The other animals in human clothing surround me, moving their bodies in seductive feline postures. I can hardly contain myself, thrusting my pelvis in every available direction.

A Chinese beauty moves in on me. Long dark hair, shapely waist, she swings her tush against my groin, and turns to wrap her lips around mine. One kiss and she is gone, a feline scout to suss out the new boy in town. Where race relations revel in the mutual attraction between the white barbarian and Asian women, bars and hotels are like the new world court tribunals, cocktails the conciliation.

Yet lurking just out of view, on the peripheries of Shanghai's bubble, forever daunting and most definitely felt, lies the old China; the world behind the Wall. Barricaded from view by the allures of women and enticing fashion, it cannot be forever forgotten. How long can I possibly hide?

It is going to be a while. I have decided to return home.

31 December 2001, Farewell Spit, New Zealand
> *He rei nga niho,*
> *He paraoa nga kauae.*
> *If you have sperm whales' teeth,*
> *You must have a sperm whale's jaw to carry them.*
>
> Ancient Maori Proverb

I have an eerie experience late one afternoon on Farewell Spit. The sandy spit lies at the very north-western point of the South Island and rolls out from the mainland ambling eastwards for twenty miles into the ocean. Bleached wooden bones of shipwrecks, orange fishing nets and cast-away bottles line the sands, accompanied by a section from a light aircraft missing at sea. White floats surround a rusted German mine from World

War One. The isle is a haven for travelling birds, such as white oystercatchers and pied stilts. It is the godwits' spring sanctuary before they launch out upon their 18,000-kilometre flight around the globe to Alaska.

I find a sandy pathway through the flax and toi-toi. It heads under a macrocarpa tree, sheltering me from the sun, and slithers up the side of a vegetation-cloaked sand dune. The path continues to the top of the dune face, before opening out into a wide desert plain. The silence is empowering. The windswept formations are untouched by man.

As I wander through the plain, the lowering sun casts a glow upon the intricate weaves of sand. About 500 metres across, immersed in the serene stillness, I reach the other side and look out at what lies beyond. The view fills me with awe. The ocean's waves crash wildly into the foreshore almost a kilometre away, leaving white foam from its journey across the Pacific. The air is full of mist and the smell of fresh salt.

This is not a place to go. It looks *tapu*. A place of the dead. But I go. I go because I know – 13,000 kilometres away, after 4,000 kilometres of walking – Diego Azubel is completing his epic trek along the entire Great Wall. This connecting walk, my farewell spit.

I set out for the sea despite the grinding feeling in my gut. My instincts serve me well. I walk straight into some quicksand, and have to rapidly retract my right foot from the grey puddle of death. It is a warning. Turn back. I don't. Instead, I see the warning as a test. Be careful, but don't give up. Don't stop fighting. A feeling of death pervades the entire area. Many tribal battles must have been waged on these shores.

It is then that I notice some footprints. They are lightly pressed into the sand. I take it as a safe path to follow. The footprints soon vanish, yet are replaced with a windswept path of fluffy white sand. It leads all the way out to the rumbling ocean.

I tread each step carefully, rotating my leg 90 degrees upon touching the earth, like the pukeko. Feeling each movement in all my muscles, I walk like a Maori warrior, alert and ready should the earth again sink.

Now only 50 metres before the crashing ocean, I think again to Diego's journey along the Earth Mother, *Papatuanuku*, from the Gobi Desert to the Pacific Ocean, *Tangaroa*. Sea mist rises from the rolling waves. *Tawhirimatea*, the God of Wind, howls down the beach highway, throwing sand against my shins. I go to take my video camera to film the whirling dervish's wild sandy dance.

My thumb begins to go numb. I persevere with the strange sensation and push the red record button, but the numbness spreads through my hand like some sort of demonic possession. I hastily put the camera away lest I find myself again overwhelmed. I have already been drained by my recent decision to remain in New Zealand: it left my body limp, and I was forced to recover in bed for two months.

It was dangerous to walk the Wall without the protection of my white bone-carving; it left me open to the many presences I felt along the Wall's path. When I gave the carving to Jack before starting my second walk, the bone fell off the string from around his neck the very day I reached Beijing. When it happened a second time, the day I returned from Shanghai to catch my flight home, he put the bone into my hands, and a shiver of reunion ran up my spine.

I continue the pukeko *hikoi*, my walk mimicking that of a warrior holding a *taiaha*. Conscious and respectful, my muscles reawaken and the alien sensation leaves. The ancient spear provides the first point of the pyramid that extends back through the body, encapsulating all my ancestors and beyond. I walk in reverence, each step towards the ocean.

The sea crashes loudly 10 metres from my feet. The sand blows painfully against my legs, and my grief grows steadily as a lost dream haunts my soul.

'Imagine walking to the end of that fuckin' Wall,' Diego had said as we sat around the fire over a year ago in London.

'And the full moon rising out of the ocean,' I added, the

fusion of Great Spirit tickling both our spines. Indeed, we had been right. An orange full moon pierces the giant waters on this fated day, the day before Sumana's fiftieth birthday. Tears run down my cheeks as I imagine Diego finishing his walk. I cry and I cry, until my stomach convulses and the ocean comes. Everything goes quiet, the peace of the chilling waters upon our feet. *Noa.*

It becomes clear to me in this moment that we are to live our lives in great heart. Live out our truth and follow the path, grateful and giving. *Whai-koha.* I salute Diego for completing his walk along China – for facing his fears and, despite all the odds, walking for over nine months in solitude to remain true to his dream.

Giving up the race across China has changed me. It is hard on my proud ego at first, to acknowledge defeat. But now that I have lost, everything seems okay. The race is solely with myself.

And like a baby who falls flat on his face when learning to walk, the most important thing is to get back up and try again. The Maori – a warrior race, renowned for never giving up – have a similar saying: *Whitu ki raro, waru ki runga.* Seven times down, eight times up.

There is no such thing as failure. There is only success and learning. My river's pause has ended. It is now time to finish the Great Wall forever.

The men launch into a hair-raising war dance – eye-whites glaring, tongues poking out – revealing the animal within. Stamping the foot on the dusty ground, slapping the chest and thighs, the men stir up a frenzy to tackle the challenge that lies ahead. My twin brother and I go in like warriors, wielding the taiaha *to lead the* Lord of the Rings *parade down the red carpet lane. The wailing chant of the old kuia greets the sun and stirs my spine – commanding me to be of this faith.*

1 March 2002, Wellington, New Zealand
Polly Greeks is a reporter for Wellington newspaper the *Evening*

Post. Graduating top in her class at Christchurch Broadcasting School, she writes a highly amusing entertainment column called 'Polly's Picks'. We meet when she interviews me about my walk across China.

'You're on a spiritual journey, aren't you?'

'Spiritual journey?'

'It's rare in this day and age – everyone driven by the race for the dollar. It must be hard adjusting.'

'Sure,' I reply, looking out across the harbour in silent reflection. It has been next to impossible to readapt. Nurtured by nature, my walk along China has returned me to my Neanderthal core – far from the values of my middle-class upbringing.

Ж

My twin brother is the first to notice. 'Boy you've changed,' he says, watching me as I crouch over like an ape, sniffing an apple I am about to eat. My brother and I are products of the same genetic source, but the divergence of our life experiences has turned us into two totally separate beings. One twin is Western, having spent the past year dancing for a world-famous aerial company in London's West End; the other is a product of the East, losing all sense of Western materialism in the wilderness of desert retreat.

Seeing people from the perspective of their true animal core, I am finding Western behaviour imprisoning. Dressing up in black suits with constricting ties – it seems like everyone is heading off each morning to mourn. Even the simple act of a woman putting on lipstick seems unnatural, the excesses of capitalism weighing heavily on my mind. Slow to think, wary to engage, I struggle to find a culture where I can successfully belong.

Ж

'I'm finding it difficult,' I continue, although it is my Maori side that is providing me with the ultimate sense of cultural grounding – tears streaming out of my eyes when I hear the strong tones of the *waiata*.

Polly, too, looks out towards the harbour. Her eyes suddenly ignite, as if she has just uncovered a magic secret. 'I knew I was going to meet you, the moment I interviewed your sister for her dance show *Wild Civility*.' She looks up to me with a demure smile. 'She mentioned your journey as the inspiration for her work.' She pauses, looking up meekly. 'I couldn't wait to see what you would be like.'

We talk like old friends, well beyond the article's mandate, and start dating a few weeks later. We fill our spare time going on hiking adventures whenever possible, making cycling and road trips all around the country. Both of us are enthused by the thought of adventure.

Four months later, unhappy with her job, Polly gives it up to apply for a documentary course with the Natural History Unit in Dunedin. When she isn't selected, she isn't sure what to do next. She certainly isn't an avid fan of the Great Wall, sick of me waxing lyrical about it every time I convince her she should listen. However, with nothing else on the agenda, my journey certainly provides her with some direction. Filming while walking the Wall is as good a place as any to learn how to shoot a documentary.

'Can I come to China too?' she asks, flicking an auburn curl from across her cheek.

I hesitate. To invite her along is to give life to a relationship that doesn't yet have proper roots. We have already broken up several times, and, although we have talked about it once or twice, I doubt I would have given up the Great Wall dream to follow her to Dunedin. Yet her support would be invaluable. I don't want to return to the wild Chinese Mainland without a sense of connection to home, and sharing the journey is better than going alone.

'Yeah, sure – why not?'

Her dimples deepen.

Polly purchases her flights and we get our visas, although the mood between us is fuelled with dread, especially given what I know lies ahead on the journey. I set up to write an email to my Internet network, announcing my intention to return to the Wall. Just before I push 'send', a blackbird flies through a tiny opening in the house and crashes into the wall beside the computer screen. The experience totally shakes me. I am no longer sure.

Polly has travelled extensively through India, South America and Nepal – predominantly on her own – and has done the two-week Anapurna trail, as well as other hikes through the Andes and Amazon. I know she possesses the will, and her mental and physical potential is clear from our hiking experiences in New Zealand; however, her mind is in no way prepared for the type of journey I intend taking. The trails she has hiked are all laid out, easy to follow. Nothing like bashing one's way through the bush across a continent. I begin to despair, toing and froing. Are we ready? Is the risk too great? Do I really love her? Sometimes she is the most beautiful girl I have ever seen. Sometimes she isn't. She looks up with her keen blue eyes, still willing to risk it all.

17 March 2002, Wellington airport
Polly and I plan to meet at Sydney airport to take the trip together to China. I accompany my father to Auckland, heading up on business en route to visiting my brother in Sydney. A man with greasy, long hair and red eyes walks down the plane aisle and sits between my father and I. His presence unnerves me.

'Why are your eyes red?'

'I'm testing out the latest coloured contacts,' he replies, his teeth flashing with a smile. 'Here, have my card. I'm shooting a vampire movie.'

The plane revs its engines to maximum velocity and takes off at full speed down the runway. Halfway down, the brakes suddenly screech, smoke careening off the wheels as we come to a halt just before the end. The cabin is silent. I look to my father. Grey-haired with bespectacled blue eyes, my father gazes at me for longer than I can ever remember him doing – a look a father gives when his son is about to head off to the trenches.

The man with the red eyes gestures down to his business card. On the back, scrawled in bloody graphics, are three words:

GO FOR IT.

The plane turns again and takes off down the tarmac towards the ancient pathway of bricks.

27 March 2002, Beijing

Polly and I meet up with Kelvin and Julia upon arriving in Beijing. Kelvin has just returned from teaching golf in Jiuhai, but can't find it in his heart to tackle the second half of the Wall. That lonely trail does not equate with his life's search. Kelvin and Julia have caught a train to the Wall's end instead.

'We had such an amazing day – heading out on the jet-skis at Shanhaiguan.'

'Must've been so nice to have shared the end with the person you most love.'

'The two people,' Kelvin replies, raising his shoulders proudly.

'Two?'

'Yeah, Julia is pregnant with our daughter, Elena.'

Kelvin had come to China in search of his son, walked half the Wall and come to its end with a daughter.

'It's not really the place to take Polly, mate,' Kelvin lectures.

'We're here now,' I reply defensively.

'Oh well, what doesn't kill you can only make you stronger.' He pauses. 'Remember, though, you're taking a beautiful lady out onto the Wall – be a gentleman.'

One of China's most famous legends talks about Meng Chiang-Nu, who went in search of her husband to clothe him warmly while he built the Wall. By the time she made the journey, her husband had already perished in the harsh winter. While mourning at the base of the Wall, legend says her tears caused the Wall in the area to crumble, revealing her husband's bones.

MOON 10

THE HEART OF THE WALL

Day 151, 29 March 2002
Death hunts you — there is no time for regrets or doubts — only decisions.

Carlos Castaneda

'I'm glad I came with you. I can't imagine you walking here on your own. It would have been so lonely,' Polly says, compassion shining from her light blue eyes.

The conglomerate of granite marches out into the grim grey battlefield, weaving ancient and modern tales of cowardice and courage. It splits north and east. Polly and I follow the 3-foot rampart of rocks heading north. It is overcast and windy. Polly wears her Gore-Tex anorak to keep warm. The rocks seem to slither silently across an empty paddock, undulating towards a grassy hilltop. There are one or two patches of snow.

I slip in behind to watch Polly tackle the next hill. She places her walking sticks awkwardly, thrusting her blue pack up the slope. She is of small stature but has determined bones. We reach the top.

'How are you going?'

'I'm just trying to find a rhythm.'

'You're doing a great job. Let's head up to the next hill.'

We continue to walk, entering the trance of the Great Wall meditation. The wind gradually increases as wisps of fog waltz in and out of the curving ridgeline. It gets colder. Polly puts on her blue woollen hat and ties the hood of her blue jacket, as light sleet sweeps across her face. We continue along the Wall, but the wind picks up, drawing the clouds closer. Where ten minutes ago visibility had been several kilometres, now we are in a white-out. Polly is barely visible 15 metres away. My eyes scrunch up as the wind hurls sleet and grit.

Polly is scared. There are no towers with entry points to shelter in and the tempest is getting violent. I rush along the Wall to find an alternative shelter, almost losing sight of her. She emerges through the mist as powerful gusts of wind pound snow against the opposite side of the Wall. It blasts over the top like a fire extinguisher, and we crouch low to escape the skin-piercing particles. A watchtower appears through the mist.

'This is it!' I shout, racing towards the tower, but again there are no entry points. 'We are going to have to bunk down in between it and the Wall! Get out your sleeping bag: we'll sleep in the one bag to keep warm.'

Polly's eyes turn mournful. Her hands are trembling, too cold to untie her laces. I quickly untie them for her and blow up the ground mat.

'I'll put my orange survival bag over our sleeping bag. It's waterproof,' Polly suggests.

'Good thinking.' This will keep the lower part of the bag dry. Having ditched the tent 1,000 kilometres back, we are going to have to use everything we have to keep warm. I arrange the packs to cover us from the direction of the wind and attach my jacket as a roof from the snow. I don't notice that Polly has taken off her trousers and thermals. When I enter the sleeping bag I find her half-naked. Indeed, this is far from the romantic outing I'm sure she had imagined for our first night out on the Wall. I know we can survive, though, because I have experienced far colder conditions in the Gobi. The key is to remain positive and stay awake. If we fall asleep, we will join the builders forever . . .

Day 152

Snow impales my coat jacket, the rooftop above our heads. We are being buried alive. Polly's face is pressed against my chest, constricted by the tightness of our sleeping bag. There are

5 inches to breathe through, a small gap I've clawed out with my hands. I manoeuvre my arms upwards to adjust Polly's cotton hat. It has slipped from her head and her arms are wedged into her sides. She is looking pale and cold. I reach around to rub her uncovered legs. They are starting to shiver.

I begin to sing the Elton John lyrics to *Your Song*. My attempt is raspy, but Polly locks on.

We give in to a resigned smile and begin to laugh at the hopelessness of our situation. Slowly, however, we fade back into silence. I turn off the torch and the storm takes over.

Time goes by, methodically measured by the snow that slowly builds. Our shelter is growing strong. My thermals are keeping my legs warm, but Polly's legs are stone-cold. I reach around with my legs and rub hers. It is exhausting, but it keeps me awake and it is all I can do. The storm rages outside as Polly drifts in and out of dreams. 'A passing caravan . . .' she mumbles. 'Mongolian couple waving me in . . .' She knows that if she goes, she can never return.

I thank God that Polly is wedged into the sleeping bag and can't act on her hallucination. If she escapes into that storm, there is nothing that can be done. How can I possibly explain her death to her parents?

'We're gonna get through this.' I rub her legs harder – forcing us both awake. Snow surrounds the jacket upon our faces. My black gloves are saturated, so I have just my bare hands to scrape away the mini-avalanches closing in the air gap above our heads.

Time labours. I tick the seconds past in my mind, willing this night to be over. I'm guessing we have been inside the bag for several hours – although time is an unknown quantity. All I know is our darkened cave. Suddenly the wind changes direction. It sounds like a Boeing 767 engine pointing down our sheltered channel. The blast shreds our snowy shelter and latches onto our jacket rooftop like a frantic burglar, launching it into the night. By some unconscious reflex, my hand catches the jacket in mid-flight. Snow pounds my face and the wind screeches in my ears as I wedge my upper body out of the sleeping bag, holding onto the jacket for dear life. My hands begin to freeze as I drag the packs around to protect our heads from the storm's deadly new advance. I feel the rip of fat and muscle as my left shoulder semi-dislocates from dragging Polly's heavy pack through the snow. I wince in pain but manage to maintain my clutch on the jacket. To lose it now will mean certain death.

Shoulder limp, I retie the jacket to the straps, locking it securely between the newly placed packs. Snow and wind continue to pound my face, the night storm hungering for my flesh. The jacket flaps wildly, but the roof repairs hold. Again I sink back in towards Polly, who is cowering in the sleeping bag. Holding the jacket steady while the snow re-secures the fort, I patiently await the night demon's next move. *Tawhirimatea* doesn't return, so I again focus on rubbing Polly's legs . . .

Ж

Light pierces the tiny gap. I lift the frozen roof, which is heavy with snow. The storm has gone. A blue, crystal sky is filled with fading stars. Snowy peaks surround us, garnished by the sun's honey glaze. Above the golden temples lies the full moon. It looks like a medallion of hope – solid and strong. Polly awakes, blinking timidly.

'I'm gonna shift us to the other side of this tower, shelter us fully from the wind.' The mountains' scarred skin lays exposed. We leave the sleeping bag and reset camp where the sun shines a golden square of light beside the sheltered side of the tower. As we resettle to thaw, there isn't anything else to say. Polly sits there staring, quiet and vulnerable. I leave our shelter to see if it is still possible to walk this subsidiary loop of Wall. It weaves like a winding line of cocaine up and down the next three mountain ranges. I yearn to follow its course, but the icy wind blows hard into my face. This journey will have to be done with the mind. I sigh within, and return to Polly who is finding refuge behind the watchtower's shade.

Warm and ready, we drop 3,000 feet of altitude into the dry, brown plains. The day is already hot, nearly 30 degrees. We lay out all our gear to dry, and I blow up my green sleeping mat. Polly stays awake, looking to the surrounding mountains in awe, happy to be alive. I fall asleep, exhausted under her watchful gaze.

Day 154

The rickety bus heads up a tarseal road towards a series of mountains woven with grassy scrub. On the other side lie the Beijing plains. Surrounding us lie remnants of an ancient beast. She stretches her gigantic scales sumptuously over the mountains – watchtowers studding the land like vertebrae. We have arrived again at the main trunk line of the Great Wall.

Polly looks up in wonder, shifting her walking sticks impatiently. She is eager to climb up onto the Great Ming Wall. She shuffles ahead, taking the lead along a hard-baked mud path up to the mountain's crest.

'Stop!' I grab Polly's shoulder as a cloud of dust rises before her feet. Polly stalls, startled. A light brown snake wriggles rapidly in retreat.

We watch on in silence. Its movements are mesmerising, a million tiny muscles weaving its way across the land.

'Don't be afraid. Watch it go.'

She looks back blankly, her face white with fear. I squeeze her shoulder with my right hand.

'Snakes force us bigger animals to tread the earth with respect. It's a guardian to the Wall.'

Polly remains deadpan.

'I'm going to do a *karakia*. I stupidly neglected to do so at the subsidiary loop of Wall.'

I breathe in solemnly. Sixteen lines of kilned limestone lay out before us, the Wall at chest height. I call out the first line of the prayer to our hot and hazy surroundings. The world around us is silent.

Whakataka te hau ki te uru

A cooling wind comes in from the north upon utterance.

Whakataka te hau ki te tonga.

A cry from the shriku bird echoes from the Beijing plains to the south. My spine shivers. It's as if Nature is listening.

Kia makinakina ki uta.

Calling to the shore, I hear seagulls crying out far, far in the distance.

Kia mataratara ki tai

A bee buzzes by my ear, flying off in the Wall's opposite direction, towards the desert.

E hi ake ana te atakura:
He tio, he huka, he hau u

I call to the different elements to guide us in our lessons on our way to the shore, celebrating in the breath of life.

Tihei mauri ora.

A pheasant scampers out of the bush and scurries up the path leading straight onto the Wall. We are to follow. The builders have invited us on.

Days 154 and 155
The Wall serenades us in and out of brick watchtowers, Polly following closely behind as we wade our way through a hot, humid day. Surrounded in valleys by white spring blossom, our steps are chaperoned by a background of ginger peaks,

whose Oriental sheerness transforms to bright orange in the setting sun. It leaves me breathless with its beauty, as we walk along ingenious pathways that Chinese shepherds have devised through the mountains where the Wall no longer trails. By night, we reach a fully intact watchtower with eight arched windows. It looks out to a crimson lake, reflecting the purple starlit sky above.

We lay out our bedding, enter our separate sleeping bags, and prepare a meal of two-minute noodles left to soften in cool water. Scroggin of nuts, raisins, apricots, pumpkin seed and chocolate is saved for dessert. It isn't exactly top-quality travel – however, the Ming watchtower feels warm and secure, and a tiny mouse has even taken up residence, busying itself by scampering over our sleeping bags. We feed it some cold, space-wrapped baked beans as a diplomatic peace offering, but it turns up its nose at our budget cuisine, continuing to scramble over our heads in pursuit of the ultimate prize: the box of Kit-Kats I bought Polly for her twenty-eighth birthday.

Indeed, my romancing skills leave a lot to be desired. Dragging her out into this insane snake-infested terrain, almost killing her on the first night, and refusing to have sex with her while walking on the Wall – this is far from the hand-holding 'honeymoon' that Polly has in mind.

The view of the lake glistens with golden fragments in the morning light. It is paradise.

We trace a trail down the side of the Wall the next morning, bashing through thick bush laced with thorns. Polly begins to slip further and further behind.

'Stop going so fast!'

I pause to wait as a Chinese man sees us heading down the hillside and comes out in his blue row-boat to take us across to a white shanty hut. He is young, with a bowl cut, and gives us a reserved smile. The oars squeak as he rows to the guesthouse; the family are fixing up fishing nets on the wharf. We settle in for the day and his wife feeds us a plate of small fish, duck eggs, rice, tomatoes and small grey twigs.

'You okay, mate?' I ask, despairing at the forlorn expression that has yet to leave Polly's face today.

'I can't communicate with these people.'

'Just look them in the eye – try and engage. It's a different way of talking, but you've got to at least try.'

'Let's head off.'

'Chill out, Polly. Take a look around you. This place is amazing.'

The lake is surrounded by an amphitheatre of green, cascading mountains, grey bricks traipsing over the peaks. The temperature is also well over 30 degrees. I sign on as deckhand and pretend like I am helping the old fisherman, my heroic jubilations resonating through the valley every time he brings out a fish. Polly waits and watches, but as yet can't share my enthusiasm for the Mainland, preferring the magic of India or the wonders of the Himalaya. It's going to be a challenge to marry our differing conceptions of the journey.

We head off to find a new mood later that afternoon, walking towards dusk through a range of molten mountains which crystalise like toffee in the setting sun. Polly soldiers ahead while I film her walking. She enters a watchtower at the top of the next peak just before dusk. To her surprise, she finds a German couple from Berlin setting up to sleep. It is the last thing we are expecting to see, given the isolation of the terrain. They have come from a newly opened tourist section over in the next valley, escaping the ticket collectors to experience their first night on the Wall. We line up to sleep beside each other in an open watchtower, stars twinkling through the collapsed roof. I wake up at midnight to find the couple shivering, and cover them with my fleece and jacket. They, too, are having a chilly first night up on the Wall.

Day 156

Feel the fear and do it anyway.

Susan Jeffers

The worst still looms ahead. An afternoon's walk away, right at the peak of the next mountain range, the Wall vaults a cliff face at an 80-degree angle. I am filled with pure dread heading towards it, and can't even begin to imagine what Polly must be feeling. We say nothing, our attention brought swiftly to the present by a Chinese man sitting in a watchtower, sheltering from the stifling heat. The watchtower is filled with ticket butts, Buddhist prayer mantras and other bits of rubbish.

'*Yi kuai.*' One *yuan*, the man says, indicating with his hand his rubbish-collection services. The old woman down the hill had done the same, setting up a cardboard sign that stated *Tree Conservation, 1 Yuan*. As I pay the region's latest entrepreneur, I announce proudly that I have walked the Wall all the way from Jiayuguan.

'*Da laji, da laji!*' He responds with a look of awe, immediately jumping up from his crate. 'So you're the Great Wall walking legend,' I surmise the translation, my chest heaving in pride. He immediately rushes out of the tower with his axe in hand. I follow him curiously and watch him cutting down the only living tree left in the entire range, effectively putting the conservationist out of a job. I lift up my two walking sticks to explain that I already have two suitable aids. Unperturbed, he begins whittling the end into a sharpened point, offering it with a generous grin. I stand there confused. Such a walking stick would easily get caught in between the rocks of the Wall.

'*Da laji, chang cheng da laji.*' He looks up expectantly, urging me to take it. '*Da laji.*' He smiles again, as I take the stick off him to be polite. A month later I learn that he has just given me my Chinese name: 'The Great, Great Wall Garbage Man.'

William Lindesay, the first man to run across China, trailing on his route most of the Great Wall, had set up rubbish bins on all the tourist sections near Beijing as his part of giving back to the people who had provided him with so much on his journey in 1987. He's without question the single individual who has done the most to protect the Great Wall, and founded various non-profit organisations that work directly with the government, and influence government policy, to protect the 'Wild Wall', and the surrounding landscape. I, too, walk the Wall, picking up rubbish left strewn on its route. Yet New Zealand's passion for the clean and green doesn't translate back to China – the job is generally left to the 'plebeian classes'. It is the reason the country is generally a littered mess.

We recommence the climb towards the hideous granite peak that even Dr Seuss would have been proud to draw. Had we started here first, I probably would have suggested we pack up and leave. Looking at Polly's fear-stricken eyes, I think she would quite like that option. I take a photo of Polly harnessing a brave smile; the Wall towering forbiddingly behind. At the very least I can take a photo for her prized Wellington newspaper, the *Dominion Post*. She is certainly putting up a brave front, even though I know she doesn't really want to be out here. It has shown from the very beginning in the way she made no effort to help out with preparations.

'Right, Polly, I don't think it's gonna be safe for you to make this climb, but I'd like it if you could film as I try. Afterwards you can carry both bags around the side, and I'll meet you down the other side to bring them up.'

'Fuck off.'

'Look, I invited you here, and part of your responsibility is to act as support crew to make my journey successful.'

'Your journey?'

'You said you wanted to come here to learn how to film. Now here's your chance. Do as you're told.' I am beginning to sound like Diego.

'Go stuff yourself.'

We continue to rant and rave, but the lovers' tiff isn't going to get either of us to the top of that Wall. The way the Wall has crumbled on the steep slope has created a fierce-looking face which leers down upon us both. We change tack, sharing a meal of rice and what can only be described as boiled grass. We gathered it from a tourist restaurant at Huangechangpu earlier in the morning through lucky-dipping the menu. Polly passes across a gold-wrapped Easter egg as a peace gesture, and the cliff face seems to be looking upon us more approvingly. The only way over is as a team.

'Okay, I'll film.'

Polly films lying down, and, spurred on by the rush of caramel cream chocolate, I start the climb. It is easier than it looks. A passage of viable hand-holds and manageable terrain appears around the side of the cliff face – and I reach the top, celebrating like a monkey.

'Stay where you are, Pol, I'm coming back to get ya.' I climb back down to grab my pack, and head up again before returning for Polly's.

'Go just in front of me. I'll be close behind. You can do it.'

She is nervous initially, her hands shaking, but they gradually steady with the aid of encouraging words. Her leaden legs also soften as she propels herself more confidently up the steep cliff. At the top, her face beams with pride. We look back at the Wall traipsing majestically over the five ranges we have crossed over the past three days.

'Feels good, eh? Facing your fears.'

'Sure does.'

The Wall is now just a small gathering of bricks in high-altitude terrain, and it seems like we have just crossed from spring into autumn. The terrain is greener and filled with lush trees, and we scrunch our way through a forest of fallen leaves. Polly rests in the late afternoon sun while I climb to the next peak to assess exactly where the Wall heads next. The dragon's body criss-crosses like ribs across the land. Five peaks away lies the aorta. Blazing red in the setting sun, feeding blood to the other veins, it is a sight I have dreaded for ten months. Jiankou. We have passed the Ming Wall's initiation, and are now ready to take on the heart of the Wall.

Day 181

Polly and I have been walking for three weeks through the mountains, gradually finding a walking routine and sense of confidence in each other's ways. It has been an exhausting affair, walking peak after peak, and Polly is in need of a break, so we have decided to leave the Wall and hitch-hike to a small village to rest during the full moon. We have found a cheap farming hostel, and, although initially welcomed with open arms, the locals think it necessary to inform the police of our presence. I try to convince them that this is not necessary – that it will only lead to trouble – but they are insistent that they have to abide by the State's rules.

Polly and I are woken up at 5.30am by a loud knock at the door. It is still dark. I lift the latch and a fat man barges in, shouting in Chinese for us to pack up immediately and get into a van outside. He waits beside our bed, leering at Polly lying half-naked under the sheets.

'Get out!' I snarl, closing the door on him and rapidly starting to pack.

'Let's get going Pol – it's induction day to the might of the Chinese State.'

Criminals, genuine or simply members of the Falungong, are often paraded in trucks through the city streets. A loudspeaker draws everyone from their shops to watch the modern-day crucifixion. The two criminals on each truck are dressed in orange and surrounded by ten policemen in dark blue uniforms. Each one has a hand placed on the perpetrator's shoulders in a showing of State strength. A red van with darkly tinted windows waits outside with its engine running. As soon as the escort leads us out into the van, the peasants begin viewing us with suspicion too.

'Don't let them see that you are scared,' I urge Polly. 'And, whatever happens, treat him with respect.'

Polly and I take a deep breath and get into the van. The driver is smelly, and scratches his balls, spitting through the window before setting off. He drives hastily through the mountain roads, cutting corners, inconsiderate of young children riding their bikes to school.

'Put your packs on your laps,' the driver shouts half an hour later. He stops to pick up a woman waiting on the corner for a ride. I am beginning to get confused. This van is becoming a taxi service, not a police escort.

'60 *kuai*,' the driver shouts, ordering us and the last remaining passengers out at the bus station of Miyun city, two hours' drive later. I can't believe our luck. We aren't being taken to the police station at all, and a bus bound for Huairou, our walking base over the past month, rolls up behind the van that very second. I pass over 16 *kuai*, the same price the other passengers have paid, grab my pack and Polly's arm.

'Come on, let's go. We're heading back to Huairou.'

Our 'eviction' is perfectly timed for the 1 May Chinese holidays and the chance to meet up with Michael Gresham for the next walk. After a month of trailing the Wall, we are beginning to let the journey walk us, rather than us it.

Huairou is a construction site, its skyline punctuated by cranes. Even as jackhammers chip through old concrete, more concrete is being poured to form the foundations for new shops and apartment blocks. Bulldozers crunch their way down old alleyways, flattening brick walls and homes and leaving knots of bewildered men and women in their wake.

History isn't allowed to take root here. There isn't room for traditional lifestyles when there are highways and malls to be built. Out with the old, in with the new. Teenagers with dyed red hair and designer footwear hang out at McDonald's or around computer screens in Internet cafés. Or they shop. I have never seen such shoppers. Every time I walk down the street, I see hundreds of people clutching their latest purchases in plastic bags. There are clothes shops everywhere – thirty alone built on the street parallel to where Nathan and I sleep in our hotel.

Musings from the Wall: Polly Greeks

PROVINCE 6: BEIJING
30 April 2002, Huairou
Consumers are enticed by loud techno and clapping attendants

– China doing all it can to enter the hunt to become middle-class. Polly and I have set up camp-base in Huairou, to store the bulk of our gear and return to after each section of walking to recuperate. Our hotel is 60 *yuan* a night for a double room that contains washing-machine facilities, a warm shower and a television, and is close to our favourite restaurants, Internet café and Polly's masseuse. The hotel's custodians are friendly – a band of hard-working women who take us under their wing. The room, albeit bland with light green walls and a view of a grey industrial courtyard, provides a good escape from the rigours of walking through the Mainland.

It has been a taxing month, especially encouraging Polly along. Tackling Jiankou is just like the Dr Seuss climb. I head up the steep mountain peak on my own, spending the night at the top while Polly remains safely in a tower below. Once I assess that it is safe, I leave my gear at the top and come back down the ridge to collect Polly and her gear. Sometimes, it is like walking the Wall three times.

En route through the mountains Polly suffers from intense period pain which grows into a mega migraine, rendering her almost blind. I do not recognise the severity of her illness, and we spend the rest of the day in a watchtower while she recovers. Perched on a steep mountainous ridge, low-lying mist comes in the next morning, rendering it too dangerous to leave. We are forced to spend an extra day before escaping to the safety of civilisation.

The journey is simply a matter of learning to compromise. Giving up walking sections of the Wall to cater to Polly's idea of how the journey should go is an incredibly difficult thing for me to do, especially considering how much I have walked. However, our compromises are teaching me some important things: like sticking together despite the tough times, and learning to enjoy the sections of Wall that we do walk. Polly is slowly beginning to learn that it is the journey, not the destination, that matters; I am learning to smell the roses rather than tread blindly over them. As long as I get to a place high in the mountains where I can see the Wall's majesty unfold, I am okay with not walking every step of those parts. Diego had warned me just before we set out that much of his journey had to be walked with the mind.

I also make sure to give myself breaks when we have settled safely in a nice hotel. I sleep out in the mountain-tops alone, scaling crazy mountains as I wish – the time apart is healthy for our relationship. Polly has purchased a Chinese phrasebook, and is making a concerted effort to learn some Chinese. Looking in the same direction as we both take in the peace of the mountains, the unity we are beginning to forge is going to be vital as May arrives with its consistent 40-degree summer heat.

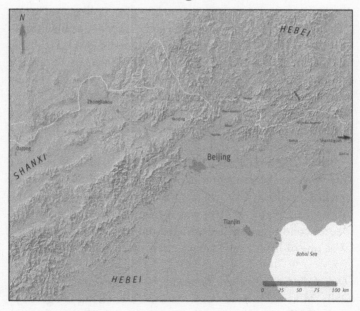

The Great Wall continues uninterrupted across the provinces of Hebei and Beijing, where the main tourist sections lie. It continues onwards towards the Bohai plains and terminates at the sea (at Shanhaiguan).

MOON 11

THE STAIRWAY TO HEAVEN

Not every mountain needs to be climbed to understand its height.

Anon

I have known Michael Gresham since I was nine. We were batting together one Saturday morning for Collegians Cricket Club when I lost my middle stump in the throes of a ninety-nine-run partnership. The experience cemented a good friendship which continued through our time at Wellington College and a stint at Victoria University. One day, however – completely out of the blue – Mike left to teach English in China. In those days no one we knew went to China, so his act was pretty legendary. Our connection soon whittled away into the pit of global anonymity.

Kelvin and I emailed 'Gresh' upon arriving in Beijing. All we knew was that he was somewhere in the Mainland. We eventually tracked him down in the far northern reaches of Harbin, famous for its ice sculptures. Mike was teaching English in minus-40-degree conditions and had settled into a relationship with Wang Wei, one of his former students, before settling in Beijing.

Day 187, Gubeikou and Simatai, Hebei Province
Polly, Mike and I head out by train to Gubeikou, the gateway to the Wall's most renowned section, Simatai. We pass through the countryside, passing brick villages and figures on bicycles, the Wall trailing across a thin line of ridges. Polly looks to me and grins.

'We've walked all of that,' she says proudly. 'Look, there's the peak where we had the massive fight.'

'There's the one where you were crying with fear.'

'Look, there's the section I did on my own while you were resting.'

'It's like our own private timeline.'

One hundred and twenty kilometres north-east of the capital, Simatai is an absolute Great Wall masterpiece. Trailing over a massive mountain range, the wall rises up like a striking cobra, scaling a sheer precipice only one brick wide. With a 2,000-foot drop below, the pathway is aptly named the Stairway to Heaven.

It is getting late in the afternoon. Mike, Polly and I have just finished walking 20 kilometres along the Wall at Jinshanling to the base of Simatai. We bathe in a clear green reservoir to cool off in the sauna-like heat. Chinese visitors watch us swimming, sweating away in their Sunday best. A few daredevils take off their shoes and socks to touch the water, but that is as adventurous as they get.

Other European tourists lie about the lakeside. It is strange to be walking amongst tourists dressed in the latest fashions, some reeking of perfume. Many look completely bewildered, unaccustomed to the Mainland experience. We are smelly, with twigs through our dishevelled hair, and I realise how far Polly has come since beginning her quest. She can speak some of the language, is no longer afraid to engage, and has even ventured out into the Mainland on her own. As the sun dips behind the mountain, shrouding the lake in shadow, the tourists get back on their buses bound for their hotels. We set off instead to scale Simatai.

The Wall is immaculately built with large kilned bricks, and the gradual alignment of steps makes it surprisingly effortless to scale despite the steepness of the terrain. Built under the Ming reign of Wang Hu, the builder of this Wall was killed by the authorities because he completed it well after the intended deadline. When the authorities saw his creation, the body was posthumously pardoned, dug up, and buried beside his work of genius.

The real test of Simatai is actually getting the opportunity to scale the summit. Kelvin and Sumana had been turned away by policemen stationed to ward off overly zealous tourists from putting themselves in danger. Yet everyone knew this was a ruse to extract the 100-*yuan* bribe to get past. A group of young Chinese students with army packs and sleeping bags walks back towards us, heads down in disappointment. 'You can't walk through to the sergeant's tower. It's closed. The guards have already turned us back.'

Sure enough, a young officer in army uniform comes down from his post as we head on up. I had hoped we were timing our walk late enough to just miss them.

'The path is closed,' the young officer states.

'I'm walking the Wall from Jiayuguan to Shanhaiguan,' I reply, enunciating my Chinese tones slowly, 3,300 kilometres of conviction in my eye. He sizes me up for a second, then nods and lets us pass. The young students leap up from behind, taking their chance to rush off towards the next line of watchtowers that trail perilously towards the top. The Stairway to Heaven has invited us to her test.

The first part of the climb is challenging. It presents an 80-degree cliff of waist-high steps specifically designed to keep the sane at bay. With her red hair tied back, cheekbones defined after a month of walking, Polly takes a brief sip out of her water bottle and eyes up the crumbling stack of white bricks.

'Go for it, Polly – take the lead.' Without hesitation she leaps up the first chest-high step, placing herself delicately to the side of the anorexic ledge. I am impressed at her growing ability to scale the steeper Walls. We had done a lot of work in the earlier days just standing on rock sides to work out how to balance with our packs. She grabs Mike's pack as he claws his way up the Chinese python, careful not to slip over the ledge that falls away several hundred feet to the left. Next it is my turn.

My legs are shaky and I can't get up on my own. Polly and Mike grab my pack, and lift me up. Standing tenderly on the narrow ledge, we continue our way as a team – the tune of this ancient trail.

'Let's go for the century, Mike,' I exclaim as he lifts me up to the next level by the shoulders. As we get higher up the narrow channel, the bricks become looser.

'Take the lead, Nath?'

'Sure, Pol.' I squeeze my way carefully past, grabbing her walking sticks, and head towards the top; the others close behind. A giant red sun sinks into a bed of grey cloud, marking our moment of triumph as we hit the summit. We make our way to a small watchtower which lies just before the actual stairway. The lights of the villages around Beijing are lit, visible for miles as the sky fills with fireworks. China is celebrating its 1 May Labour Day national holiday. We are celebrating our newly forged team.

Day 188

The next day we are five.

A young Chinese boy wakes us from our slumber, sitting at the doorway to our watchtower, dispelling any illusions we may have held about making such a valiant climb.

'*Yao shui ma?*' You want to buy some water?

'*Bu yao, women you.*' No thanks, we've got plenty.

He whisks off towards the sergeant's tower, taking a safe trail through the woods towards the top of the hillside. I am relieved. The thought of taking the actual stairway – zig-zagging precariously beside a 2,000-foot cliff – has haunted me all night. In fact it has haunted me the entire journey. So many fears are unfounded: fantasy blurring all sense of reality. Mike and I take a few steps along the stairway to get some photos, but testosterone's addiction to bravado gives way to maturity – we return to follow Polly up the safe path through the woods. The sergeant's tower lies on top of the final crest, providing a view of fields and steep green mountains for miles and miles.

Builders are renovating the inside, lugging loads of water and bricks up a 3,000-foot jagged pathway. They carry plastic containers that are attached to their backs by wooden braces. The reconstruction of this one tower has taken several weeks. I have never really fathomed how long it must have taken to build the Wall. One of the builders has set up his home in one of the towers, with a mattress, rickety stick gate, cooking fire and larder to hang up his white bread (*mantou*).

'*Ni hao*,' pants a short, skinny man wearing a pink-and-white hat. He wears glasses and has buck teeth. '*Wo jiao Ming Xiaodong*,' he says, informing us of his name. His friend comes up shortly afterwards and looks upon us silently. He is taller than his friend and in his early forties. He wears a black-and-red nylon jacket.

'My name's Zhao Weiguo. Are you the Kiwi guy who knows Ma Pangfei?' he asks in Chinese.

'Diego?' I reply, aware of Diego's 'flying horse' nickname, given to him by the Chinese.

They nod simultaneously. 'Di–e–go.'

Diego had spent a night at their home in Zhangjiakou, en route. Ming Xiaodong and Zhao Weiguo have heard that there are some foreigners walking the Wall, from the guide who had taken us safely around an army zone the day before. They have rushed to catch us up.

'Let's all walk together, then,' Mike replies in perfect Chinese, translating the words Polly and I can't understand. The Stairway to Heaven has provided. For the first time since Day 11 of the journey, we are again five.

Day 193

My body is racked with churning guts and a particularly dehydrating strain of diarrhoea. Polly and I are back in Huairou. Our last day on the Wall has been an extravaganza as we dragged our tired and ailing bodies up the reconstructed slopes of Huangyaguan. Yellow Cliff garrison – a fort built by the Ming between 1528 and 1619, and restored in 1984 – is surrounded by thick stone cliffs. It lies on the last major invasion route by which the Mongols would attack Beijing from the north-east. Containing a maze in the middle, each of the fort's intricately designed guard towers is built in accordance with *feng shui*.

Thunder grumbles in the distance. The Wall often attracts lightning onto its rocky hide, demolishing towers, filling the construction with electric energy. As we head towards the top of the next range we drag ourselves wearily to a forlorn tower to escape the rain. The lightning storm closes in, the wind changing direction to keep the embankment of clouds firmly lodged within the amphitheatre of mountains. The storm circles us like a shark, lightning scattering across the sky, but we are far too mesmerised with the display of electric veins to consider our safety.

Suddenly, a brilliant ray of purple-and-white light comes down from the heavens and smashes into the cliff face beside us. There is an almighty explosion and then an avalanche of boulders cascades from where the cliff has been struck. The shock of the explosion reverberates through our bodies, and the thick smell of sulphur permeates the air. It's all over in a few seconds, a plume of dust rising to the summit. My ears are deafened but I do not feel afraid – just privileged to have been a witness. Given that this cliff is the next place we are heading to along the Wall, it seems clear that our decision to take a break from walking is in accord with the will of the gods.

My stomach aches.

Polly's growing grasp of Chinese and my sickness have changed our roles on the journey. Polly is now camp mother. Without her help I am a piece of waste. As I lay curled up in bed, skin pale and stomach convulsing, Polly learns the words for hospital and escorts me to the local medical centre.

'Amoebas, Nath. I'm sure of it,' she explains, unable to disguise her grateful smile. It means at least a week of relaxation before being forced back out to march the Wall. She waltzes up to the hospital counter and explains her prognosis to the hospital clerk.

I am sent upstairs immediately and enter a room where a doctor is tending to a long queue of patients. My foreign skin paves the way for her instant attention. The doctor looks me over with a frown. Putting on a pair of white plastic gloves, she points to my fly: 'Unzip them,' she gestures.

I go to untie my belt, but, confused, point back to my stomach, shaking my head. Polly has sent me to the venereal disease clinic.

I deserve it.

Ж

It has been a week of Great Wall walking lunacy. Upon meeting the other Chinese walkers – Zhao Weiguo and Ming Xiaodong – we follow their journey along the Wall for five days. They traverse it with the aid of a Chinese guidebook which shows the best sections to walk, which sections to skip because of the danger, and which mountains to cut across. I soon give up my need to lead, and begin to get trained by the best. These guys know how to carve up mountain ranges in a matter of hours, taking hidden chasms and reconnecting with the Wall in mystical ways before diverging off again down a different valley to find the best views.

Talking with the locals to ascertain routes and secure daily feasts of noodles, meat, vegetables and beer, their break away from their respective families is a time to pretty much drink themselves silly. Mike and I join in the revelry as the weather consistently reaches 40 degrees. Without shade to shelter us, throats parched like dry gorse, the Wall is like a desert of stone. I even lower my hygiene standards, drinking from Zhao Weiguo's cold water bottle when out of hot water. After almost a year now in and around China, I presume my stomach will be cast iron like those of the locals. It isn't. Polly the Wise stays on the hot water and lemonade.

Zhao Weiguo carries a small axe and a rope outside his aged army rucksack, and sends Ming Xiaodong ahead to pace out the trail for us all to follow. This is good, given the influx of snakes. Mike almost stepped on one yesterday, and with Ming Xiaodong beavering away keenly at the front, they will all be scared off by the time we come along.

Some of the sections are steep with overhangs. Zhao Weiguo uses his rope to take our packs up while we rock-climb to continue the Wall's line. It is still scary to tackle such sections, but we know now just to do them, focusing on each manageable hand-hold after another.

On our third night camping out together, we stumble across a fat Chinese lawyer from Beijing who is walking on his own to escape the stresses of the city. At night we talk around the fire, taking shots of white spirits while Mike and I converse with the others in Mandarin. Polly is finding herself increasingly left out.

'I want to leave these guys now, and rest. I'm shattered,' she says exhaustedly.

Mike left us yesterday to head back to his fiancée in Beijing. I don't want to let the others go, knowing they are on their last day of walking too – but Polly is adamant: it is a choice between her or them.

'You head east, while we head west,' the lawyer says philosophically as he bids us both adieu. Zhao Weiguo and I look over one another emotionally. We have grown close over the past five days and I know he shares the same gut feeling that it is too early to sever the connection. It is eerie how we have met, the extreme coincidences that have brought us together. He had started walking towards the sea at Shanhaiguan from Zhangjiakou, the very same point I had started walking on my own.

I embrace the others, who head up the next hill while Polly and I abandon the Wall to head down a road out towards the next town. We walk for five minutes, but I can't help feeling remorseful, my instincts imploring me to head back to the others. A blue truck approaches. I decide to wave it down.

'Let's go back and walk with them, Polly – stick to the Wall.'

'I'm not coming, Nathan – you'll have to go on your own.'

'Come on, just this last day. We've come this far.'

'No, Nathan – I've really had enough. Do what you want, I'm no longer coming with you.'

I wave the truck away and we walk in silence. A taxi-van comes up the road a minute later.

'Don't even think about it.'

'I'm off,' I decide. 'I'll meet you back in the hostel in Jixian. We'll find each other.' I open the van door as Polly walks down the street in defiance. I look inside. The van is full of Chinese people, looking at me curiously. All of a sudden it doesn't seem a good idea any more. I can't bring myself to do such a selfish thing. I let the Wall go and walk after Polly. She is sitting beside a tree, crying.

'I'm sorry, mate. I've given it up. Let's have a proper break from all this madness.'

Day 194
Rural Chinese pillows bring out sighs on the best of days. They look plump and generous, but their stuffing of sand and wheat grains make them as comfortable as resting your head on a brick.

Musings from the Wall: Polly Greeks

Treacherously close to my second anal examination of the journey – the first being when I was suspected of narcotic laundering and was strip-searched at Auckland Airport on the way home – Polly has a good chuckle, but I am infinitely grateful for her presence. Having a penchant for lying in bed, she is a great mate to spend the time with recovering. We do normal stuff for once, like watching movies. *The Two Towers* is showing at the local cinema, Frodo and Samwise slogging it out in Middle Earth speaking Chinese. Their journey seems to emulate ours. Polly, with her curly red locks, out to save her master with this horrible curse to finish the Wall.

I am given some yellow pills by a doctor with Elven eyes, and, after a full recovery, head into Beijing for a feast of domesticity at Mike's apartment. DVDs, soft beds, all-you-can-eat Pizza Hut, and street upon street of clothes shops for Polly. Nothing enhances one's love for Western capitalism than an enforced six-week diet of scroggin, cold two-minute noodles, baked beans and tuna.

Paolo gets in touch while I am in Beijing. He walked the Wall for a week with his wife, Zaotijie, starting just before Polly and I set out from New Zealand. We had hoped to walk some sections together as a group of four, but they found it too challenging once they saw the section at Jiankou. Instead, they headed to Shaolin for two months to partake in Qi Gong classes.

Paolo eagerly pores over the maps as I show him where Polly and I have walked.

'I'm gonna return one day with an adventure travelling group.'

'It's not as bad as it looks,' I reply. 'Polly managed it with a 20-kilogram pack, and there was a group of thirty young students being guided along the section in just sneakers and jeans.' I pause, reflecting on our good fortune to follow the experienced guide's trail which took us through all the safe diversions to conquer the fairytale Wall.

It is hard to walk 3,000 kilometres of a journey and let it go altogether, although Paolo is now strongly connected to China through Zaotijie, and will be able to complete his journey throughout his lifetime if he so wishes.

After a week's rest, sick of the Beijing heatwave suffocating us in a sauna of concrete, smog, exhaust and fried food, Polly and I set out for our last walk for the season, to celebrate my twenty-eighth birthday in China.

Day 203
China specialises in never-ending mountains, the sort that transform victory cries into anguish as yet another furtive peak rises on the skyline.

Musings from the Wall: Polly Greeks

Polly isn't keen to come out with the increasing heat – but I am determined for us to try to at least reach the next major dam as a place to finish for the summer. We jump into a taxi to drive to where the lightning struck the cliff face, and from there we follow the Wall deeper into the mountains. It takes us through dense jungle for the next few days.

In search of food, we find a valley which leads to a dilapidated brick house. An old grandmother and one of her daughters invite us in to partake in what looks like strips of slimy brown seaweed. The sustenance slithers its way down my gullet, and I wonder how long it will take before it makes its way out. Looking at Polly's tentative prods, she is no doubt thinking the same thing.

The other dish is pig's ears. Polly takes a bite of one and places it at the corner of her plate, pretending it never existed. I give up on the brown sludge, but hunger compels me to try an ear – the one delicacy I have yet to try. It is very chewy, almost impossible to swallow, but I finish it up, Polly urging me off before I can ask for any more. She looks like she is about to vomit. I pay our hosts 10 *kuai*, who in turn rush around the property making a big fuss, gathering handfuls of sour green apricots for us to take.

'You must return if ever in the area.' They smile as if they have never seen so much money.

'Hmmm. Hardly likely,' Polly mutters, sucking in breaths of fresh air. The day is blisteringly hot, so we abandon the Wall as it rollicks over the mountains and take the easier path through a natural canyon. I lie down to rest in the shade on a flat, dusty ledge, blowing up my air mattress and inviting Polly to sleep beside me. I lift a rock to make room for her, only to find an angry scorpion rearing its tail. It extinguishes any desire we may have of resting.

We stumble instead across a group of men chiselling rocks from a quarry – just as would have happened thousands of years ago. Hammering sounds echo through the valley as the younger workers break boulders in half by hammering metal nails into the middle with sledgehammers. Once small enough to transport, the rocks are carried down the line to an older worker who continues the paring-down process. It is hard work, and the men are paid 50 *yuan* a day for their efforts. We are picked up by two men passing in a van and taken to their guest home for dinner, beer and peanuts.

Day 205

The next day, dropped off by our kindly hosts who will have nothing whatsoever to do with our money, we begin the major climb over the biggest mountain range in Hebei province. On the other side of the range, according to the maps, lie the Bohai plains. At 1,000 feet above sea level, it is the last step in a gradual drop of altitude which begins at the Himalayan plateau. There are actually four major drops in the land from the original 6,000 feet above sea level where the Gobi lies. The second occurs in the loess land from Shaanxi onwards after the deserts at 3,000 feet; the next in the mountains around Beijing to where we are now; and the last, a trench lowering 200 metres below the ocean level itself. After this range we are on the long home straight to the sea.

The vista from the top silences us. Small, rounded hillsides peep out amongst the dry golden plains – islands in days gone by. The mountains are engorged with bluffs which were once perhaps deep sea fissures and underwater canyons. Far out into the east, ancient temples and villages dot the landscape. Our weary eyes have discovered a lost Atlantis realm.

Polly leads us down the Wall, now only a foot high, snaking through green bush. The dense foliage shelters us from the harsh sun which reaches 40 degrees by 10am. Clambering down cliffs that make our earlier climbs seem like child's play, the jungle opens up into a basin where we are presented with a clear green lake.

We head towards it to escape the heat, and two Chinese peasants beckon us to enter a dilapidated shed to replenish our water supplies. They invite us to sleep on one of the workers' beds, with folded newspaper and cardboard boxes constituting the mattress.

An hour later, a well-dressed man in grey trousers and black skivvy comes in to see us.

'Come with me,' he says, rousing us from our bed. We follow him up a tarseal road, past fields of apple trees. Each separate apple is covered in a plastic bag. The searing heat reflects off the concrete pavement as we rise higher up the hill towards his brick domain, where we are greeted by the barks of two German shepherds.

'Don't be afraid. My name is Li.' He pats his dogs on the head as they happily circle us.

Li Beng is one of that very rare breed of Chinese who actually own land. His house lies secluded from the rest of the villages in the valley, a brick castle without turrets. The view sweeps out over a valley of oak trees and terraced fields, while his compound out the back contains two enclosures for deer. Li's deer are raised for their antlers. Ground to dust and imbibed for medicinal purposes, the antlers sell for up to 200,000 *yuan* a year.

His six hired hands float around the estate, cooking and doing the daily chores. One young boy comes in with some tea and beers, as well as a plateful of tomatoes, cucumbers with vinegar, and rice.

'Stay with me Pol Lee, Nay Than, please – for long as like,' he says, showing us to a washing-machine so we can scrub our clothes. After we have showered with a bucket, Li offers his oversized shirts for us to wear. He seems to have no love interest in his life.

On the dawning of our third day on the farm, Li drives us to the Wall at 5am to tackle the last mountain before the dam. He is saddened by our departure and gives us sixteen foully fermented eggs to take with us as nourishment. Polly and I had both struggled to politely stomach one when invited to a meal at Li's neighbours'. Polly surreptitiously manages to leave the eggs behind in our bedsit; however, Li notices our folly and insists we put them into our packs. Standing there, alone by his brown Cherokee Jeep, he is almost in tears, waving at us until we are out of sight.

We climb the next range, following the skinny trail of rocks as the sunrise bleeds through the trees. Sweat pours through our clothes: it is almost 30 degrees even before 8am. Polly secretly places the eggs up ahead to see which ones I can find. I manage to miss every single one – an unexpected Easter surprise for the next group of *laowai* mad enough to walk on through. Over the peak and into the oven-baked plains of the Bohai basin, I take a dip in a goose-shit-infested stream, and lie beside Polly under an oak tree. I rise just a minute before a branch comes crashing down just where I have been lying. A grey taxi-van drives past the dusty road, and, even though the Wall parades over the next hill, we agree to catch it to find a nice place to sleep for my birthday. Five kilometres later, the taxi drops us off, without payment, in front of a marble stairway that leads through automatic doors into a plush air-conditioned hotel.

Thanks China.

Day 207, 26 May 2002, Malanyu'er, Hebei Province
Polly is sick now. A local girl kindly takes us through the streets of Malanyu'er village to find a hospital. Riddled with fruit stalls, the streets are strewn with rubbish and dust.

'Take her upstairs,' the young doctor says, after a cursory examination. He seems to know what he is doing. We enter a spartanly furnished room which contains two spring-less beds. The green paintwork is peeling. Polly is immediately laid on a bed beside a contraption for dispensing intravenous fluids. It shocks me to see the difference between the medicines used in the cities and in a Mainland village, no further than 150 kilometres away. Where I had been given a couple of yellow pills for a similar gut complaint, Polly's arm is being filled with a jar full of clear liquid.

'Sorry, Nathan. I know you want to spend your birthday out on the Wall.'

'Don't worry. We've got to get you right,' I reply, gazing out at an orange full moon which is slowly rising over the plains outside the hospital window. I must find us a guesthouse for when she gets out of hospital.

We are still 500 kilometres from the Great Wall's end, and I don't even want to show Polly the map, given how many quadrants still remain. It is unlikely we are going to finish the Wall together, if at all. After two months of walking, I know Polly has reached the end of her adventuring tether and wants to finish as soon as possible. In the extreme heat my will is waning too, and I can't help but feel concerned. My third attempt is coming to an end, and still I am as far from the ocean as I felt when I actually began my journey. What is it that drives me to dedicate so much of my life to this vague, ancient and unreasonable quest?

Day 209
It is market day. An old man playing a flute attracts me to his stash. He is selling old Kuomintang and Communist badges, as well as an ancient Tibetan artifact which shows an engraving of the Buddha. The image is visible only when caught by the sun. I've never before seen such invisible artistry. What lay behind the minds of the ancient Tibetans?

We continue along the Wall over a series of small grassy hillsides and reach a long-awaited lake by midday. We rush down a side track to throw our sweaty bodies in for a swim. We sleep on the banks as a man hoses the fields to prepare for the next harvest. A host of thick, tropical clouds passes overhead and I suggest we set off quickly while the piercing sun is under cloud-cover. We do so, but Polly is decidedly unhappy and storms off in the lead.

'Help!' she soon screams.

Shit: she's been bitten by a snake. I rush to her side – her hand is already swelling. Oh God.

'It's a hornet. I'm allergic.'

I feed her some antihistamines and we make our way slowly down the last mountain range towards the lakeside road. Her hand is too swollen to climb down the slippery gravel with her sticks, so I inch her down carefully. Her journey, once we reach the lake's end, is finished. It is now only a question of whether I want to continue on my own.

I take Polly into my arms and guide her into the soft cool waters. We wash the sacred *tapu* from our bodies and I look upon her fondly. A strong woman nestles in my arms. Few on this earth would ever give up their lives to follow a man across 500 kilometres of some of the planet's most dangerous terrain. Growing from a timid wee creature, afraid to engage, even to look the Chinese in the eye, Polly has transformed into a veteran of the Mainland experience.

Across the lake, a rampart of grey bricks emerges from the waters like a kraken's tentacle from the deep. Its raw beauty still haunts my soul. A lightning storm fills the night sky as we head by van to take a holiday at the Emperor's summer palace in Chengde, 300 kilometres up north. I sigh with relief: it has been an exhausting journey. After a quick break in Beijing, we collect up all our belongings from Huairou, and take the train to the beach coast of Qingdao. We make a deal.

Walk three complete.

I take a last look at the rough ribbon of rocks trailing over the faded brown land. Suddenly the wall is alive again. For a moment I hesitate. Already I'm remembering the sunrises and sunsets I've watched from its back, the warm velvet nights studded in starlight, the unspeakable beauty of it snaking across bizarre twisted mountains, the certainty of its guiding me through the days. Do I really want to give all this up?

An old excitement returns and I know my answer is 'yes'. It's as if we've been untethered. Now we can go in any direction. Now we can jump into the unknown and let the current take us anywhere.

I stick out my thumb as we walk up the road.

Musings from the Wall: Polly Greeks, 'Embracing the Dragon'

MOON 12

THE RETURN OF THE MONK

When we begin to renounce our dreams and find peace, we go through a short period of tranquillity. But the dead dreams begin to rot within us and infect our entire being. We become cruel to those around us, and then we begin to direct this cruelty against ourselves. That's when illnesses and psychoses arise. What we sought to avoid in contact – disappointment and defeat – come upon us anyway because of our cowardice.

Paulo Coelho

15 August 2002, Independence Day, New Delhi, India
'Look at this,' Polly says, passing me the newspaper. 'It's got your horoscope.'

> Gemini
> Organise travel schedules now.
> Go back and complete what you started
> two months prior. Don't give up.
> What you are doing is worthwhile.

'Finish the bugger off,' she continues with a steely stare. I look out on a vista of kites flying freely from the open rooftops as the locals celebrate India's Independence. The day is symbolic for us, too: Polly and I are heading our separate ways. After five months attached at the hip – two months on the Wall, three months resting in Korea and travelling through Polly's beloved India – she's heading off to fulfil her own dream of writing a novel in the Himalayan highlands.

I feel somewhat dislocated, and it takes some days to find the will to continue alone. China for me is a place where in each city, each village, there is no one waiting — only the completion of my dream. On my own, I walk down the grimy, cow-filled streets of Delhi, waiting for my flight. The key for me now is the Wall. My *turangawaewae,* or sense of being. Like the middle beam of the meeting-house on the *marae,* although branches weave off like a ribcage providing insights into new paths and worlds, it is important not to lose sight of the overall goal.

My first step is to commit. This is always the hardest step, as I know full well the loneliness that lies ahead. I yearn instead to follow Polly up to Ley, but my gut instincts implore me not to follow her — internal instructions I now follow at all costs.

I fly out over the white peaks of the Himalaya, across the Gobi Desert and mountainous Mainland where I have walked. Tears roll down my cheeks as I sit humbled by my body, that it still has the strength to attempt this final challenge. A hall-length mural of the entire Great Wall greets me at Beijing Customs. I trace the mural from Jiayuguan right to the Wall spilling out into the sea at Shanhaiguan. The universe is helping me to stay inspired.

Day 215, 1 September 2002, Malanyu'er, Hebei Province
The Wall crawls out of the still blue lake. It is hot. I am now on the other side of the dam from where Polly and I finished our last walk. This is a new journey, and I must focus on what lies ahead. The Wall wraps its gentle, grey tentacle across the distant peaks as I circle the lake, complete my *karakia* and trail the Ming kraken deep into a kingdom of mountains. It is lonely but peaceful, and the pack on my back gives me strength and direction. Lietzle trees along the Wall give me a constant supply of nuts. It is harvesting season, just as it was two years ago when I set off like a naïve child through the Gobi. What lies ahead now is no longer an expectation of the imaginary; I am tackling the final 500 kilometres fully aware of my mortality.

I trail the fading light to rest at a spot where I see the sun set behind the diminishing lake. Thousands of steep peaks surround my being – I am a mere ant. The thought of the ocean draws me closer, each new step speaking of the person I am. I am Hoturoa – a man who walks many worlds. Drawn from the Tainui chief who steered his people's canoe from the Pacific Islands to Aotearoa, my Maori name is one of sacred significance. Sometimes I walk the pathway of despair, sometimes the pathway of passion, sometimes the trail towards lust and fame, and sometimes the road of giving. Like a stream that shapes a valley, there is no reason for its trail. I walk through these mountains, alongside this Wall – simply because I am willing.

Day 225
Sometimes it's better to remain on the journey in hope, than to finish it at all.

Robert Louis Stevenson

Wu Shilei drives me on his Nifty 50. His Chinese name means 'I am tired' – apt, given the state of my body after walking the mountains for ten days solid. He drives me along a narrow, winding road set amongst towering green peaks. We are visiting disconnected sections of Wall that I am unable to walk because they are so steep.

I am living off pure instinct now – surviving off the land in ways only an ancient aspect of me knows. I walk day and night under the glow of the decreasing moon, sheltering in towers like a lone wolf as thunderstorms enforce their *mana* upon the land. I howl to summon courage, as the Walls I am now facing are the most telling of all. I am timeless, stamping my feet on the ground, beating my chest and doing the *haka* to the empty constellations above. The Wall is lit like bone under the moon and I continue my way through the night, sniffing out my next port of food. It scares me sometimes, the beast that resides in us all.

My mother once told me that you start to get special powers when you travel on your own. I've learned to read the journey. The path dictated by the language of my heart. It's warning me to stop pushing, to stay away from the perfectionist's art.

We pass by a river which flows at the base of a steep mountain range. The flowing waters dazzle my soul, and I know its sparkling beauty is calling me to recommence my walk.

'*Dao shuiku you dou yuan?*' How much further to the dam?

'*Yi dao liang tian neng dao.*' One day, two days maximum, Wu Shilei replies, with a caring smile. I hug him and take a photo of his handsome young face and checkered red shirt. He has taken me 30 kilometres out of his way to bring me back to the Wall. I left the Wall yesterday to find a town from which to send an email to Polly – a day before she was due to enter the imposed silence of her ten-day meditation. Four consecutive hitch-hike rides manifested to enable me to get there. It's amazing what the universe allows with matters concerning the heart.

A group of bikers pass by and stop down the road. Wu Shilei smiles and turns his attention towards his next life flow. I head off on mine. Two days. I breathe deeply, allowing the oxygen to enter my weary brain. I am shattered, and don't think I can go another day. Panjiakou dam is only the halfway point between Beijing city and the sea.

It is the goodness of China that fuels my will to keep going. I have purposely not been in contact with anyone via email on this last walk. No external pressure or influences – I just want to see how far I can get on my own. I'm only going to talk once I've done the hard yards.

I cross the river with my pack and bare feet, and make my way up the next mountain slope. The trail is thorny, my trousers pocked with prickles and holes. They have already been repaired several times by caring mothers en route. Cobwebs line the path, and I respectfully skirt around towards a well-worn ridge. Watchtowers line the tips of the next seven northward peaks before the Wall arches back east towards my desired ocean. It's looking like at least another day's walk.

I retreat into my thoughts – oh to be relaxing with Polly. This only serves to make matters worse, so I force my gaze outwards to face my present. A sheer rock cliff fills the northern horizon, a tiny village lying below. Humans hoe the fields like small ants, so small compared with Nature's immensity. I can't let another person's existence so consume my present flow.

The Wall rolls sumptuously over a gentle, grassy summit and I follow her kind path, inching myself closer. My eyes melt: blue, velvet waters lie peacefully, surrounded by cascading limestone cliffs. It's the dam, my first big walking goal. My body sighs with relief. I drop my pack and lay out my sleeping bag to rest. The lake turns orange in the setting sun. It may as well have been the ocean.

11 September 2002, Panjiakou Shuiku
When drinking water, think to the source.

Ancient Chinese proverb

The Mayan calendar, which has been used for thousands of years, terminates on the shortest day at 21 December 2012. No one knows for sure why the calendar stops on this date, although ancient Mayan scripture states the planet's entry into the fifth great age: The Age of Fire.

When the planet turned three, an asteroid smashed into Earth. This annihilated almost every species, including the dinosaurs during the Mesozoic Era/Cretaceous Period.

When it turned four (the Cenozoic Era, and the beginning of humanity), the planet was struck with the hugest ice-melt ever recorded. After 40,000 years of an Ice Age, which brought the polar caps halfway towards the equator, a significant temperature rise occurred, melting the ice in just over 1,000 years. Archaeological remains show beasts and trees merged together during the massive glacial floods – many of the animals still in the process of gestation when caught in its flow.

The land surrounding Panjiakou dam is dry and inhospitable. Six years without rain and the dam's original waterline has lowered 4 metres. Watchtowers, once submerged, are now in full view. Irrigation schemes keep farming going, but are depleting most rivers, which are already grey with pollution from industrial effluent. The locals say that the Yellow River now only trickles into the ocean. They also say the region's wells need to be drilled to 40 metres instead of the original 10, especially since 1998, which was recorded as the hottest year ever in human history.

In the intense 40-degree heat, my mouth suffers from a putrid, dry thirst, which creates an unbearable pressure at the back of the throat. A small store, set up at the edge of the dam, sells water bottles and hires long-tail boats. I count my lucky stars that I am able to afford the price of a bottle of water, and think I can understand why the Mayans are calling 2012 the Age of Fire.

MOON 13

DEATH: NO SELF

*I am encompassed by a wall, high and hard and stone, with only
my brainy nails to tear it down.*

Keri Hulme

18 September 2002, Beijing

Diego has returned to China. Reuniting with his Thai girlfriend
Nadia, whom he met towards the end of his walk in Beijing,
he is preparing for a gallery showing in Hong Kong. I walk up
to him in Tian'anmen Square. He wears a grey polar-fleece
and looks strong and healthy, fully recovered after his walking
mission.

'Hello, bella,' he says, looking upon my battered body with
compassion. 'Come sit.' He points to a pole beneath a picture of
Sun Yat-Sen and we watch a group of children fly their kites in the
square. 'He should ask us before taking those,' Diego continues,
pointing to a photographer taking shots from a distance.

'He's recording our history.' I pause, reflecting. 'Remember
when we first met up here for team photos?'

'Yes, I wondered then how it'd all turn out.'

'What happened when you finished? How did it feel?'

'My ending wasn't what I had imagined. Shanhaiguan's just
another one of them dull industrial cities.' He looks out wistfully
into the distance. 'I walked into the city at night, slept, and then
walked out to the ocean the next morning with my brother.'

'I'm glad he was there to accompany you – to share in your
achievement.'

Diego looks again at my battered body with compassion.
'One day I was filming myself with the tripod and in my haste
to walk back, I tripped and fell off the Wall.'

'You fell off?'

'It was a 3-metre drop – all caught on film.' He smirks proudly. 'I landed on the only piece of land without a tree stump – no injuries except for my thumb!' He pauses again, reflecting. 'The fall taught me to stop pushing, Nathan – to have faith in myself that all things have their right time and that I would be able to keep my commitment.'

'How did you keep going?'

'You know me: I like to be on my own. I'm also very stubborn. I had been walking through knee-high snow for days, and towards the end my knees were almost crippled. The pain was excruciating, but I continued because my soul would not be happy unless I finished.'

'I fell off the Wall too, sliding down the rocks and dislocating my shoulder. I lay there for about thirty seconds, just breathing, then I got back up and continued to hobble along.'

'There's something about following your dreams.'

'What's that?'

'You're driven by the desire to arrive.'

We both look out towards the Forbidden City in silence. Sitting across from the traffic-filled highway, we note that Beijing has seen many changes since we arrived in China. Almost all the shanty brick cottages have been flattened to make space for four-laned highways and tall apartment buildings. It is common to see the locals crying on the pavements as the bulldozers demolish their childhood memories.

'I was angry for a long time about the separation,' Diego continues, 'but I eventually came to accept that if you really want to do something in life, you can only get help so far.' He pauses, looking straight at me. 'I'm proud of the decisions we made – if anything, because we made them.' He pauses again, wiping some sweat off his forehead. 'It took courage to give up the walk where you did – to return home. Having you on the journey gave me the impetus to finish.'

'We have a Maori saying that you should only ever bow to an almighty mountain. And if you bow you have to know that you have done your best, and grown as a result. I've just reached Panjiakou dam.'

'You're close. It took me two weeks from there to the ocean. You may as well finish.'

'Thanks for the encouragement.'

'Relish the search, Nathan, and remember, there is nothing more powerful than that virgin walk. She'll be waiting for you on the other side.'

We look out into the distant mountains surrounding Beijing like two hawks scanning for prey; this time, however, towards our separate futures. The final photo is taken and the last circle has been closed. I have one last relationship to address – the one with myself. One that will not rest until I have completed what I have set out to do.

Day 230

Only Love, Only Service

Yogi Sharma

I set off by motorised row-boat across Panjiakou dam. Below sheer limestone cliffs, the crystal waters are calm and reflect the mountains ahead. My guide sits at the back of the long-tail boat, directing the engine. The passing wind blows his wiry black hair across his face. He has a grey moustache and wears wide-rimmed glasses. He lives on his own in an abandoned brick village and invites me to spend the night. We laugh merrily as we cook up a meal of fresh eggs and noodles.

A cool mist rises from the waters early the next morning. Chinese fishermen awake from their slender wooden boats and feed breadcrumbs to their fish stocks, which are farmed in large, round nets. The water ripples wildly. My guide drops me at the edge of the lake.

'Follow along the side of the mountain range, and you'll meet up with the Wall again on the other side.' I listen to my next instructions, pay him and leave, wandering through grazed farmlands, watching a farm boy herding cows with a whip. I walk for two days along the flat fields before spotting a watchtower atop a rocky saddle which calls as a place to sleep for the night. Six students also take the path up the same mountain pass. Clasping onto chains fixed into the rock, we help each other to the steeper sections, reaching the top just in time to witness the orange ball sinking into the horizon. My friends leave me to sleep beside a crumbling watchtower, and I awake to the sound of a screeching owl. A blood-red full moon rises between two watchtowers on the next range. It is the thirteenth, and final, full moon of my journey.

The Mayan calendar is set out in accordance with the thirteen twenty-eight-day cycles of the moon. Marking out 364 days, this leaves one day left over which the Maya call 'a day lost in time'. This extra day forms the basis of their religion, a day of celebration and forgiveness, a day to acknowledge the passing year and celebrate the new one coming. It also reminds humanity that 'time' is purely a manufactured art.

Humans' natural time sensibility has been captured since 50 AD by an artificial measure of twelve-month periods. The Gregorian calendar was first implemented when Julius Caesar used it to schedule taxation upon his conquered (indigenous) peoples. The calendar fell outside the normal biological cycles, the twenty-nine-, thirty- and thirty-one-day months falling out of sync with a woman's twenty-eight-day menstruation. In 1933, the League of Nations voted to restore the thirteen-moon calendar, naming the thirteenth month 'Tricember'. Before implementation, however, the Vatican City argued that the 'day lost in time' would lead to confusion, calamity and eventual war. Humanity was easier to control with the twelve-month system that had been so effective over the past 2,000 years.

I had been living my every day in accordance with the dictates of the moon. It was a source of comfort. A friend I could always rely on. The times of greatest action were from half to full moon and back again to half. These were the times when I could walk for two weeks solid. The times for resting, reflection and love-making fell within the waning quarters of the new moon. With energy at full peak, I head off early the next morning to tackle this next deadly peak.

Day 234

> *Ah, but a man's reach should exceed his grasp.*
> *Or what's a heaven for?*
> Robert Browning

A shepherd rushes into the watchtower where I sleep. He looks around anxiously, gives me a quick glance and then rushes back out and up the mountain. I get up immediately. My motivation: no water.

I have spent two days crossing this last mountain range. Small villages are scattered throughout the plains below – small brown specks on a farmland quilt. They are too far away to head down to ask for food. I am relieved to see a road at the bottom of the next peak. I also only have one day left in which to extend my one-month visa.

A diagonally-roofed watchtower sits near the base of this last slope. It is the first of its kind I have seen on the journey. On the next range lies a brilliant white section of Wall. It is made out of limestone, but looks like it is made out of bone. A Chinese man is working down below, laying a line of red bricks along the roadside. It's as if this is the new Wall I must follow. I enter the tower. It has a feeling of immense comfort and I see many names scribbled in Chinese – past walkers perhaps. I have a gut feeling that I too must sign; that from this point on, there is no more need to walk every step to the sea.

I don't.

I leave the Wall at the road and catch a bike, and then a bus, to renew my visa in the nearest big town. The officials only grant me fifteen days, not enough time to walk every step to the end according to the maps. My last day is two years to the day from when the walking commenced. Even the Chinese State has imposed the deadline. I feel pressure from my stubborn self to still try to walk every step. Even though my body cries out for another night's rest, I plan to head back out immediately.

The old lady at my guesthouse looks at me with concern. She frowns. She can see the exhaustion in my eyes and shakes her head scornfully when I explain I won't be staying the night. I also decide to leave my camera behind to save on weight, catching the last bus out and then a taxi back to the wall.

The lesson is brutal.

The taxi driver doesn't stop at that glorious section of limestone Wall as I had hoped. Instead, as a grey darkness looms over the mountains, he drops me off half a kilometre down the road.

'Take that path up there,' he states forcefully.

'But the Wall's further up the road.'

'Take that path,' he repeats, his eyes narrowing.

I get out of the cab, cross a wooden bridge over the river, and follow a gravel path up the hill. I cross paths with a Chinese lady making her way down. She has short, dark hair and is carrying a bunch of gigantic incense sticks.

'*Yi kuai,*' she smiles, handing me one. It is 2 centimetres thick and 15 centimetres long. I purchase it for 1 *yuan* and head slowly up the path. Animal statues of the Chinese calendar line both sides of the path. Twilight diminishes, and I round a corner to stand mesmerised before a gigantic Buddha statue. It is sitting in the lotus position, etched out of the mountain rock. I approach the structure as a strong gust of wind blows into my face. Suddenly, I feel an unseen presence leap into my body.

'Ohhhh . . . fuck,' I moan, shaking my body, violently trying to rid myself of the possession. The sensation is despicable, like being forced to place my mouth around an exhaust pipe and suck in the fumes. I shake my body again, focusing all my mental strength on evicting the alien presence. It seems to leave. I shiver in disgust, as one does when spitting out a chunk of mouldy apple. I feel violated, but remain alert in case whatever it is returns. My white bone shines brightly.

I walk cautiously towards the Buddha statue, reaching its feet. My full height just reaches its big toe. I break the incense stick in half, and light both halves. To me, the statue's message is clear: I'm to change my stubborn ways. Surrender to the flow of the journey and survive to tell the tale. I am to take the middle way along the Wall.

I head up to a watchtower on a peak above the statue, but can't sleep. A fierce wind rages through the open windows, shadows flicker ominously around my wavering candle. When I finally sleep, I am visited by a girl I had fallen in love with when living in America. She comes towards me with her loving blue eyes, returning my camera, but when she hands it across her beautiful face transforms into an angry monster. I wake up, shocked, and pick up *The Pilgrimage*, a book by Paulo Coelho which accompanies me on my road. The book opens at a page which talks about the protagonist finding his long-lost and treasured sword, and needing to transform his journey across Spain to maintain his passion for the trail.

Motorbikes, I think.

A flicker of hope re-enters my eye.

Day 238
Wisdom is knowing what to do next. Skill is the ability to do it, and virtue is actually doing it.

Anon

I walk out of the mountains the next day. It is raining heavily. A Chinese student sees me walking towards his town and picks me up on his motorbike. He shows me round his city and takes me to the local showers. It is nice to have a friend for the afternoon, and we visit the local pool hall to play with two other friends. I am taken to a small hotel with a Great Wall painting displayed outside.

An hour later there is a knock at the door.

I refuse to answer, pretending to be asleep. I'm too tired to be playing the clown. The door opens and a policeman enters.

'Come with me.' I am escorted into a red van and we race through the darkened streets. The van slows to pass a truck that has stopped on the side of the road. Its hazard lights are flashing. I see two splattered Chinese cyclists. Blood and guts lie all over the road, and on the truck's grill bars. A month now of solo walking and I've finally had enough. My tormented soul has reached its limit and my eyes are about to explode with what feels like years of grief. I have to do something lest the floodgates burst. The van drops me off at a registered hotel and I ring Michael Gresham to ask if he can find my old black diary at his home. Inside is a phone number I need if I'm going to make it to the end of the Wall. Michael finds it and I call it.

'*Ni hao?*' Hello?

'*Wei, ni hao. Wo jiao Nathan. Ni zou lu dao Shanhaiguan ma?*' My voice is teetering on the brink of tears.

'*Ni zai na'r?*' Where are you? a quiet voice replies.

'*Tiannan.*'

'*Ni deng deng deng, san tian zhi nei wo neng dao.*' Stay put. I'll be there in three days.

I pass the phone to a Chinese man to give exact directions to my hotel and run through the dusty streets with my arms raised in the air. China's angels are coming to take me into the ocean.

Day 246

For two long years I have thought about what it will be like to actually reach the Bohai Sea. Whether cycling along when resting back in New Zealand, or walking in ambitious hope through the Gobi Desert, the thought would stir me with the most deeply felt emotion.

I walk with two Chinese brothers, Zhao Weiguo and Zhao Weidong. Zhao Weiguo is dressed in an army jacket, and scours the terrain with his battered binoculars, holding command. He is in great shape for his forty-four years. Zhao Weidong is the complete opposite. Dressed in a blue-jean dress-shirt and tan business trousers, he is chubby and far less prepared for the epic. We meet in Qian'an, embrace like old friends, have a quick meal and set off immediately on our bus towards the next section of Wall. Passing a white statue of Genghis Khan on his horse, his sword at the ready, we are making one last surge to conquer the Wall. I recall Nostradamus's prophesy that from 1999 until 2030 China is going to experience world domination unheralded since the times of Genghis Khan.

We walk together for four days along mountain-tops and through valleys shrouded in autumn's red and gold. Nature always saves its most beautiful for its dying last. Zhao Weiguo speaks with the locals to ascertain the best routes, and as we reach the mountain-tops the brothers sing ancient Chinese tunes. It's like we're flying over the continent. The tunes transform into monkey cries as they make the most of their freedom. We call out to each other from distant peaks and watchtowers. This is the way the Great Wall of China is supposed to be walked. Love and friendship between nations – the Wall's builders are overjoyed.

We take a short-cut up a valley filled with red maple and onwards to the next mountain range where the Wall again trails. Upon taking a step back on top of the Wall, the view ahead causes me to freeze. Behind China's last range lies a hazy blue mirage. After hundreds of desert and mountain vistas, the view is unmistakeable – we've reached the ocean. It lies there, silent, mist rising from its depths. Strangely, I feel no significant emotion. In fact, it is just like any other day on the journey. However, it is what happens next that feels special. Two children, a boy and a girl, emerge on the Wall, walking towards us hand in hand. They are walking in slow motion.

'Come with us,' Zhao Weidong says kindly, securing their trust. Bristles grow on his chin, but the goodness of his intention is unmistakeable. I am in the presence of two very special fathers.

Zhao Weiguo takes the lead, trailing the reconstructed Wall that winds along a ridge as the kids file in behind, with me and

Zhao Weidong at the back. Again we are five, the sea out in front. I look to the tiny children with adoring eyes, attentive to their every step. Their presence gives me a sense of life's purpose. More than any ocean that lies out ahead. More than any Wall I have been traversing for two years. I finally understand the journey's destination. Diego was wrong when he said you can only get help so far. One can get help right to the very end so long as you are the one that is doing the helping.

The Great Wall of China is a trail of self-initiation. A one-man path that tests the very threshold of your mental and physical exhaustion, makes you believe in the guidance of the divine, and, when you are ready, graduates you towards the journey unto the other.

A photographer with short black hair takes photos as we approach. It's as if China has been with me every telling step. Zhao Weiguo tells them about my journey, but I am not interested in the fame. My eyes never want to leave the children. They continue past the group, through the other side of the watchtower, and take a pathway of concrete tourist steps off the Wall. A hawk sits atop a dome of rock to an alternative pathway of life where the crumbling Great Wall heads. There is a warning sign in red, warning mortals from continuing.

I return to get the others, and we follow down in the path of the two children. Zhao Weidong is due to head back home to Zhangjiakou the next day, but I am not ready to catch a bus to the end if it means missing out the last two days of Wall. We spend the night at a small peasant home and embrace each other the next morning as we head our different ways.

Day 247

Zhao Weiguo remains to accompany me to the end. I am immediately sad about my decision. Slightly overweight, with big puffy cheeks, Zhao Weidong always wanted to walk around the ranges taking the comfortable flat routes, while I had wanted to remain on the tops with the Wall. It has been challenging being a team again. Our compromises have had us taking all sorts of elongated rectangular routes, but we have stuck with each other, swapping packs and battling away with our sacrifices to keep the connection strong.

As Zhao Weidong walks away down the gravel road, never to be seen again, I understand again that it is all about connection rather than simply finishing.

'You're lucky we both didn't leave you,' Zhao Weiguo says quietly in Chinese. He is also sad his brother has gone. 'You'd be feeling pretty lonely if that was the case.' He pauses to let the lesson sink in. 'No regrets! We've come all this way – let's make our way to the end.'

By nightfall we have made our way to the base of the last mountain range. We sneak through the gates of the now-closed tourist section and walk up the mountain to find a suitable place to pitch our tent. Shanhaiguan's city lights flicker in the plains below, a ship's foghorn blares through the mist of Bohai Bay. The ocean's presence can be felt out into the horizon.

We head up the reconstructed Wall, essentially walking the trail of my journey backwards. I feel like I am walking the very first mountain range of a 4,000-kilometre journey. I bound up the slopes passionately, just like those first steps out into the Gobi. The sea behind is like a gigantic mirror reflecting all the mountains, deserts and valleys trailed, not to mention all the emotions encapsulated within the ocean's depths. Yet in some ways it symbolises a new journey. The rest of my life now lies out ahead.

I am exhausted by the time we reach the top of the mountain, stalling immediate plans on making the return trip. However, I feel honoured to begin Zhao Weiguo's new journey. His plan is to spend the next six years heading west from his home in Zhangjiakou towards the western-most terminal in Jiayuguan. I wonder whether I will be there to *utu* his finale in 2008, reciprocating the enormous act of giving he has displayed. It's a great way to celebrate one's fiftieth and falls in the same year as the Olympics. Indeed it is something new to dream about. We enter the tent, waiting excitedly for the sun and the sea.

Day 256
All rivers and streams run down to the ocean, because it is lower.
Herein lies the power of humility.

Ancient Tao saying

A host of monks adorned in white run past our tent, chanting with shortened breath. I get out to see an aged local taking the same path up the Wall but with a more lackadaisical approach towards his morning's austerities. He paces up the hill, his dog tugging at him excitedly. The Wall zig-zags to the summit and continues across a host of razor peaks before disappearing into a distant embankment of clouds. To the south lies a blue, crystal lake.

Zhao Weiguo and I climb to the top and sit before the view of the sea. The sun reflects its orange rays along the smooth waters towards the shore. I have never felt so relaxed. Zhao Weiguo and I trade grin after grin. Today is a very good day. It's as if all the stress that has gone into worrying about not making the journey has been a complete waste of time. Anything is achievable. It is purely a matter of being patient and present, and enjoying the journey unfolding.

We head down from the jagged foothills and out onto a vast coastal plain. It is green with wasteland grass and sugar cane. A rock lies in the fields, emblazoned in red characters with the famous words of Mao: *You are not a man until you have got to the Great Wall.*

Stumbling brokenly across grass fields, the Wall erupts into the parapets of Shanhaiguan Fort. *The First Pass Under Heaven* stands out, etched in red characters on the ancient city's main temple. The fort contains a moat soiled with flung-away vegetables, surrounded by curio markets that sell knives, clocks, fans and medallions. Stoked to be the third member of the original team to see the journey right to the end, I buy myself a bronze medallion of the Wall, my Chinese Tiger sign engraved on the back.

Statues of all the brains behind Great Wall construction line the main palisade. Some of the Wall masterminds are dressed like wizards, intellectual giants in full-length silvery-blue cloaks wearing pointy orange slippers, asserting their influence with the pen rather than the sword. Others are adorned in loincloth and bear skin, wielding lofty swords or clubs to demonstrate their preferred manner of reign.

Zhao Weiguo urges me to walk the ramparts twice to properly pay our last respects. I can't believe that they built this Wall across an entire continent. I feel I have been as loyal to it as I can. We eat lunch and then leave the ancient fort, crossing a motorway and four railway lines before the Wall re-emerges beyond modernity. Camouflaged by rubble and grass, it passes peasants living in grim corrugated hovels. They wave us onwards towards Laolong Kou, the Head of the Dragon; their smiles mirroring those of the thousands of folk who have carried me from the very beginning.

The ocean vista grows with every step, salt permeating the air. My two-year flight from the desert ends where the ancient dragon dips her head into the ocean, connecting the material with the immaterial, and marrying the earth unto the sky. My guts cave in as Zhao Weiguo and I climb the back of the last tourist section, now only 500 metres from the sea. Zhao Weiguo looks to me and gives a knowing smile. Both our ancestors are here to celebrate the end of this trial.

Zhao Weiguo beats the drum at the back as I make my way through the very last tower. There're just 10 metres left of Wall before the ocean crashes violently against her mouth . . .

I place my hands on that last brick and scream six screams so completely inhuman – I evict from my soul the fuel of a billion angry men.

The dragon is alive, and through our dreams we still can learn.

A DAY LOST IN TIME

In the end what matters most is:
How well did you live?
How well did you love?
How well did you learn to let go?

Helen Keller

21 December 2002

'Look at the rainbow,' Polly says, pointing out of the window as our plane heads into Wellington. A spectrum of colour weaves along the top of the ridgeline, ending where the ridge dips into the Cook Strait. I wouldn't have even noticed had she not been there to point it out. It is like a rainbow version of the Great Wall of China. Polly and I exchange smiles as the plane lands smoothly at the edge of *Te Upoko o te Ika a Maui*, the head of the great fish.

COPYRIGHT ACKNOWLEDGEMENTS

We acknowledge copyright for the quotes used in *First Pass Under Heaven* and thank the copyright holders for permission to reproduce their work:

Greeks, Polly. *Embracing the Dragon: A woman's journey along the Great Wall of China*. Awa Press, Wellington, 2004.

Hawken, Dinah. 'The Harbour Poems' in *Small Stories of Devotion*. Victoria University Press, Wellington, 1991.

Hulme, Keri. *The Bone People*. Spiral/Hodder and Stoughton, Auckland, 1985.

Jeffers, Susan. *Feel the Fear and Do It Anyway*™. Ballantine Books, New York, 1987.

Lindesay, William. *Alone on the Great Wall*. Hodder and Stoughton, UK, 1989.

Thubron, Colin. *Behind the Wall: A Journey through China*. Heinemann, 1987.

Waldron, Professor Arthur. *The Great Wall of China*. Cambridge University Press, 1992.

Thanks also to the extended family of Rewi Alley.

PHOTOGRAPHIC ACKNOWLEDGEMENTS

Thanks to Kelvin Gilbert Jones for the use of his images in this book.

Visit www.greatwalldvd.com for colour slide shows and edited footage of the journey.